JOHN L. LEWIS
LABOR LEADER

TWAYNE'S TWENTIETH-CENTURY AMERICAN BIOGRAPHY SERIES

John Milton Cooper, Jr., General Editor

JOHN L. LEWIS
LABOR LEADER

Robert H. Zieger

TWAYNE PUBLISHERS • BOSTON
A Division of G. K. Hall & Co.

Copyright 1988 by G. K. Hall & Co.
All rights reserved.
Published by Twayne Publishers
70 Lincoln Street, Boston, Massachusetts 02111

Twayne's Twentieth-Century
American Biography Series No. 8

Book Production by Janet Zietowski
Copyediting supervised by Barbara Sutton
Typeset in 11/13 Goudy by P & M Typesetting, Inc.

Printed on permanent/durable acid-free paper
and bound in the United States of America

First Printing

Library of Congress Cataloging in Publication Data

Zieger, Robert H.
John L. Lewis / Robert H. Zieger.
p.   cm.—(Twayne's twentieth-century American biography
series ; no. 8)
Bibliography: p.
Includes index.
ISBN 0-8057-7763-6 (alk. paper). ISBN 0-8057-7782-2 (alk. paper :
pbk.)
1. Lewis, John Llewellyn, 1880–1969.   2. United Mine Workers of
America—History.   3. Trade-unions—United States—Officials and
employees—Biography.   I. Title.   II. Series.
HD6509.L4Z54 1988
331.88'33'0924—dc19 87-31553
[B] CIP

*To Sam Merrill
and Marion Galbraith Merrill
with gratitude and affection*

CONTENTS

FOREWORD

No one who saw or heard John L. Lewis ever forgot him. A large, solidly built man, he exuded an aura of physical strength that was appropriate to a leader of multitudes who made their living by manual labor. Fittingly, he once indulged in a well-publicized fistfight with another labor union leader at a national convention. His jowly face was topped by a thick mane of hair and punctuated by unnaturally thick, bushy eyebrows. The most famous photograph of him showed him wearing the clothes and lighted helmet of the workers he led—the miners—smudged with dust and dirt, scowling grimly after inspecting the scene of a disastrous coal mine accident. But the most memorable of all Lewis's characteristics was his voice. It was appropriate that he rose to national prominence just when radio was making the sounds of famous people's voices as familiar as newspapers and magazines made their photographs. Lewis spoke in a deep bass, with a slow, ponderous delivery that made everything he said seem weighty. Moreover, he studded his speech with flowery phrases and archaic words that were deliberately calculated to remind listeners of the cadences of Shakespeare and the King James Bible. Withal, Lewis made a powerful impression.

That public image both helped and hurt him, as Robert Zieger demonstrates in this shrewdly insightful biography. In the mid-1930s, when Lewis broke with the conservative craft unionist leadership of the American Federation of Labor, his visibility lent a stature to the movement that he started, the Congress of Industrial Organizations, that it would not otherwise have enjoyed. Lewis delightedly dramatized his conflicts not only with the management of some of the nation's biggest businesses, such as the steel and automobile manufacturers, but also with successive presidents of the United States, especially Franklin Delano Roosevelt in the late 1930s and Harry S. Truman at the end of World War II. This penchant for well-publicized confrontation undoubtedly helped reap gains for Lewis's own union, the United

Mineworkers, and for the CIO. Yet his antics also lent themselves to humorous caricature and often to sinister depiction of him as a menacing, possibly revolutionary force. Lewis succeeded in making the labor boss an even more feared figure than the business tycoon and himself a symbol of irresponsible economic power to replace an earlier generation's fixation on such "malefactors of great wealth" as John D. Rockefeller and J. P. Morgan.

The positive and negative poles of Lewis's reputation contained paradoxes that Robert Zieger explores with great sensitivity in this account of the labor leader's life and career. He was a mine union leader who worked only a short time in the mines; the head of a movement of modern, industrywide unions whose base was in one of the most old-fashioned craft unions; an associate of big-city leftists and immigrants who was himself a small-town conservative who embraced traditional American morals and values. He spoke and fought for millions of ill-paid, boss-ridden toilers, but he lived in luxury and ruled his own union with the proverbial iron hand. No single career better illuminated the achievements and the defects of the trade union movement in the United States during the twentieth century. To read this exciting, thought-provoking biography of John L. Lewis is to begin to grasp some of the central problems of modern American labor.

John Milton Cooper, Jr.

PREFACE

Where are the working-class heroes? Recently, an interviewer asked Oklahoma autoworkers whom they admired. The filmed responses shocked veteran labor activists. One worker thought long and hard, at last settling on John Wayne. Another chose Superman. A third named Martin Luther King, Jr., but most of them just shook their heads.

An earlier generation might have responded more eagerly. In the 1930s and 1940s, an expanding labor movement propelled a cadre of gifted leaders to the front rank of public attention. Philip Murray of the Steelworkers inspired trust and affection among thousands of industrial workers. The Auto Workers' Walter Reuther was fast building his reputation for intelligence and leadership.

During this heyday of the labor movement, however, one leader towered above the rest. In the pages of the nation's newspapers and magazines and over the country's radio broadcasting network, the bushy-browed chieftain of the United Mine Workers, John L. Lewis, rivaled movie stars and comic strip characters, to say nothing of politicians, business tycoons, and religious leaders. By no means universally acclaimed, even among his own United Mine Workers (UMW), Lewis nonetheless projected power and dynamism in a thousand speeches, organizing campaigns, strikes, and confrontations with capitalists and politicians alike. True, public opinion polls sometimes showed that as many working people reviled as revered him, but it is hard to imagine any representative group of workers ignoring him. In the crisis-ridden 1930s and 1940s, enough endorsed his claim as their champion to put him in the front rank of American heroes.

Indeed, for over forty years, John L. Lewis embodied the best and worst in the American labor movement. He mixed authoritarianism in his rule over the miners' union with service to democratic labor organization in launching the CIO. His association with industrialists, politicians, and publicists sometimes verged on sycophancy and collaborationism, yet he was also the consummate organizer, bargainer, and critic of corporate America and of the emerging national security state. His tenure at the center of American public attention coincided—and not fortuitously—with the peak of laborite activism. Worshipped and hated, Lewis dominated public attention as no labor leader before or since has done.

Thus, the invitation to write a biography of this giant of the labor movement, a man whose life and work are central to the understanding of twentieth-century political economy, offered a splendid opportunity. Lewis had appeared in my earlier books, first as the beleaguered leader of the UMW in the 1920s, then as the militant warrior of the New Deal years. Confronting him directly would take time from the history of the CIO that I was preparing, but he looms so large in twentieth-century labor history that writing his biography hardly seemed a digression.

The Lewis whom I discovered in focusing specifically on his life and work was both more and less than I had anticipated. His hunger for wealth and recognition often seemed demeaning and even pathetic. His condescension toward working miners, his contempt for critics and dissenters, and his vilification of opponents stood out. So, too, however, did his boldness in the 1930s, his genuine determination to build a powerful working-class movement, and his warnings about the militarization of American society. Emerging from this bundle of jarring impressions was the common thread of Lewis's intense American-ness. In all his diverse activities, he was a child of the native heartland, an exemplar of so many national traits. In his individualism, his isolationism, his privatism, and his attachment to the unique blend of economic and political values that defines our commercial republic, John L. Lewis was a quintessential native son.

This book attempts to put Lewis into the context of a rapidly changing corporate and political order. It seeks to re-create a time when the labor movement was a central force in American life. Lewis wrestled with basic problems, most notably the governance of popular organizations in a bureaucratic society, the claims of the state upon individuals and the private bodies that they create to advance their interests, and the efforts of essentially propertyless working people to find a collective voice and make themselves heard at the centers of power. These matters have hardly been resolved. Perhaps Lewis, so obviously a Victorian figure in so many ways, remains relevant even as the incessant struggle for power, voice, and influence takes on forms unanticipated in the laborite idiom in which he thought and spoke.

Even a short book requires help and encouragement. Barbara Hudy Bartkowiak gathered information in her inimitably prompt and careful way. Le Roy Ashby read almost all the manuscript and provided that much-mentioned but ever-so-rare commodity, wise counsel. Warren Van Tine was a cheerful guide to sources and an invaluable critic of the finished product. John Cooper offered the chance to include Lewis in Twayne's Twentieth-Century Biography Series and provided good advice throughout. Anne Jones's editing and Cecile Watters's copyediting were outstanding. Ginny Corbin and Mern Johnston-Loehner typed the manuscript with skill and speed. My good wife, Gay Pitman Zieger, helped, encouraged, and advised in about equal—and equally needed—proportions.

INTRODUCTION

Although two generations of opponents and detractors often depicted John L. Lewis as the veritable Antichrist of the American Dream, his life in fact exemplified some of the most enduring American myths. Born on 12 February 1880, Lewis exhibited in his own career important elements in the Lincoln story. Both men used keen intelligence and powerful oratorical skills to compensate for impoverished origins and lack of formal education. Both led broad, popular movements while learning to live and flourish among the nation's well-born and powerful. Both men, seventy-five years apart, settled in Springfield, using central Illinois as a stepping-stone to the achievement of power in Washington. Indeed, the last remains of the two men lie in the same cemetery, only a few yards apart.

Equally striking is the congruence of Lewis's life to the Horatio Alger myth. It was not merely that Lewis overcame early disabilities and rose to eminence through intelligence, hard work, and good fortune. The Horatio Alger hero always won out as much through proximity to the powerful as through personal qualities. So it was with Lewis. The patronage of established leaders in the United Mine Workers (UMW) and American Federation of Labor (AFL) in the 1910s permitted the young miner to climb to the presidency of the UMW in 1920 at the comparatively youthful age of thirty-nine. Loyalty, ambition, and cultivation of the elite were hallmarks both of Alger's youthful nineteenth-century heroes and of Lewis's rapid rise to the presidency of the nation's largest labor union.

In the 1930s and 1940s, corporate leaders, irate editorialists, and embattled politicians often denounced Lewis as un-American and unpatriotic. Indeed, a life spent in the labor movement—especially a life so filled with dramatic achievement and pointed controversy as Lewis's—ensured charges of betrayal of the American Dream in a country whose identity is so overwhelmingly capitalist. But in reality Lewis, both in his origins and in his career, was as American as the farmlands and coalfields of central Iowa from which he

economic independence
or self-sufficiency.

came. Isolationist in his politics, autarkic in his economic philosophy, possessed of the practical American's distrust of theories and ideologies, Lewis was a son of native soil. Although his Welsh-born father and mother linked him to the epic story of immigration, he paid little attention to his European ancestry and had little patience with the European frames of reference—the international rivalries and political ideologies of the Old World—so central to many of his contemporaries in the American labor movement.

Lewis's life exhibited paradoxes aplenty. It spanned the period of profound industrialization of the American economy and the assertion of American power in the world arena. No labor leader played a greater role in the public events that surrounded these two developments. Yet Lewis's power and influence derived not from leadership of the workers who manned the assembly lines or produced the gleaming new products that reshaped twentieth-century life but rather from his position at the head of the country's coal miners, whose conditions of employment and whose methods of production were, for much of this period, traditional and even primitive. Similarly, though he and his miners achieved their greatest victories during periods of intense American involvement in world affairs, Lewis never strayed far from his isolationist mid-American roots.

Paradox also characterized his involvement with corporate America. No twentieth-century labor leader more stirred the wrath of businessmen or unsettled the defenders of the status quo than did the chief of the UMW. Especially in the generation after 1930, editorialists and conservative politicians spoke of a power-hungry, radical Lewis, exploiting popular unrest, defying the government, heaping contempt on the representatives of the business class. Yet in reality, as his shrewder opponents soon realized, Lewis bowed to no one in his commitment to capitalism, his contempt for the Left, and his genuine delight in intimate association with the business and social elite.

Within the labor movement itself, contradictions abounded. During a critical decade—that of the 1930s—no American spoke more eloquently or spurred organization more effectively in behalf of democratic values. Yet this same man dominated the UMW with an iron hand. Even as his public speeches and his skillful maneuverings advanced the cause of industrial democracy, he tightened his grip on his own union and systematically choked off democratic stirrings within the ranks of the miners.

Lewis's career was so long and so tempestuous that it inevitably touched upon virtually every significant theme in twentieth-century public life. It embraced transformation of the UMW from a congeries of grass-roots miners' organizations to a sprawling Lewis-controlled machine. The fate of the UMW reflected both the rise of bureaucratic governance in private institutions and the tenacity of institutional feudalism in the labor movement. Lewis's relationship to the federal government, which he alternately used and reviled just as its leaders used and reviled him, highlights the complex interaction of the emerging national security state and the modern labor movement, itself partaking of the character of both mass movement and narrow interest group. Indeed, this man who spoke for labor at the height of its twentieth-century struggles contained multitudes.

If Lewis's life exhibits paradox, his legacy is likewise ambiguous. Today, organized labor faces the twin problems of internal ossification and organizational stasis. The Lewis legacy of top-down leadership, discouragement of rank-and-file activism, and sycophantic hero worship has little to offer a labor movement struggling against inertia, careerism, and charges of abuses of power. Nor is the Lewis record in collective bargaining edifying, at least in its latter stages. For some observers, the growth of a cooperative relationship between the UMW and management, as reflected in the contracts of the 1950s, points to the future in an economy generally affected by international competition, technological innovation, and limited employment opportunities, problems that prevailed in coal thirty years ago. On the other hand, UMW contracts in the fifties, far from attempting to empower workers at the local level or provide employment guarantees for displaced miners, simply underwrote the rapid mechanization of the industry. The rapid disemployment of miners helped deepen the poverty of the mining regions. Labor-management cooperation soon degenerated into union-operator collusion, while use of union funds to buy coal properties did nothing to challenge the environmental and human chaos of the area. This late phase of the UMW legacy, it would seem, has little that is positive to offer a labor movement beset by the problems of a shrinking industrial base, international competition, and declining employment.

The other Lewis legacy, however, could still inspire. The Lewis of the 1930s broke the rules. He violated ancient principles of craft autonomy and internal loyalty, shattering the house of labor. Although in the long run he functioned within the limits imposed by the history and character of American unionism, he nonetheless stretched those limits. He placed himself at the head of rebellious rank-and-file workers and boldly dramatized their grievances. Under Lewis's leadership, a labor movement seemingly moribund soon pulsed with new life and moved, if not as Lewis hoped and expected to the center of national power, at least far from the ghettos in which it had been constrained. These years, the years of the mid-1930s when he was nurturing the industrial union movement, were the years of Lewis's greatest glory and most positive contributions to American life. This moment in his life provides the American workers' movement with John L. Lewis's most heartening legacy.

It is easy to document the contradictions and controversies of his life. A comprehensive public record—along with the correspondence files, oral histories, and newspaper articles of two generations of labor leaders, journalists, and government officials—makes it no particular challenge to establish Lewis's public position on virtually every important labor, economic, and political issue through most of the first two-thirds of the century. The record of John L.

Lewis, business unionist par excellence, is clear: his ardent enthusiasm for free enterprise capitalism; his ready acknowledgment of the economic and technological realities of coal mining; his hostility toward socialists and other radicals; his pre-1933 defense of the status quo within the labor movement. It is no trick to document the career of the John L. Lewis who upheld and defended the conventional wisdom, both within the economy generally and within the labor movement.

Nor is documentation of Lewis's authoritarian behavior within the United Mine Workers difficult. Even before his rise to power, he aligned himself with the UMW leadership and defended it against rank-and-file dissidence; indeed, it was this identification with the upper echelon that earned for him the series of administrative appointments that put him, essentially without popular mandate, at the head of the UMW in 1920. Thenceforth, whether during periods of famine, as in the 1920s, or prosperity, as in the 1930s, he ruled the UMW with high-handed panache. He removed democratically elected officials. He closed the UMW *Journal* to dissent. He red-baited his opponents mercilessly, employed plug-ugly tactics on the convention floor, and systematically destroyed regional autonomy in the UMW. He eagerly sought contract language that had the effect of stifling rank-and-file activism and leached power away from the union's grass roots.

Moreover, even during his lifetime, the sad results of this authoritarianism became plain to see. He lived to witness ample evidence of the degeneration of the UMW, as its leadership's resort to collusion, fraud, and murder became public knowledge in the 1960s. Chroniclers of the union's dismal state pointed trenchantly to the Lewisian roots of these pathologies.

But if the record of Lewis the business unionist and autocrat is clear, so is that of Lewis the champion of industrial democracy. If his taste for wealth and power is an open book, so are his powerful and incisive warnings about the dangers to working people inhering in an all-encompassing national security state. If in the end he upheld corporate America, he also challenged it as few others have been able to do. His speeches and press conferences of the 1930s and 1940s stand out not merely as inspiring rhetoric but also as articulations of the demands and aspirations—and not merely the material demands and aspirations—of working people. Through the 1940s and into the 1950s, Lewis's bitter controversies with the federal government brought from him a powerful and telling critique of the powers claimed by public authorities in the modern state. The student of Lewis's life, by immersing himself in the labor leader's speeches and statements, can, in short, chart the career of one of the ablest defenders of traditional American union conservatism and at the same time one of the most pointed and perceptive challengers of the emerging modern capitalist state in the United States.

Ultimately, however, the biographer feels a need to bring these divergent themes into some sort of harmony, to trace them to a common seat within the man himself. But it is in this pursuit that one finds the record falters. Intensely private, Lewis left few personal letters or revealing documents. What few did survive his son, John, destroyed. He permitted virtually no one into his inner life. "My father can't have any friends," declared his daughter, Kathryn, in 1949. "No great man can have friends."[1] Product of a Victorian world, Lewis remained aloof even when, as in approaches to his grandchildren, he sought to cultivate intimacy. Few of his associates in the labor movement were ever invited to his home. He rarely committed anything beyond the most formal statement or tactical polemic to paper. He telephoned his wife, Myrta, daily, but, of course, nothing survives of their conversations. Several times in 1949 and 1950, during the final illness of his ninety-one-year-old mother, he drove through the night from bargaining sessions to be by her side. Seventy years old himself, he would arrive exhausted. Once he had to sleep on a cot in a hotel banquet hall, with the kitchen staff, unaware of the identity of the rumpled old man, continually interrupting his rest. Yet Lewis left virtually no record of his feelings about his mother. Nor, apart from a series of stock stories about youthful heroics and physical prowess, did he ever speak or write frankly about his early life.

Thus, the place where the contradictions of Lewis's public career might be reconciled, or even merely understood, remains beyond reach. This inability to find the root is, of course, disturbing. At the same time, however, it is not fatal to an effort to bring Lewis's life to the attention of modern readers. For Lewis had no unified theory, no consciously articulated creed by which he sought to reconcile opposites or explain an inexplicable world. A man largely lacking in speculative taste, a man whose reading was largely confined to daily newspapers, trade union documents, escapist and light historical books, Lewis asked only to be judged on the public record. "Questions as to motive," he once told a journalist, "will be purely speculative. . . . the pursuit of motives is the most elusive task in all the world."[2] On several occasions, reported long-term associate and critic John Brophy, Lewis would lapse into musings about his own behavior, wondering if even he could fathom his reasons for taking a particular course of action. In short, since Lewis articulated no integrated public vision, since he, by his own evidence, responded to opportunity, and, especially, since he rarely sought to amplify or explain, we are then justified in taking the story as it is given. The facts, pace Lewis, do not and cannot speak for themselves. But in Lewis's case, they provide ample material for examining a long and eventful life, a life rare in its duration and centrality over sixty years of convulsive national history. If we cannot ultimately trace the wellspring of Lewis's public behavior, we can at least bring his rich public life and the still-timely concerns around which it centered to the attention of a rising generation, born long after the labor wars of the Lewis years had twitched to an end.

1

BEGINNINGS

In 1920, at age thirty-nine, John L. Lewis gained the presidency of the United Mine Workers of America (UMW). He achieved this office not through his direct leadership of rank-and-file miners but through his services to the established elites of the UMW and the American Federation of Labor (AFL). His first two decades, spent in the mining region of south-central Iowa, provided him with the rudiments of an education, a fierce determination to rise in the world, and an intense sense of family loyalty. Five years spent working in mines and construction sites throughout the American West helped round out his practical education and left a permanent impression of the country's vast and self-contained abundance. Returning to Iowa in 1906, he strove to carve out a niche for himself among the petit bourgeoisie of Lucas, a small mining town. In 1907 he married the schoolteacher daughter of a local doctor. In that same year, he offered himself as candidate for mayor and ventured into a business partnership. Defeat at the polls and financial failure, however, stifled his political and entrepreneurial ambitions. In 1908, he, along with his entire family, moved from the marginal mines of Iowa to the booming central Illinois coal fields, settling in the thriving immigrant community of Panama.

In Illinois, Lewis, backed by his fiercely loyal father and brothers, rose quickly. Appointment in 1911 as a national representative for the

AFL provided a rich opportunity for a man who in his youth had exhibited little indication of pursuing a career in the labor movement. Expansion of the UMW during World War I provided stepping-stones for Lewis's rapid ascent. Appointment as the union's vice president in 1917 stemmed from his knowledge of the UMW hierarchy and his services to union influentials as much as from his demonstration of ability in the jobs he had held. He assumed the presidency in 1920 on the resignation of the incumbent and gained election in his own right later that year. In this meteoric rise, Lewis exhibited shrewd intelligence, ruthlessness in quest of his goals, and astute cultivation of the patronage of his superiors.

Lewis achieved power at what seemed a particularly auspicious time in the history of the labor movement. During World War I, both the AFL and the UMW expanded rapidly. The nations's 750,000 coal miners, most of whom still practiced highly skilled traditional methods of digging coal, had a reputation for militancy that put them in the vanguard of an expanded labor movement. Wartime developments permitted the UMW to make impressive inroads into organizing the hitherto nonunion fields of the southern Appalachians. Though personal rivalries, regional differences, and ideological controversies continued to affect the UMW as they had done ever since its founding in 1890, the union that Lewis took command of seemed poised to transcend its heritage of internecine conflict and to solidify its leadership in a newly confident and successful AFL.

From Lucas to Panama

As a boy John Llewellyn Lewis knew both advantage and struggle. Born on Lincoln's birthday, 1880, he was the eldest in a family that eventually came to include four brothers and one sister. Neither his birthplace, Cleveland, Iowa, nor the other small coal-mining towns in which he spent much of his youth offered much in the way of diversion or variety. His father dug coal, hired out to farmers, and served a stint as a policeman. His mother, barely into her twenties when John was born, spent her young womanhood in the endless round of cooking, cleaning, sewing, and tending youngsters that was the lot of a coal miner's wife. Home was usually a company-owned house, cheaply hammered together of raw lumber and covered with tarpaper. Two bedrooms, an all-purpose kitchen, and an outdoor privy provided for the growing family. The towns in which Thomas and Louisa Watkins Lewis reared their children—Cedar Mines, Oswalt, Cleveland—were little more than appendages of the harsh coal camps that speckled south-central Iowa in the 1880s and 1890s. With Thomas Lewis's work irregular and with the family dependent entirely on the earnings that his labor and that of his young sons provided, life was hard and insecure.

At the same time, young John enjoyed some important advantages. A healthy, strapping lad, he quickly grew tall and handsome. Despite the family's wanderings, it remained intact, and if Thomas Lewis had to relocate frequently to find work, he did not fall victim to the injuries and illnesses that maimed and sickened so many coal miners. Although the poor mining towns offered little in the way of intellectual stimulation or community activity, it was John's good fortune that as he entered his teen years, Thomas Lewis left the mines and took the family to the bustling state capital, Des Moines. There Thomas joined the police force, and for four years the Lewises were urbanites, free at least temporarily from the nomadic life of the coal miner. Young John attended high school, eventually completing three and a half years of the course, an impressive achievement for a working-class lad in the 1890s. Thus, when the family moved back to its starting point, Lucas County, John brought with him a wider experience and a broader education, both formal and practical, than was usual for a coal miner's son.

The young man quickly became something of a leader upon his return to his birthplace. Like his father and younger brothers, he worked in the mines. In 1901 he became a charter member and secretary of the new local of the United Mine Workers. At the opera house, he performed in talent shows and doubled as its manager, bringing in traveling companies and exhibits. In all, observe his biographers, by the time he reached his majority, "he seemed a young man of many talents and interests, a typical small-town striver, yet a person whose future promised no spectacular accomplishments."[1]

Throughout his youth, John Lewis had occasion to observe the important role politics, religion, and ethnic and fraternal matters played in the lives of his fellow Iowans—to observe, that is, but never really to participate. Both the Lewises and the Watkinses had migrated from Wales after the American Civil War. His grandparents spoke Welsh, and especially in his earliest years, John was exposed to the highly distinctive and vibrant culture the Welsh clung to in America. Yet his own family was too frequently on the move, too often among the non-

Welsh, perhaps too absorbed in the struggle for survival for the powerful Welsh culture ever to seize his imagination.

Late nineteenth-century Iowa bubbled with political rivalries. Democrats, Republicans, Prohibitionists, and agrarian reformers competed for votes. Political campaigns provided comradeship, community, and diversion. Voter turnouts regularly surpassed the 80 percent mark, and for many youngsters, politics became an absorbing interest. Not so, however, for the transient Lewis boys. In the coal towns, the companies simply ran things, with the merest nod to democratic participation. The fierce partisan loyalties characteristic of late nineteenth-century America seem not to have captured the Lewises. Public issues, beyond the narrow confines of the mine or village, had little part in the family agenda.

Religion may have touched young John more forcefully. Although not a churchgoer himself, he had difficulty avoiding the implications of his mother's faith. For Ann Louisa Watkins Lewis belonged to the Church of Latter-day Saints (Reorganized). Amid a militantly Baptist and Methodist Welsh population, Louisa's allegiance stood out. It may have created problems on the school yard and streets of Des Moines for John and his brothers. Yet Louisa seems not to have pressured the children to follow her path, except, perhaps, in the matter of observing the Mormons' stringent rule against alcohol and their firm disapproval of sexual adventure. Sweet-tempered and loving, Louisa may have exerted a firmer influence upon her eldest son through her example than she could have through insistence on formal observances. In any event, though John rarely went to church, he never lost his sense of reserve when it came to women and never succumbed to the temptations of drink that lured many a lonely labor organizer.

Despite his membership in the Lucas miners' local, young John did not grow up in a household in which union affairs figured prominently. It is true that labor unrest may have forced Thomas Lewis's decision in 1882 to leave the Cleveland-Lucas area. In later years, John L. Lewis's account of the family's departure featured a leadership role for his father in a strike at the Whitebreast mine and a resultant blacklisting. There is, however, no independent evidence for this episode, and it is entirely likely that his departure had more to do with a rebellion of Whitebreast Welsh miners against the company's employment of blacks. Thomas Lewis's subsequent relocations never featured active involvement in the local unions he no doubt joined in the well-organized soft coalfields of the Des Moines area in the 1880s and early 1890s.

This largely apolitical upbringing contrasts sharply with the youths of John L. Lewis's subsequent associates and rivals in the American labor movement. The boyhoods of many of the eventual leaders were steeped in labor activism. George Meany, president of the American Federation of Labor and the AFL-CIO in the 1950s and 1960s, was born into a union household in the Bronx. From his earliest days, the family home served as a gathering place for plumbers and union officers who looked to his father, Michael Meany, for leadership. George's earliest memories were of talk of the "or-gan-i-za-tion," the Bronx plumbers' local, and of Irish Democratic politics. Unionism and politics of a more dissident character permeated the household of Walter Reuther, Lewis's antagonist in the Congress of Industrial Organizations (CIO). An Old World radical, Valentine Reuther raised his sons on a diet of socialism and unionism. Young George Meany remained rooted in the Bronx while Reuther left Wheeling for Detroit, but throughout their lives both carried with them the legends and martyrology of labor's struggles.

But if John Lewis lacked this intense laborite upbringing, he did not lack objects of attachment. The years of wandering and the demands of the family economy bred a fierce familial loyalty. Father and sons worked together in the mines. John as the eldest defended the younger boys in the street brawls that broke out in their Des Moines neighborhood. He grew especially close to his brothers Alma Dennie and George. His was the intense loyalty of common experience and common struggle, the product of a family environment in which the claims of church, community, and even union were abstract and insubstantial in contrast to the claims of blood.

Powerful family ties fed equally powerful personal ambitions. Young John Lewis left no youthful record of his dreams and aspirations, but the testimony of his actions speaks eloquently. In 1901, now twenty-one years old, he struck out for the American West. Blessed with a strong back and a rugged constitution, he readily found work, certainly in coal and hard rock mines, perhaps also on construction crews. Did he regularly write his family to report on his adventures? If so, no correspondence survives. Did he once single-handedly slay a killer mule? Did his wanderings take him to Hanna, Wyoming, in 1903 to help dig out the remains of 230 miners killed in a ghastly mining disaster? If so, we have only later, rather imprecise, recollections, buttressed by an even fuzzier folk memory among UMW functionaries, to rely on. Did he always plan to return to Iowa? Nothing in the contemporary record speaks of plans and intentions. Late in 1905, however, nearing his twenty-sixth birthday, he did in fact come back and showed every intention of making his life in Lucas.

There he displayed a strong, if unformed, ambition to rise above his coal-mining origins. He took up amateur theatricals again and for a time went back into the mines. Indeed, he later boasted that his workmates chose him as their delegate to the 1906 UMW convention. He joined the Masons, a bastion of Lucas's tiny middle class, and even gained election to a minor post. In 1907, he ran unsuccessfully for mayor of the town. He also entered into a partnership to establish a feed and grain distributorship, a venture that quickly fell victim to the severe depression of that year and deadbeat customers. Clearly, Lewis was struggling to move out of the mines and to take a place among the town's bourgeoisie, but failure and, no doubt, frustration dogged every effort.

Despite these setbacks, 1907 was an auspicious year. On 5 June he married Myrta Edith Bell, daughter of a local doctor, John C. Bell. Also aged twenty-seven at the time of the wedding, Myrta Bell Lewis brought a prestigious lineage and impressive educational credentials to the match with the young entrepreneur. The family traced its roots to colonial America. Myrta, the eldest of seven children, had not only completed high school but had attended summer sessions at Drake University, thus qualifying for public school teaching. Demure and soft-spoken, Myrta had been on the verge of spinsterhood, a prospect that may have made John, the coal miner's son without an established calling, more atttactive a mate than he might otherwise have been. The Lewis legend of later years cast Myrta in the role of single-handed tamer and educator of an inarticulate miner; through her, ran the story, he gained knowledge of Shakespeare and the classics, thus enabling him eventually to find the language with which to become a remarkable public speaker. His authoritative biographers are more skeptical, crediting Myrta with providing a stable and nurturing home life but awarding *Bartlett's Familiar Quotations* the credit for the ostentatious literary references that came to characterize the public utterances of Lewis, whose reading tastes rarely went beyond western adventures and popular historical works.

Marriage was followed by another decisive move. In the spring of 1908, Lewis and his new wife left Lucas County for good, taking the Chicago, Burlington, and Quincy Railroad two hundred miles eastward to settle in the new mining town of Panama, Illinois. Later that summer, Thomas Lewis and his entire family followed. Within weeks, all the Lewis men had found work in the Sandy Shoal mine, one of the largest and most mechanized in Illinois, a vastly more important coal-producing state than John's native Iowa.

The move to Illinois was decisive. There Lewis's two enduring attributes—his family loyalty and his powerful ambition—fused to launch his career in the labor movement. In Iowa, his plans had unraveled, but in Illinois, he rose rapidly—almost ruthlessly—to positions of trust, influence, and power. No sooner had the Lewis clan completed its move in the summer of 1908 than they began to dominate UMW Local 1475 in the raw mining town thirty-five miles south of Springfield. In 1909, John was elected president of the local, while younger brother Thomas became a city police magistrate. Perhaps because the mine and the town were new, perhaps because the English-speaking Lewises had an advantage in the largely Italian community, or perhaps because the family was experienced and cohesive, they soon achieved status and power beyond anything imaginable in Iowa.

Indeed the Sandy Shoal mine and Local 1475 provided a stronghold for John in the turbulent world of Illinois mining and UMW affairs. One of the nation's leading coal-producing states, Illinois employed ninety thousand coal diggers. The Sandy Shoal mine stood thirty-first among the state's two thousand mines in terms of tonnage produced. Only a handful of local unions in the state counted more members than Local 1475. Thus as John ventured into the hectic and often sordid world of UMW politics, he had a firm foundation on which to build a career.

The Miner and His Life

At the time Lewis gained his first substantial union post, over 710,000 men toiled in the nation's coal mines. In 1910, a record year, they dug 417 million tons of soft coal (bituminous) and 85 million tons of anthracite, or hard coal. Their efforts supplied 75 percent of the nation's energy. The steel mills of Gary and Pittsburgh, the growing automobile factories of Detroit, and the nation's offices, schools, hospitals, and railroads drew their sustenance from the magnificent coalfields that lay in some thirty of the states.

The men who dug the coal were unique. They and their families typically lived in isolated valleys and crude coal camps remote from the cities. Poverty was chronic. Housing often consisted of hastily assembled pine-and-tar-paper shacks. Indoor toilets were rare, paved streets, running water, and electricity luxuries. In a book that he published shortly after he became UMW president, Lewis drew upon his personal knowledge of the miners' hardships. He invited his readers to observe the rough coal towns of western Pennsylvania and to peer back into the river valleys of West Virginia and Kentucky as the sleek passenger trains carried them through the gleaming plenty of modern America. The miners' "shanties lean over as if intoxicated by the smoke and fumes of nearby mills. . . . They cluster higgledly-piggledy in some gulch, along the banks of a polluted little stream, or squat on a pile of slate."[2]

Many factors conspired to perpetuate this poverty. The boom-and-bust cycle of coal production drew too many into the fields. Once engaged in coal mining, men found it difficult to leave. Company housing and company stores encouraged indebtedness. Mining, though a dangerous and demanding calling, provided few skills useful in modern industrial or clerical employment. The mining areas' very isolation bred feelings of solidarity and mutual support, but the coal towns lacked the schools and opportunities to prepare mining people for the outside world. Daily wage rates might be adequate, but even in good years regular employment escaped most miners. In 1910, for example, despite booming coal markets, miners averaged only 217 days of work out of a possible 308. In slack 1914, they worked only 195. In the newly opening fields in the South, Lewis declared, powerful mining interests had created "scattered feudal states exercising dominion that no private power should have over the life of citizens." Throughout the coalfields, Lewis asserted, miners suffered from "loneliness and [a] sense of helpless subjugation."[3]

Yet coal miners were not merely poor and victimized. In their impressive skills and their long record of militant unionism they exhibited pride and tenacity. About 70 percent of the mine workers actually dug coal. The rest served as auxiliary workers, performing hauling, maintenance, construction, and custodial tasks. These workers, called day men or company men, were paid on a daily wage basis. Most miners, on the other hand, were compensated on a tonnage basis. That is, their earnings depended on the amount of coal they dug.

Actual mining was typically carried out beneath the earth's surface in "rooms" extending from tunnels perpendicular to the vertical shaft that provided entrance to and egress from the mine. Each miner was assigned a room, its earthen roof supported by pillars of unmined coal and wooden timbers muscled into place by the miner himself. The miner chopped away the lowest three or four feet of the room's wall (or "face") to a depth of several feet. To do this, he often had to lie on his side and swing his pick horizontally, though increasingly advanced enterprises such as Panama's Sandy Shoal mine relied on teams of specialized cutters employing power-driven machines to perform this task. Once this "undermining" was completed, the miner used a long steel auger to drill holes for explosive charges to be placed in the face above the cut. He then packed in the powder, affixed the fuse, and, retreating to a safe area, lit the charge. The resulting explosion loosened the coal, which the miner then loaded (after separating out the rock and other refuse) onto tram cars mounted on tracks extending into the room from a main line, and in turn leading to a hoist that lifted it to the surface.

This was hard and dangerous work. Well into the twentieth century, the annual death toll from fires, cave-ins, explosions, and other accidents averaged 1,600. An additional 12,500 were maimed each year, many crippled for life. Between 1890 and 1917, 26,434 miners were killed, 3,242 of them in 1907 alone. Spectacular explosions, such as those in Hanna, Wyoming, in 1903 and Monongah, West Virginia, in 1907 killed hundreds of miners at one time. In the fall of 1909, a disaster at Cherry, Illinois, wiped out virtually the whole adult male population of the town. On the whole, however, it was the small-scale cave-ins, burying a miner and his helper or trapping a few miners and tram men in an ill-timbered room, that took the majority of the lives. Peter Urban, the sole survivor of the Monongah tragedy which claimed 361 lives, died in a cave-in in the same mine nineteen years later. The refrain of one of the many songs that sprang from the rich oral culture of the mining camps contained a grim reality: "Watch the rocks, they're falling daily. / Careless miners always fail."

Whatever his dangers and hardships, the coal miner enjoyed great autonomy. He punched no time clock and set his own pace of work. Since his income depended on his own efforts, as measured by the tonnage he produced, he resisted close supervision. Traditionally, miners ignored rules stipulating working hours, often leaving the mine when they had dug the quota they had set. The dozens of rooms into which even a moderately sized mine was normally divided made supervision hard. Even day workers often toiled in remote sites, laying tracks, reloading cars, shoring up timbers, and repairing machinery. Nominally more subject to scrutiny than was the miner himself, they nonetheless shared his sense of independence and autonomy.

9

Although the coal miner derived most of his income from the coal he produced, he did perform auxiliary tasks for which the mine operator compensated him directly. Track laying, timbering, gaining access to unusually difficult veins, salvaging coal from collapsed rooms—these tasks were known collectively as "dead work," for which the miner negotiated compensation with the mine boss. The miner and the supervisor dickered over payment for each episode of dead work. Observed Lewis, "Coal mining . . . is vastly different from any manufacturing or transportation activity . . . ; it simply cannot be standardized because nature has refused to standardize rocks, slate, coal or men."[4]

If a union miner found the compensation offered by the mine boss unsatisfactory, he called upon his local's "pit committee," a body of fellow miners elected to negotiate with management in behalf of individual miners. A system of appeals culminated in arbitration of disputes through UMW district officials and regional operators' representatives. Bargaining was collective in its general character and it partook as well of individual negotiations. In Lewis's words, it was "impossible to negotiate a district or sub-district contract . . . [to] serve as a yardstick . . . for all forms of work performed by the coal miner."[5] The omnipresent pit committee, the individual miner's jealous defender, asserted the workers' power at the point of production and helped preserve the "miner's freedom," an almost preindustrial sense of independence and autonomy.

Freedom from close supervision, possession of unique skills and experience, and the sense of common danger helped sustain solidarity and pride among mine workers. They put in a lot of time waiting—waiting for the hoist to take them into the shaft; waiting for the "man trip" to bring them to their individual rooms; waiting for tram cars to appear for loading. They lounged near the "gob pile," where refuse, rock, slate, and debris were dumped, forever discussing the conditions of the mine, the incessant dead work negotiations, and the secrets of the trade. "It's the *gob pile oration*," declared one union activist, "that makes the miners less submissive than other workers." Should a boss bawl out one worker, "the men get together on the piles of slate . . . and talk it over." Veterans took new hands in tow. An anthracite miner explained the system to an academic observer. Whenever the mine boss appeared in his room, he told his helper " 'Come here, Frank. . . . Here's the boss. Don't work. Always sit down when the boss is around.' "[6]

The Union

These, then, were the men who formed the rank-and-file of the United Mine Workers of America. The miners' relatively independent status nurtured traditions of democratic and autonomous local unionism. The election of the pit committee and of the checkweighmen—miners' representatives charged with ensuring honest measurement of tonnage—affected every miner. Local unions often reflected the solidarity and rough-and-tumble democracy of the miners' communities and working lives. They played a significant role in the everyday lives of mine workers, for it was through the local union that the miner gained the strength to bargain over dead work and could feel assurance that his output was being fairly weighed and credited to him. "Union miners, stand together," counseled a mine workers' anthem. "Heed no operator's tale / Keep your hand upon the dollar / And your eye upon the scale."

Vigorous local unionism in turn encouraged autonomy and independence among the various districts into which the UMW was divided. Indeed, the United Mine Workers' birth in 1890 resulted from the decision of a number of regional mine workers' organizations to join together to create a national organization. By 1920, the UMW was divided into some thirty districts, three of which contained Pennsylvania's 150,000 anthracite miners. The twenty-odd bituminous districts were diverse, extending as they did from the long-established fields of Illinois, Indiana, and Ohio southward into Virginia, Maryland, West Virginia, Kentucky, Tennessee, and Alabama, and westward into Iowa, Colorado, New Mexico, and Washington State. In addition, there were two Canadian districts, representing soft coal miners in Alberta and Cape Breton Island.[7] Every district—and the subdistricts into which they were in turn divided—reflected the unique characteristics of each mining area. Veins of coal were richer and purer, for example, in southern West Virginia than in the older mines of Ohio's Hocking Valley. Western Pennsylvania fields produced for a relatively small handful of large-scale industrial and utility consumers, while Indiana and Illinois coal found more diverse markets. Geological formations dictated the size of the pieces of coal coming from the mines, which in turn dictated the industrial, commercial, or domestic purposes to which the coal would be put. Payment scales depended heavily on local conditions, so that the international union could at best hope to establish

11

uniform rates of pay only for the 30 percent or so of mine workers who were not paid on a tonnage basis. Thus, observed Lewis, "the very great degree of local self-government and regional autonomy" of the UMW flowed directly from "the physical, geographical, and marketing differences of the coal fields."[8]

Throughout its history, the UMW had struggled to accommodate both the imperatives of local and district autonomy, on the one hand, and the need for broader-scale collective bargaining, on the other. The logic of soft coal mining, with its thousands of coal operators producing in a bewildering array of conditions and selling to diverse markets, drove decision making down to its most basic level—hence the importance of the daily on-site negotiations between miners and pit bosses over compensation for dead work. This same logic, however, impelled operators to attempt to cut costs through paying the lowest wages and tonnage rates possible. With operator competing against operator for markets, in effect a miner in one mine competed against his counterpart in another mine. Since wages comprised about 70 percent of the cost of producing coal, miners, for all their autonomy and pride, continually faced the threat of wage and tonnage rate slashes. Especially was this true because from the late nineteenth century onward overall economic growth drew more and more men into mining, while the periodic depressions quickly translated into gluts of both coal and miners. During downturns, soft coal operators chopped wages, and in boom times new operators and mine workers flocked to the coalfields. Miners found it hard to leave the pits. The intermittency of employment, the difficulty of transferring skills gained in mining to other occupations, and chronic indebtedness kept the men in and around the pits, even when widespread unemployment stalked the mining regions.

Since at least the 1880s, mine workers' unions had struggled to change all this. Early efforts to achieve broad regional agreements between the UMW's predecessor unions and a combination of bituminous operators in the so-called Central Competitive Field (Illinois, Indiana, Ohio, western Pennsylvania, and parts of northern West Virginia) collapsed in the 1880s. The UMW, nonetheless, continued to promote the adoption of formal labor agreements as a means of stabilizing the industry. In 1897, as the country began to emerge from the terrible depression of the 1890s, the UMW backed its program with a strike call in the midwestern soft coalfields, which then accounted for over 70 percent of bituminous production. Although fewer than ten thousand of the country's quarter-million soft coal miners belonged to the UMW, thousands

saw the walkout as an opportunity to halt the cycle of poverty and underemployment that victimized them. Response to the strike call in the
central fields was overwhelming. In 1898 operators representing most of
the tonnage in the Central Competitive Field (CCF) signed an agreement with the UMW, establishing standard day rates and providing for
tonnage rates that were negotiated on a district-by-district (or subdis-
trict) basis. Miners and operators alike hoped that this innovative
agreement would stabilize the industry, taking wages out of the competitive equation and discouraging fly-by-night entrepreneurs from starting
up operations. Employers agreed to collect union dues and turn them
over to the UMW, while the union pledged to use its disciplinary power
to enforce work rules and to discourage work stoppages.

In the hard coal mines of northeastern Pennsylvania, a different
set of factors prevailed. All of America's (and much of the world's) anthracite was mined in this 464-square-mile wedge of the Keystone
State. In contrast to the bituminous industry, which by 1910 had over
five thousand operators, a handful of railroad and mining combines
controlled virtually all of the hard coalfields. Yielding an astonishing
amount of thermal energy, hard coal was a magnificent fuel for domestic heating purposes, and it had significant industrial and commercial
uses as well. Still, in the twentieth century, anthracite faced increasingly stiff competition from soft coal and from fuel oil. Having crushed
early hard coal miners' unions in the 1870s, an oligopoly of anthracite
operators controlled the mining towns closely and fought the UMW's efforts to gain a foothold there.

The breakthrough for the union in the hard coalfields occurred as
a result of two impressive strikes in 1900 and 1902. Under the leadership of UMW president John Mitchell, miners and mine workers bridged
the sharp ethnic and national cleavages that characterized the social
and geographical world of the Pennsylvania hard coal–mining valleys to
challenge the railroad and mining combines. The long 1902 strike
aroused intense national interest. President Theodore Roosevelt intervened and the resulting settlement gained the mine workers a wage increase.

Pennsylvania mining interests, however, were less impressed than
their soft coal counterparts with the possibilities of using unionization
as a means of stabilization. They refused the UMW recognition and
sought to convince the southern and eastern European mine workers
that the UMW was an Anglo-Irish-dominated intrusion. Immigrant mine
workers did indeed have historic reason to feel resentful of the treat-

13

ment they had received at the hands of English-speaking coworkers, but the strikes of 1900 and 1902 established once and for all the virtues of mine worker solidarity. Mitchell soon became a folk hero in the hard coal region. "Me Johnny Mitchell Man," went a song attributed to the immigrant mine workers. "Whistle blow, me no go. Me Johnny Mitchell Man." Lacking the dues checkoff and contractually enforced union security, the UMW did have to struggle to maintain its membership in the hard coal region, but after the turn of the century there could be no doubt that it was solidly entrenched and that the 150,000 hard coal miners would be a bastion of UMW strength thenceforth.

For the first twenty years of its existence, the UMW had achieved an impressive, but still limited, success. Its grip on the CCF remained shaky, as new entrants into soft coal production there and in neighboring fields that were only partially organized continually threatened to destroy the regionwide bargaining agreement. A combination of continued employer obduracy and rank-and-file impatience with the union's unwillingness to contemplate another long strike made it vulnerable in the hard coalfields. Continuing tribulations in the realm of collective bargaining were reflected in the UMW's contentious internal politics, with international presidents continually under assault and with powerful district leaders defying the international's efforts to impose greater discipline and higher standards of contract compliance—the keys, international officials believed, to establishing the credibility needed to gain enduring regionwide agreements—on the independent-minded and sometimes parochial mine workers.

John L. Lewis's experiences as a miner and local union leader gave him perhaps an atypical perspective. Less provincial than most miners and more acquainted with modern mining methods by virtue of his stint in the large and mechanically progressive Sandy Shoal mine, Lewis was less wedded to traditional practices than many of his coworkers. He had scant sympathy with the unemployed or underemployed miner. Had he not roamed the West, living off his physical strength and ingenuity? "I have always found that if I could not make a living in one place," he told a convention of Illinois miners in 1909, "I could in another. . . . Many men do not hunt work if they can make a living without it," he warned delegates about to vote on a plan for providing unemployment benefits.[9] His, and his family's, activities in Panama departed from those prevailing in UMW local unions. Here was a large local, substantially mechanized, employing a high percentage of relatively unskilled Italian immigrants. Clearly, it was no bastion of the miner's freedom, nor did it conform to the model of gob pile democracy common to older mines. The able Lewis men quickly dominated its affairs. Indeed, both his father and his brother Dennie eventually came to view the local's treasury as interchangeable with their own finances, leading to charges of financial peculation. Thus, as the young man from Iowa began to ascend the UMW ladder, he had seemingly little in common with the traditional miner and every reason to find the broader—and inevitably more hierarchical—perspective of the UMW's international leaders particularly congenial.

To the Top

It took only a decade for the obscure young miner to rise to the presidency of the nation's largest labor union. His rapid ascent revealed that a man of vigor, intelligence, and opportunistic instincts had emerged from the Iowa boy he had been. Certain of his attributes, notably his keen intelligence, his silver tongue, and his ability to juggle loyalty and ruthlessness, made him a favorite of the men in the labor movement who dispensed patronage and controlled opportunities. Cultivation of John Walker, president of UMW District 12 (Illinois), led to Lewis's appointment late in 1909 as a lobbyist at the state capital in Springfield. The next year, Lewis turned on Walker and supported his successful rival, John White, for the UMW presidency, earning for himself a key role at the union's convention in 1911. There the imposing young miner spoke up for White and his running mates against insurgent charges of election fraud. Moreover, his stout defense of AFL president Samuel Gompers, under assault from black coal miners who accused him of racism, brought him to the attention of the labor movement's most powerful figure. Thus, it was no surprise that White and other UMW leaders warmly recommended him to Gompers when a position on the AFL organizing staff opened in the fall, and even less of one when Lewis eagerly snapped it up. Meanwhile, brothers Thomas and Dennie tightened the family's control of Local 1475.

The labor movement of the 1910s in which Lewis so surely made his way seethed with activity. The American Federation of Labor, founded in 1886, boasted 2 million members in 1913, and with the coming to power of the Democratic administration of Woodrow Wilson it began for the first time to exert influence in the national political and legislative arenas. The outbreak of war in Europe and the increased

15

tempo of industrial production—first to feed the Continental war machines and then to build America's military power—stoked rapid expansion. Unemployment dried up and newly confident workers rebelled against low wages, harsh conditions, and arbitrary managerial practices. Between 1913 and 1919, AFL membership swelled to 3.2 million. And no union benefited more from the wartime prosperity than did Lewis's UMW, which expanded from 250,000 to half a million members in the same six years.

But the teens were not merely years of growth and achievement. The decade was one of the most turbulent in the bloody annals of American industrial conflict. Although some employers, enticed with lucrative military contracts, acceded to their employees' demand for organization, many resisted fiercely. In the summer of 1914 civil war raged through southeastern Colorado, as powerful mining interests, aided by the Colorado National Guard, crushed UMW hopes, gunning down miners, their wives, and children at the strikers' tent colony in Ludlow. In the great mass production industries such as automobiles, rubber, and steel, efforts to organize led to savage reprisals and ended repeatedly in failure. During the war itself, great strike waves rumbled through the heavy industry and munitions sectors, as wartime inflation and relentless production schedules propelled workers into confrontation with employers and, sometimes, U.S. Army troops.

Laborite radicalism peaked during these years as well. In 1912, the Socialist party mounted its most successful campaign, gaining almost 900,000 votes for its presidential candidate, Eugene V. Debs, and electing scores of municipal officials. In this decade, voters sent two Socialist congressmen to Washington. Moreover, through most of the decade, unions with strong socialist affiliations or influence represented about 35 percent of the AFL's membership. In response to the economic system's gross inequalities of income, chronic industrial conflict, and increasingly severe cycles of prosperity and depression, radical ideologies, some vastly more revolutionary than the program of the Socialist party, claimed wide support. It was in the teens, for example, that the Industrial Workers of the World (IWW), a revolutionary mass union movement that rejected the cautious policies of the AFL and vowed to "build a new world from the ashes of the old," launched its bold, and occasionally successful, campaigns to organize harvest hands, hard rock miners, longshoremen, timber workers, and auto, rubber, steel, and textile workers.

On the shop floors, in the mines and mills, and at the picket lines and voting places, conflict rocked the nation. New production methods pitted production-obsessed employers against proud skilled workers. Masses of immigrants and northward-migrating blacks formed a complex kaleidoscope of industrial demography, at times confronting each other as strikebreakers and scabs, but, though more rarely, sometimes putting aside racial and national rivalries in the heat of industrial conflict. As the war ended and strikes swept through the economy in 1919, American society seemed fractured, some feared beyond repair. Thus warned William Jennings Bryan, so bitter and violent was the industrial conflict, it threatened to become "a war of extermination."[10]

For the mine workers' union, the 1910s were years of growth and power. True, the defeat in Colorado rankled. Still, the union expanded from its previous core—the coalfields of the Middle West and the anthracite mines of Pennsylvania—to previously unorganized districts in West Virginia, Kentucky, Tennessee, and elsewhere in the South and West. World demand for American coal soared, and employers who in the past had fought the union without quarter now signed contracts. Eager for industrial peace during wartime, officials in the Wilson administration cultivated UMW officers and often encouraged operators to accept unionization.

If, however, the UMW's relations with most employers were relatively peaceful (always excepting the bloody episode in Colorado), its internal affairs roiled with conflict. Powerful district leaders jockeyed endlessly for the union's presidency. Its election campaigns featured fist fights, espionage, smear tactics, and charges and countercharges of duplicity and sellout. Vocal rank-and-file miners, often with the backing of outspoken and ambitious district officers, lashed out repeatedly at the international leadership.

Lewis's appointment in 1911 as an AFL organizer provided the ambitious young man with ideal opportunities to expand his knowledge and broaden his contacts. Besides, the pay was good, for an organizer earned at least five dollars per day and enjoyed a substantial expense account. Moreover, the work was steady, unlike employment in the coal mines. Thus, for six years John served Samuel Gompers and the AFL, crisscrossing the eastern three-fourths of the country, spending most of his time on the road, and serving in the trenches in this hectic decade.

Actually, being an organizer did not always entail literally attempting to organize workers into unions. Lewis, did, of course, perform this work. He logged time in Akron, Ohio, in 1913 assisting striking rubber workers, and 1915 found him in western Pennsylvania, seeking fruitlessly to bring steel and electrical workers into the organization. He saw at first hand the primitive living and working conditions, the ethnic rivalries that often divided workers from one another, the fear that employers' reprisals created among union-minded workers, and the limitations of the AFL's poorly funded and decentralized organizing campaigns when confronted with powerful and determined employers. Though he gained a broad experience of industrial America and visited hundreds of towns, mills, and factories, he recorded no great organizing success.

But organizers had other tasks, and at these the young union functionary excelled. He routinely visited mining towns and UMW locals, getting to know the influentials and building his reputation in his own international union. He did political work, lobbying for the passage of a progressive state constitution in New Mexico and stumping throughout the Middle West for Woodrow Wilson in 1912. He did legwork for Gompers, making discreet inquiries in their hometowns about federal judicial prospects. He accompanied Gompers on a speaking tour through Illinois and Indiana in 1916, introducing the AFL chieftain to his audiences and gaining from this proximity to power.

The inner world of labor in this period was self-referential. That is, it had its own pecking order and power structure, its own rituals of deference and authority. The UMW, as the AFL's largest affiliate, naturally merited the careful scrutiny of the canny Gompers, who had not remained at the AFL's head for thirty years without intimate knowledge of what was going on behind the scenes in the various unions that composed the Federation. Thus, it was natural that among Lewis's most important duties would be serving as Gompers's eyes and ears in UMW circles. Which officers liked the bottle too much? Who owed poker debts to whom? How would the large locals and powerful district leaders behave at the forthcoming convention? Gompers thrived on such information, relying on his vast experience to sort out the gossip from the hard news, and Lewis fed him a steady diet of both.

While working for the AFL, Lewis did not neglect his UMW roots. In 1915, he campaigned actively in behalf of his patron, President John White, who was seeking reelection. Indeed, the young organizer earned White's gratitude—and the enmity of insurgent forces—by forging a series of incriminating telegrams, written by Lewis but "signed" by

White's opponent and Lewis's erstwhile patron, John Walker. This performance earned Lewis a key role at the UMW national convention early in 1916. Chairing the resolutions committee and presiding over important floor debates, he impressed even his critics with his knowledge of parliamentary procedure and his harsh tongue-lashings of opponents. He spoke as a loyalist, deflecting the complaints of black miners about locals that practiced segregation, defending White and the incumbent secretary-treasurer William Green against criticism, and clashing repeatedly with insurgents irate over the international union's questionable expenditures and accounting procedures.

The convention in turn led to other opportunities. Lewis was appointed to a key Pennsylvania district negotiating committee. Late in 1916, he ran for one of the UMW delegate slots for representation at the 1917 AFL convention, losing in his first effort at international union office but gaining the encouraging total of 49,000 votes. The biggest plum, however, came in 1917 when the grateful White named Lewis the UMW's statistician, a key office in the development of the organization's collective bargaining posture. In the summer of the same year, White also appointed Lewis business manager of the UMW *Journal*, giving him a golden opportunity to keep his name constantly before the 350,000 union members who received the paper.

Now with almost incredible speed, Lewis shot to the top of the UMW. The outbreak of war in April 1917 injected the union into endless rounds of negotiations not only with coal operators but with government officials as well. Lewis participated in some of these in the summer and fall of 1917, earning his spurs as a forceful and well-informed negotiator. In October, federal officials appointed UMW president White as a member of the newly created Federal Fuel Board and as an adviser to the government's fuel administrator. White resigned the union presidency, which immediately devolved upon international vice president Frank Hayes. Who would succeed Hayes? With the unanimous approval of the union's executive board, the new president tapped Lewis, the able young statistician and negotiator. On 15 October, with his appointment to the UMW's second spot assured, Lewis scribbled in his travel diary, "Our ship made port today."[11]

Nor did he have to contemplate a lengthy apprenticeship in the vice presidency. The popular Hayes, as was well known, suffered from a variety of physical ailments and had begun to drink heavily. Lewis, who until now had scrambled up the UMW ladder through preference and appointment, ran for election to a full term in 1918, linking his candidacy with that of Hayes, and was elected overwhelmingly. By 1919 Hayes's drinking had intensified and he sank into despair and lethargy. In effect, from March of 1919 onward, Lewis ran the union. On 1 January 1920, Hayes resigned, leaving Lewis officially in charge.

How had Lewis managed to achieve so much so soon? Undoubtedly, native ability counted for much. He was intelligent, articulate, and hardworking. Aside from the labor organizer's inevitable poker playing, he had no interests outside his family and the union. He attached himself and made himself useful—even indispensable—to White, Gompers, and eventually Hayes. The route he followed to the presidency—a series of appointed offices in both the AFL and the UMW—while lacking in democratic mandate, protected him from the harsh internecine warfare of the UMW and gave him access to miners all over the country. While district presidents such as John Walker of Illinois, Alex Howat of Kansas, and Robert Harlin of Washington bruised each other in head-to-head competition for national repute and office, Lewis worked his way through the bureaucracy, using his positions as statistician, negotiator, and *Journal* manager to promote himself everywhere.

Lewis's sudden rise aroused controversy. Critics charged that poker debts had led him to intimate association with a shadowy Pennsylvania coal operator, Al Hamilton. Indeed, even before the election of Hayes and Lewis in December 1918, John Walker predicted that Hamilton, his associate K. C. Adams, and Lewis would "depose"[12] Hayes, gaining the presidency for Lewis, a scenario compatible with what eventually happened. Since Lewis had his close UMW associate Philip Murray appointed as his vice-presidential replacement, and since Murray in turn was also an intimate of the questionable coal operator, Walker's denunciation seemed more than just the ranting of a victimized union politico. Whether Lewis in fact had engineered his actual rise to the presidency through such cynical maneuvering, a vocal minority of UMW insurgents and opponents surely believed that he had. But two additional facts are clear as well: in the cruel and shoddy world of UMW politics, whatever the facts of the particular case, Lewis had quickly become a master; and whatever the circumstances of the thirty-nine-year-old Lewis's ascension to the presidency, his combination of ruthlessness, precocious savvy, and sheer ability would make him difficult indeed to dislodge.

Entrenched officers, never secure in the chaotic democracy of the UMW, shamelessly used union funds, connections with employers, and control of the union press to manipulate and stifle opposition. In this dog-eat-dog world, friendships forged in the underground dangers of mining crumbled in the brutal test of political rivalry. Loyalty was as precious as it was rare. This was the world into which John L. Lewis had plunged and in which he flourished.

In 1920, Lewis was elected to the presidency in his own right. The young man from Iowa, a failed businessman and amateur thespian, had in little more than a decade gained control of the nation's largest and seemingly most powerful labor union. He had beaten the hard-boiled politicos of the UMW at their own game. Some critics worried that he had built his career on bureaucratic string-pulling rather than on popular choice by working miners. Others searched the Lewis record for evidence of any distinctive vision of the broad purposes of the labor movement that the new leader might articulate. But they searched in vain. The road to the top had been a hard scramble, leaving little opportunity for philosophizing. Perhaps in time that would emerge.

2

CRISIS

The decade after Lewis's accession to power was a bad one for the mine workers but a good one for their leader. He took over the union's helm just as vast changes engulfed the coal industry. Rapid geographical expansion, heightened employer hostility toward the union, and dramatic changes in mining technology and manpower utilization sapped the UMW's strength. Membership figures fell drastically, wage standards eroded, and massive unemployment and underemployment brought a new round of poverty to mining regions. Costly strikes and chronic internal conflict rocked the union. Even as the UMW's fortunes sagged, however, its leader purged his rivals and dominated the union's affairs as none of his predecessors had been able to.

Indeed, the 1920s brought Lewis to the fore as one of the nation's preeminent unionists. Efforts to translate his newly won stature into a wider role for himself in the labor movement and in public life generally, however, succeeded only marginally. In 1921, he sought to unseat Samuel Gompers as president of the American Federation of Labor but suffered a resounding defeat. His vocal support for the Republican administrations of Warren Harding and Calvin Coolidge and his enthusiastic endorsement of Herbert Hoover's presidential bid in 1928 earned him great public recognition and apparent entry into the councils of government. His efforts, however, to enlist public officials in campaigns to bolster the union made little headway, and hopes that he may have entertained for public office fared even worse.

War

World war had brought unparalleled opportunities to the UMW. Demand for bituminous and anthracite soared. Production leaped from 513 million tons in 1914 to nearly 680 million tons in 1918. In anthracite, with its finite production region and inherently limited employment opportunities, the number of mine workers actually declined slightly during the war, but bituminous employment in 1918 surpassed the 600,000 mark for the first time. Of greater importance, however, was regularity of employment. In 1914, soft coal miners averaged only 195 days work, whereas in 1918 only shortages of railroad cars and other transportation difficulties prevented them from going beyond a record-setting 249 days. Membership in the UMW, which had struggled for a decade to sustain the 250,000 mark reached in 1904, soared to over half a million by the end of the war.

In his capacity as UMW statistician, Lewis played a significant part in the union's key wartime settlement with coal operators, the Washington Agreement of October 1917. With U.S. Fuel Administration officials prodding the two sides, they arrived at an understanding that provided high tonnage and wage rates throughout the Central Competitive Field. Federal authorities insisted on expansion of coal production. They pressed operators to settle with the union and avoid labor disputes. Union leaders thus enjoyed government backing in their successful efforts to apply the Washington Agreement scales to other districts and to extend organization into previously nonunion fields to the south. "It is a purely business proposition," said Lewis of the agreement; "it is devoid of all sentiment."[1] Coal operators got high profits, the government got increased tonnage, and the UMW got an opportunity to achieve its basic goals.

Among miners, however, the Washington Agreement quickly began to spur discontent, for its economic provisions proved inadequate in the wake of wartime inflation. In addition, the contracts signed with coal companies under the agreement imposed harsh penalties on miners who struck during the life of the contract. For coal miners, the spontaneous strike or informal job action was a necessary adjunct to the formal collective bargaining agreement. These work stoppages protected

23

mine workers against arbitrary settlement of dead work controversies and compulsion to work in areas they deemed unsafe. True, the contractual grievance procedures in theory dealt with these matters, but miners learned from long experience that without the ability to exert power at the point of production—at the mine face or at the checkweigh station—formal procedures could atrophy. The Washington Agreement's disciplinary provisions, however, fit neatly into the agenda of the international union, for the UMW's leadership had continually attempted to persuade operators and the public that its contracts were solid and that only by dealing with the union could operators secure a disciplined and responsible work force.

By the end of the war, rank-and-file grumbling over the harsh no-strike provisions joined with bitterness over grossly inadequate wage and tonnage scales. In effect, the 1917 agreement froze wages for the duration of the war. Meanwhile, inflation drove prices upward, especially in the company stores that monopolized the retail trade in so many mining towns. Some operators agreed voluntarily to modest wage and tonnage improvements, but the great majority insisted that the letter of the Washington Agreement be observed. Meanwhile, miners saw at first hand the effects of the wartime boom in coal. Prices (and hence profits) soared, and operators encouraged miners to load rock and slate ("dirty" coal), so eager were utilities, munitions factories, and other buyers to increase fuel supplies. Throughout 1919, pressure for wage adjustments mounted, but even after the November 1918 Armistice had ended the fighting, both government officials and coal operators argued that the war was not officially over, thus keeping the Washington Agreement's wage freeze in effect. In late October 1919, responding to massive rank-and-file pressure, Lewis and the UMW executive board issued a strike call, effective 1 November.

Coal operators moved willingly to the sidelines now as the federal government, the UMW's ally during the war, turned against the union. Attorney General A. Mitchell Palmer secured an injunction, ordering Lewis and his fellow officers to call off the strike and threatening them with lengthy jail terms and steep fines if they disobeyed. The Department of Justice infiltrated the union's ranks, tapped its phones, and intercepted its telegrams. Immigration officials threatened noncitizen strikers with deportation. Federal troops prepared to descend on the mine fields to escort strikebreakers, and government officials encouraged newspapers in the harsh antiunion reportage of the strike.

But the federal government did more than assail the union. Even

as Department of Justice agents tapped phones and harassed UMW officials, Secretary of Labor William B. Wilson sought a compromise settlement. Eventually, threatened with jail terms, Lewis and other UMW
officers submitted to the government's onslaught, suspending the strike
call on 14 November and, the following month, urging still-rebellious
miners back to the pits. At the same time, Lewis used government intervention to the miners' advantage, for returning miners received an
immediate 14 percent wage increase. In addition, in February 1920, a
government-appointed commission eventually awarded the miners additional increases of over 20 percent, bringing the overall wage and tonnage hikes to over 30 percent.

For Lewis, the 1919 strike was a critical test and bore important
lessons. It occurred just as he took over the union's reins from Frank
Hayes. Although some UMW militants criticized him for failing to defy
the government—on 7 December he had declared "I will not fight my
government, the greatest government on earth"[2]—the union's executive board backed him solidly. His ringing denunciations of the government's high-handed actions solidified his support among rank-and-file
miners, while his ultimately conciliatory response to the injunction
convinced government officials and many coal operators that here at
last was a restraining influence in the tempestuous UMW.

The strike provided Lewis with a pointed lesson in the power of
the modern industrial state. When turned against the union, it acted
ruthlessly to compel submission. At the same time, however, it had
been the federal government that had broken the path for the UMW in
extending organization during the war. And, despite the harsh repression, it was through a government commission that miners won substantial wage increases in the aftermath of the strike. Clearly, the
modern state was an inescapable force in collective bargaining; the
trick was to use it to advance the UMW's goals while avoiding the lash
of repression.

All in all, the UMW had done exceedingly well during the war and
even in the aborted 1919 strike. Wages and tonnage rates were high.
The union had extended organization beyond the traditional midwestern stronghold eastward into central Pennsylvania and southward into
the rich fields of West Virginia, Tennessee, Kentucky, and Alabama.
The wartime emergency had permitted the international union to
tighten control over its districts and to bind rank-and-file miners with
rigorous contract compliance measures. As a budding union apparatchik and now as a high-ranking officer, Lewis embraced these goals and

accomplishments. At the UMW's 1918 convention, when he was on the verge of de facto control of the union, he exulted over the gains in membership and wages: "In no two year period in the history of our organization has equal progress been accomplished."[3]

Postwar Tribulations

But the war's end brought a sharp drop in the demand for coal. Renewed employer antagonism, increased mechanization of coal mining, and massive development of new fields began eroding the UMW's wartime gains even as Lewis and his supporters celebrated their formal accession to power in 1920. It quickly became apparent that the extension of the union into Kentucky and West Virginia in 1917–18 had resulted from unique wartime circumstances, not from any conversion of Appalachian operators to the UMW program. Even important operators in the Central Competitive Field, unable to oust the UMW from their established mines, began buying up coal properties in the South and exploiting them on an antiunion basis. Indeed, the rapid expansion southward began to erode the miners' traditional freedom. New entrants into the southern fields often introduced the latest machinery and subdivided and redefined the tasks of the coal miner as a means of establishing greater control over the work process, thus destroying the traditional source of worker power. As miners lost autonomy, pit committees grew feeble. Jobs were routinized and subdivided. Specialists now did the undercutting, timbering, drilling, and shot firing, thus permitting greater supervision. As new machinery was introduced—powerful new cutting machines, for example, and elaborate conveyers that eliminated the hand loading at the heart of the miner's work—mine workers could be brought under the kinds of industrial discipline that Henry Ford and other innovators were perfecting in the mass production industries. Less skilled and less experienced workers could be employed; union activists could be weeded out; a more disciplined and docile labor force, operators anticipated, would permit more efficient production of coal and greater control over the workers.

The employer offensive began in West Virginia. Since the Mountaineer State's southern coalfields had opened up in 1905, miners had battled with mining interests over the right to organize. During the war, West Virginia operators and their pliant allies in state and local

26

government faced a renewed union challenge. Officials of the UMW protested the constant harassment and abuse of their organizers and of local activists, pointing out that the federal wartime energy authority had endorsed the right of miners to organize. The response of one mine superintendent to this appeal to governmental intrusion, however, was typical: "To hell with the Fuel Administration; I'm running these mines."[4] Yet West Virginia's coal diggers flocked into the union, which grew in this bloody battleground by over sixty thousand members in 1917 and 1918.

After the war, operators lost no time in reversing these gains. Any hopes that UMW international officers might have held that the union-management cooperation that had come to prevail in the Central Competitive Field would extend southward were quickly dashed. Dozens of miners, company-employed guards, and law enforcement officers died in shoot-outs, ambushes, and protracted guerrilla actions. In the late fall of 1920 and early months of 1921, savage warfare rocked Mingo County. Pitched battles erupted in War Eagle, Rose Siding, Kermit, Vulcan, and other mining towns tucked into the gnarled West Virginia hills. Guards and policemen forced striking miners and their families out of their company-owned houses. In May 1921 state police tore up a strikers' tent colony at Lick Creek, rounding up men, women, and children. After threatening to burn their prisoners alive, they pulled out one striker. "Hold up your hands, God damn you," snarled a policeman to one unlucky miner, "and if you have got anything to say, say it fast." "Lord, have mercy," mumbled the striken man just before he was gunned down.[5]

Miners replied in kind. "We cannot live in peace and security without our union," proclaimed a local leader.[6] Miners dynamited mine tipples, railroad cars, and powerhouses. In Matewan, they killed seven guards seeking to evict striking miners from company housing. One antiunion activist was castrated and left to bleed to death. In May 1921 a three-day battle raged along a ten-mile strip of Logan County, spilling over into neighboring Kentucky. For forty-eight hours gunfire rattled through the valleys. It took eight days to retrieve the dead from the woods and hollows. Reported a U.S. Army observer after a shaky truce had descended, southern West Virginia coalfields were a "smouldering volcano,"[7] likely to erupt anew at any moment. President Warren G. Harding dispatched twenty-five hundred troops, supported by eleven military bombers, to quell the miners' uprising. With law enforcement firmly enlisted on the side of the mine operators, the rebellion flickered out. By 1922 the UMW remained in West Virginia only as a militant memory.

Throughout the 1920s the anti-UMW onslaught continued in West Virginia, Kentucky, Tennessee, and Alabama. Large areas of central and western Pennsylvania were also battlegrounds, as the union lost thousands of recent members and drew back into its traditional middle western strongholds. Hundreds of small operators, who had grudgingly accepted the union presence during the war, now attacked the UMW. In addition, powerful corporate concerns, such as Pittsburgh Consolidated Coal Company and companies representing the Rockefeller, Frick, and Mellon interests, as well as large railroads and utilities, moved massively into these southern fields. In the coal-rich Harlan County, Kentucky, area, for example, corporations leased untapped coal resources which the companies resolved to exploit without hindrance from union rules or miners' traditions of independence. Dominating the sparsely populated county's governmental, educational, religious, and civic institutions, corporate giants created private governments that remorselessly imposed the coal interests' notions of law and order. It was a brave UMW organizer or activist indeed who dared plant the union flag in Harlan County. Throughout these southern fields, declared Lewis in 1925, "great corporate powers . . . have fastened their grip on these little valleys and gorges."[8]

These same enterprises led in mechanizing the miner's work. Eager to accommodate mining companies, southern states paid little attention to environmental, safety, or miner-apprenticing laws. By employing farmers, both black and white, who had been forced off the land by the mechanization of southern agriculture, along with hardworking immigrants and chastened veteran miners, mining companies slashed wages, often eliminated the tonnage system of payment, and increased supervision. "The best mines," declared enthusiastic managers and engineers, "are coming more and more to be organized like factories." Once the proud miner had determined the pace and character of work, but now in the newly opening nonunion mines, declared a careful observer, operators had imposed a "revolutionary change in the whole manner of supervision and discipline."[9] In the 1920s, the amount of coal produced with mechanical undercutting increased by 35 percent. In 1923, virtually all soft coal had been hand loaded; in 1930, over 10 percent was conveyer loaded. Nonunion production, which before the war stood at under 40 percent of the total tonnage of soft coal, claimed nearly 70 percent by the end of the 1920s.

As the center of soft coal production shifted southward, the UMW's position in the unionized fields deteriorated. This was especially true because the rich and accessible coal seams in vast areas of West Virginia and Kentucky were easily exploitable by new techniques, whereas the older fields of Illinois, Indiana, and Ohio were increasingly difficult and expensive to mine.

True, in this central field the UMW could claim the staunch loyalty of nearly 200,000 miners. But now even operators who would not dare to defy the UMW in Illinois or Ohio opened up properties in Kentucky or Tennessee and ran them on a nonunion basis. With the chronic glut of coal reappearing after the war, union operators could claim with some justice that rival mines to the south easily undersold their northern competitors.

Lewis's Agenda

Throughout the 1920s, Lewis tried to deal with this crisis in coal mining and in the UMW through three mutually reinforcing strategies. The union had first to maintain and even improve the standards it had won for its members in the anthracite and Central Competitive fields; there could be "no backward step." Meanwhile, since it could not through its own efforts defeat the antilabor forces in the newer fields, it had to enlist government officials, the press, and even enlightened coal operators in the campaign to extend organization southward. Finally, to accomplish these goals, Lewis believed that the international union's power, and that of its president, had to be enhanced vis-à-vis the UMW's districts and the unruly rank-and-file miners.

Traditional collective bargaining was the key to achieving the first goal. In the postwar decade, Lewis led the UMW in six major strikes in behalf of unionized anthracite and bituminous miners. He supplemented collective bargaining, however, with attempts to use the federal government to underwrite his view of coal stabilization. He cultivated special relationships with key members of the Harding and Coolidge administrations, collaborated eagerly with Secretary of Commerce Herbert Hoover, and eventually sought special legislation to protect the coal industry. In his efforts to aggrandize the international union and to consolidate his own power, he created a smooth-running machine, staffing the union with his favorites, suspending district officers, and controlling UMW conventions, sometimes with violent assaults on his opponents. In his efforts to maintain standards and to recruit government in behalf of UMW goals, Lewis failed. But in the third prong of his program, the conversion of the union to a centralized instrument of presidential power, he achieved great success.

In 1925, Lewis articulated a program in his book *The Miners' Fight for American Standards*, based largely on material developed by his economic consultant W. Jett Lauck. Lewis aligned the UMW with progressive capitalism. "Trade unionism," he declared, "is an integral part of the existing system of industry." In the past, critics had assailed capitalism, but such criticism diminished as the role of business in economic improvements became clear. This also, wrote Lewis, was true of trade unionism, "a phenomenon of capitalism quite similar to the corporation." The UMW, he argued, was *the* progressive force in the soft coal industry, attempting to bring order and stability out of the chaos and irrationality that currently prevailed. Everywhere one looked, Lewis observed, businessmen embraced modern methods; Americans celebrated the gospel of high wages; cities, seeking to attract enterprises dependent on consumer purchasing power, boasted of well-paid citizens. Yet soft coal operators sought ruthlessly to drive wages down, to "inaugurate a cheap labor system in the industry upon which all the others depend—the mining of coal."[10]

The UMW was itself a modern enterprise. It had fought to establish decent standards in the union fields. "It knows that men are being used as donkey engines in the Non-union coal fields and it does not purpose [sic] to let that system spread."[11] Hence, under Lewis, the UMW proclaimed a "no-backward-step" wage policy, refusing to contemplate in the union fields wage reductions insisted on by northern operators as a means of meeting southern competition. Wage reductions, he argued, merely spread pauperization and encouraged greedy nonunion operators to slash wages anew.

But the UMW did not merely proclaim the gospel of high wages. The union favored modern methods throughout the coal industry. It encouraged mechanization of coal mining, for Lewis believed that increased use of machinery would drive out the smaller, undercapitalized operators and thus eliminate much of the competitive wage slashing that had plagued the industry. Moreover, Lewis pointed out that the UMW had been a modernizing force with regard to its own membership.

It had tutored provincial coal miners in the need to adhere to signed contracts and educated them in the need to accept—even embrace—the technology that was transforming the miners' traditional freedom. All that the union asked, said Lewis, was that miners share in the fruits of technology and that the brutal suppression of basic human rights that kept the UMW from the southern fields be ended.

Lewis hoped to enlist forward-looking Americans in behalf of this program. Surely progressive businessmen, public figures such as Secretary of Commerce Herbert C. Hoover, and enlightened editors and journalists could grasp the centrality of the UMW in the stabilization of the coalfields. Increasingly, he believed, as the ruthlessness of the southern operators became known, they would be isolated. Public opinion would force change. Since the UMW sought only rationalization of coal production, since it welcomed the introduction of labor-saving machinery, and since it had a long record of suppressing unauthorized strikes and of imposing rigid adherence to contractual terms on sometimes unruly rank-and-file miners, it was only a matter of time before the UMW would be welcomed into the new coalfields as a partner in modern production. "The conditions . . . against which the union has had to fight . . . are fundamentally un-American," he asserted. They were "out of tune with American life and thought." Surely the union's struggle to bring decent conditions to the coal miners was in the interest of consumers, intelligent operators, and the public at large. In the long run, he was confident, the American people would slap down "those who seek to cheapen coal by cheapening men," for these benighted interests "seek to reverse the evolution of American industry." Declared Lewis, "It cannot be done."[12]

Collective Bargaining, 1920s Style

In the anthracite fields, a virtually annual cycle of protracted negotiations and lengthy strikes afflicted an industry fast losing its once-dominant position as supplier of domestic fuel. In 1922, 1923, and again in 1925–26, anthracite miners conducted long stoppages, seeking wage increases and union security provisions in an industry experiencing declining markets. Lacking other sources of hard coal, the consuming public turned to alternate fuels, as both production of hard coal and employment in the anthracite mines steadily declined throughout the 1920s and into the 1930s.

31

Anthracite miners remained loyal UMW members. In the soft coal fields, however, the union lost membership. Production shifted to non-union fields. The UMW's determination to maintain 1919 wage rates ran into stiff operator opposition, for high wages in Illinois or Indiana encouraged coal consumers to purchase cheaper nonunion coal from Kentucky and West Virginia. Central Competitive operators criticized Lewis and the UMW for failing to organize the southern fields; they argued that the UMW program for bituminous stabilization was a dead letter so long as new coal undersold that produced in the Central Competitive Field. In 1922, negotiations over a new contract broke down and a quarter of a million soft coal miners joined the 150,000 anthracite strikers, with bituminous operators hoping to force the union to accept lower wage and tonnage rates.

The UMW, for all its southern tribulations, was still powerful in the Central Competitive Field. Miners there awarded it fierce loyalty. Whole communities rallied to its defense and strikebreakers encountered savage opposition. In June 1922, for example, the people of Williamson County in southern Illinois took the law into their own hands. They rounded up strikebreakers attempting to work a strip mine in Herrin, looked on while a gang of prounion thugs murdered nineteen of them, and then refused to cooperate with authorities in their unsuccessful efforts to prosecute. Clearly, CCF operators could neither budge Lewis from his no-backward-step program nor defeat the union in industrial conflict.

In West Virginia, Kentucky, and elsewhere in the South, roles were reversed. The UMW could not crack these antiunion strongholds. Its organizers were assaulted while public authorities looked on or participated. Repression kept the UMW out of the southern fields. More and more of the nation's bituminous production shifted southward until by 1928 at least two-thirds of the country's soft coal came from nonunion mines.

The 1922 soft coal strike proved that Lewis's UMW could not be broken in its midwestern fortress. True to his boast, Lewis took no backward step, retaining the 1919 wage and tonnage rates in the face of stiff employer demand for concessions. In 1924, Lewis pulled off a seemingly even more impressive coup. In a series of conferences culminating on 19 February in Jacksonville, Florida, the UMW and the CCF operators once again agreed to maintenance of existing wage rates in a contract of three years' duration. The Jacksonville Agreement would protect the union's northern flank; Lewis and his colleagues felt they had achieved three years of stability. Exulted the UMW *Journal,* 19 February would "go down in history as one of the [union's] red letter days."[13] As the UMW delegates left the Florida city to return to their northern districts, they were jubilant. "The northbound trains rocked to their singing," reported two close observers. They chanted "'we got a three-year contract; next time we'll make it five.'"[14]

Celebration was premature. Hardly a year passed before midwestern operators began reneging on the Jacksonville contracts. Some closed down for weeks or months and then reopened on a nonunion basis, using the 1917 wage and tonnage rates. Others simply announced that in view of southern competition they would not honor the 1924 contract. Large northern operators, having anticipated their inability to defeat the UMW in the central fields, quietly transferred production to newly purchased or leased coal properties in Kentucky or Tennessee, posting shutdown notices at the pits in Ohio or Indiana. In western Pennsylvania, once a UMW stronghold employing fifty thousand mine workers, the union virtually ceased to exist.

By 1927, when the agreement expired, midwestern operators no longer feared the UMW. They refused not only to renew the agreement but even to negotiate on the regionwide basis. Once again, Lewis and the UMW struck, but by now so much coal production had shifted southward that Central Competitive operators simply waited out the miners and set operator-paid "coal and iron police" loose upon the strikers. In contrast to the 1919 and 1922 walkouts, this one was forlorn and hopeless. "Conditions which exist in the strike-torn regions of the Pittsburgh district," reported a U.S. senator, "are a blotch upon American civilization." A Senate investigating committee touring the area in 1928 "found men, women and children, living in hovels which are more insanitary than a modern swinepen."[15] In the summer of 1928, Lewis permitted the several districts within the CCF to negotiate separate contracts with the operators, thus acknowledging the defeat of both the no-backward-step policy and the UMW's historic commitment to inclusive regionwide bargaining. The foundation of Lewis's strategy, the maintenance of standards and bargaining arrangements in the central fields, lay in shambles.

Throughout these ultimately unsuccessful efforts to maintain traditional standards and to gain entry into the southern fields, Lewis sought to employ the second prong in his grand strategy—namely, the involvement of the federal government. From his earliest days as a union functionary, he had grasped the importance of government to the fortunes of the labor movement. In theory, American labor was "voluntaristic"; that is, unions were to rely on their economic strength through collective bargaining and control of the job site. American labor's position, as enunciated endlessly by the AFL's long-term president, Samuel Gompers, contrasted with that of British and European labor movements, which were often directly allied with socialist parties and looked to the state for amelioration of conditions. The American labor movement formed no permanent alliance with any political party; nor did it promote a positive agenda of social welfare or regulatory legislation. True, the AFL did ask the government to restrain the issuance of hated labor injunctions, and it did support limitations on immigration, but these were negative requests, seeking only that government not intervene against the labor movement and thus permit workers to achieve economic gains in the arena of collective bargaining.

Yet Lewis had seen that this voluntarism had many exceptions and qualifications. His first position in the UMW hierarchy was as a lobbyist in behalf of safety legislation in Springfield. Much of his work for Gompers during his sojourn as an AFL organizer had involved political tasks. During the war, of course, he had participated actively in a wide range of government-business-labor negotiations. He had seen at firsthand how cooperation from the federal government could help achieve the union's aims. Even the 1919 strike, which revealed the naked fist of government repression, had yielded benefits, for the federal panel established after the UMW injunction not only boosted miners' wages but strengthened the hand of the UMW international hierarchy and its new leader, John L. Lewis.

Lewis often fulminated against government interference in collective bargaining. He had no faith in schemes of nationalization of the coal mines that gained influence in the UMW. He supported the Coolidge administration, with its strong probusiness orientation. Yet throughout the 1920s, he turned to government as a means of achieving his goals.

Thus in the midst of the 1922 strikes, with over 400,000 miners away from the pits, Lewis supported congressional moves to establish a federal body to investigate the coal industry. When Congress created the United States Coal Commission in September 1922, Lewis cooperated with its investigators and urged that it be made permanent, as a means of collecting and disseminating basic information about the troubled industry.

In the 1924 negotiations leading up to the Jacksonville Agreement, Lewis even more eagerly embraced government involvement. In Secretary of Commerce Herbert C. Hoover, Lewis thought he had found an ideal supporter for his plans. Believing that a coal strike in 1924 would jolt the economy and perhaps jeopardize President Coolidge's 1924 election chances, Hoover prodded reluctant CCF operators to negotiate, despite their belief that maintenance of high wages would ruin them. Lewis cultivated Hoover. Here was a modern statesman, free from the dogmas of laissez-faire economics, eager to promote industrial peace, stabilization, and economic growth through high wages and mass purchasing power. Lewis collaborated with Hoover in arranging for the conferences that eventually resulted in the Jacksonville Agreement. Indeed, the UMW *Journal* even referred to the agreement as the "Hoover plan of coal stabilization."[16]

When operators began to violate the contract, Lewis called on the Coolidge administration to help him police it. If he truly expected Hoover to intervene directly, however, he was disappointed. Having avoided a strike in 1924, Hoover was not about to commit the administration to protracted public controversy over the enforcement of the Jacksonville contracts. The agreement, he asserted, was a private matter between the union and the coal companies. In 1927 and 1928, administration officials offered no substantial support for the union's efforts to extend the Jacksonville Agreement, for by now the threat of a soft coal strike in the Midwest held little peril, political or economic.

Lewis never broke with Hoover. After all, the Jacksonville Agreement had embodied the union's essential wage demands, and even as late as 1927, despite the many violations, over 90 percent of signatory operators did honor its terms. Moreover, Lewis regarded his fellow Iowan, Hoover, as a uniquely qualified and impressive public figure and in 1928 supported his quest for the presidency.

Having failed to bring government into the equation on the union side through informal contacts with administration officials, Lewis now turned to Congress. For several years, economist W. Jett Lauck, an increasingly influential Lewis confidant, had urged the UMW leadership to seek legislation that would provide federal protection for unionizing efforts in the southern fields. Chary of legislative solutions and convinced that Congress would never pass such a bill, Lewis had held off. But faced with the stark reality of defeat in the 1927–28 bituminous strike, the union leader now worked with Indiana Republican senator James E.

Watson to draft legislation. Introduced just before the 1928 presidential elections, the proposal would have created a permanent federal bituminous coal commission. A code of fair competition would regulate wages, prices, and production while embracing collective bargaining (and hence facilitating union growth). The code would regulate entry into the coal-mining business and would provide inducements for operators who accepted its provisions and who abandoned their antiunion policies.

In the political atmosphere of 1928, it is not surprising that Watson's bill, which received Lewis's support, failed of passage. Indeed, it was remarkable that the platforms of both major parties that year endorsed, albeit in very general terms, the principle of legislative relief for the industry. Lewis's willingness to turn toward coal industry stabilization legislation revealed his openness to new approaches. With UMW membership now slipping below the 100,000 mark, with his efforts first to extend, then to defend, the Central Competitive bargaining structure thwarted, and with his attempt to cut a deal with Hoover unsuccessful, Lewis forgot his theoretical objections to legislative interference with collective bargaining and thus put a dramatic new approach to industrial stabilization and labor relations on the national agenda. In prosperous 1928, the Lewis-supported Watson bill attracted little public notice, but when economic calamity struck the nation late in 1929 and privation and unemployment marched out of the coalfields to afflict virtually every economic sector, the notions embodied in the failed proposal aroused more sympathetic response.

Lewis's sporadic efforts to move beyond the UMW toward broader influence in the labor movement and public life proved nearly as unsuccessful as his efforts in collective bargaining and gaining governmental support for the UMW. In 1921, flushed with his recent election as the UMW's head, he boldly challenged seventy-one year-old Samuel Gompers for the AFL presidency. Defeated decisively, Lewis contented himself thereafter with the considerable power his position on the federation's ruling executive council afforded him. When Gompers died in 1924, the UMW chief disavowed any intention of seeking the presidency anew, but he did use his influence to secure the selection of UMW secretary-treasurer William Green as Gompers' successor. Green, who had a power base in the UMW not directly dependent on Lewis, did not fit neatly into the team that Lewis was assembling to run the UMW machine. But as AFL president, the cautious Green would, Lewis correctly believed, serve UMW interests and enhance Lewis's influence within the labor movement.

Throughout the 1920s, rumors of high political office for the UMW leader continued to surface. National magazines and newspapers portrayed him as a sensible and modern labor leader, one who had wisely abandoned the class-ridden rhetoric of the past and embraced modern capitalism. In 1924, Republican leaders appointed him to the advisory committee of the Republican National Committee and trumpeted his endorsement of President Coolidge for reelection. Indeed, preconvention rumors circulated that Lewis was being considered as Coolidge's running mate. More substantial were postelection speculations that Lewis was to be rewarded with appointment as secretary of labor, speculations that Lewis carefully deflected, however. Whatever his ambitions for public office—and Lewis always denied that he had any, claiming to regard public reports otherwise as mere journalistic filler—he seemed at the crest of the wave as 1924 ended. The Jacksonville Agreement had not yet turned sour. His candidate, Coolidge, had just won reelection in a tidal wave of votes, promising, it seemed, renewed influence for the UMW chief in the councils of government. The mainstream press praised him for rebuffing the radicals in the labor movement. And the citizens of Lucas County, Iowa, brought him back to his native soil to help them celebrate an especially proclaimed John L. Lewis Day.

Controlling the UMW

While financial journals and conservative editorialists sang his praises, however, his critics in the UMW grew ever more vehement. From the start, a disparate group of union veterans had regarded him suspiciously. He had risen to power almost entirely through appointed offices; he was the darling of UMW president John White and AFL chief Gompers. Until he ran in 1918 for vice president on the ticket headed by the popular Frank Hayes, Lewis had never been elected to office above the local level. Powerful and independent UMW district leaders, such as Robert Harlin of Washington, Frank Farrington and John Walker of Illinois, and John Brophy of central Pennsylvania, distrusted this bureaucrat-cum-union leader. Indeed, rumors about Lewis's unsavory ties with certain coal operators, dismay over the character of some of the people appointed to key union posts, and general unease over a man whose experience was almost entirely as a member of the UMW and AFL hierarchy soon began to coalesce into an opposition movement.

Lewis's challengers in the UMW were a diverse group. Some, such as District 12 president John Walker, District 10 president Robert Harlin, and District 14 leader Alex Howat, were jealous guardians of their districts' prerogatives. Walker had particular reason to distrust Lewis, as it was he whom Lewis's bogus telegrams had victimized in the sordid 1915 UMW presidential campaign. Farrington, who succeeded Walker in charge of District 12, was a man seemingly without scruple or ethics. Determined to have the powerful Illinois district retain its virtually independent status and equally determined to gain the UMW presidency for himself, Farrington would level any charge, make any alliance, or conspire with any Lewis adversary to topple his foe.

Howat and Brophy were men of a different stripe. Leader of the small but fiery Kansas district, Howat fought ferociously against Lewis's efforts to force his locals to adhere to strict standards of contract compliance. A hero of the rank-and-file miner, he led his Kansans on scores of wildcat strikes. Howat epitomized a kind of grass-roots, no-holds-barred class consciousness, long a part of the mine workers' traditions; he disdained bureaucratic niceties and formalistic procedures. For years, he traveled through the UMW's western districts, relentlessly indicting Lewis and his henchmen for their top-heavy, bureaucratic dominance of the UMW. "On one occasion," recalled UMW chronicler McAlister Coleman, "I was the sole survivor [among reporters at a marathon Howat speech]. At the end of two and a half hours of steady bellowing, Howat . . . stopped at the table to ask me how he did. 'My God, Alex,'" Coleman quoted himself as saying, "'that was a long speech.' He looked at me with surprise . . . . 'Long, nothing!' he said indignantly. 'Why, son, I made a speech in a tent at a farmers' picnic in Oklahoma last month. . . . I spoke six hours. . . . Long speech, nothing.' "[17]

At almost every one of the first half dozen UMW conventions during Lewis's early years in the presidency, Howat rallied his loyal supporters in confrontations against the incumbents. At the 1924 convention, for example, Howat, who had been expelled from the union because of alleged transgressions in the leadership of his Kansas district, defied the gavel-pounding Lewis, strode to the platform, calmly poured a glass of water, and began to address the delegates. Lewis's muscle men, his "bodyguards," threw the Kansan off the platform, unleashing a demonstration among the assemblage that a New York Times reporter declared "made everything that had gone on before [in a tumultuous two-week convention] mild in comparison." As Lewis gaveled the convention to its adjournment, Howat's supporters shouted "Mussolini" at him.[18]

Throughout the decade, however, it was Pennsylvanian John Brophy who most coherently and tenaciously opposed Lewis and his program for the UMW. Born in Scotland in 1883, Brophy had migrated to central Pennsylvania in 1893 with his coal-mining family. He began to work in the mines at age twelve as his father's helper and held his first local union office before he was twenty in the all-important post of checkweighman. In 1916, Brophy gained election as president of UMW District 2, covering the central Pennsylvania fields. Imbued with a broad conception of the functions and purposes of unionism, Brophy sponsored worker education programs, consumer cooperatives, and crusading efforts to organize miners in adjacent nonunion fields. Convinced of the need for public ownership of the coal mines, he spoke vigorously at UMW conventions for nationalization. Intelligent, idealistic, and in close touch with reform-minded journalists and activists outside the sometimes provincial world of the UMW, Brophy stood in sharp contrast to Lewis, with his Republican politics, his disdain for do-gooders and savants, and his immersion in the Byzantine affairs of the UMW.

The decisive event in putting Brophy into direct opposition to Lewis was the 1922 strike. As president of District 2, Brophy had led in attempting to extend UMW organization into the nonunion fields of southwestern Pennsylvania. He had used the slim resources of his district to support the seventy-five thousand bituminous and coke strikers there, believing that any contract gains achieved in the larger strike would be meaningless without the organization of these desperate but hard-fighting men. Lewis, however, believed that the Pennsylvania strike was a lost cause, draining UMW treasuries and impeding a settlement in the Middle West. In August, when a chance to sign up CCF operators arose, he quickly concluded an agreement, called off the strike, and, in Brophy's view, thereby abandoned the nonunion strikers. Brophy believed that in effect the fate of these nonunion miners served as a test case of Lewis's UMW's commitment to organizing the unorganized. The union, Brophy charged, "had gained tens of thousands of new members" during the 1922 strike but "it cast them aside," thus signaling to nonunion miners everywhere that the UMW was not serious about fighting for miners' rights.[19]

Nor did Brophy lack for other criticisms of Lewis. In his view, the union's strength had historically lain in its semiautonomous districts. Certainly, he used his presidency of District 2 to develop a model administration, in close touch with rank-and-file miners and open to progressive impulses in the larger environment. But Lewis, ever the international apparatchik, weakened district organizations, aggrandizing the power and authority of the international union and its president. He systematically deprived the districts of autonomy, using one pretext or another to suspend or expel duly elected officers and to invoke the UMW constitution's hitherto little-used grant of authority for the president to create "provisional" governance of the districts. Indeed, by 1929 Lewis had ousted the elected leadership in ten of the districts, imposing his own handpicked (and usually sycophantic) successors. From a once-disputatious and rowdily democratic body, the UMW was fast becoming, Brophy and his supporters believed, a one-man machine.

Provisionalism was but one of the devices that Lewis used to entrench himself. Coveted positions as international organizers became patronage plums for the Lewis administration. Lewis attempted with increasing success to handpick delegates to the UMW's conventions. At the conventions themselves, Lewis's loyal supporters, many directly tied to the UMW bureaucracy by patronage and favoritism, silenced or punished dissenters. John's brother Dennie recruited toughs who could be relied upon to intimidate or even assault vocal oppositionists. Lewis used his impressive rhetoric and his detailed, if selective, knowledge of parliamentary procedure and UMW affairs to sidetrack or cut off debate. In 1924, Lewis introduced at the convention for the first time a loud-speaker system, available to him and his rostrum spokesmen but not to protesting delegates on the floor. "Lewis's voice," noted the UMW's semiofficial historians, "roared out over the unruly delegates. . . . Multiple shouting could not prevail against this new giant voice."[20] By 1925, Lewis was, in the words of a critical journalist, "the perfect boss in American labor."[21]

In Lewis's view, these criticisms ignored the realities of modern trade unionism. The UMW was in a desperate fight for survival. It existed in a business society and had to embrace business methods of operation. What corporation would permit its various divisions untrammeled rights of criticism of its chief executives? What company would stand idly by while district managers reviled its leadership? The UMW, fighting unscrupulous forces in the nonunion fields and negotiating with astute and well-organized interests in the anthracite and Central Competitive fields, had to transform itself from a collection of disparate re-

40

gional organizations into a modern, efficient, centralized operation. Hence, the UMW *Journal,* once a sounding board for all sorts of diverse elements within the union, now promoted the union hierarchy, reminding miners of the virtues of their leader and reaching out to the mainstream press to cultivate a favorable image for the UMW. The union, Lewis lectured convention delegates repeatedly, had no room for the communists and daydreamers who sought to create dissatisfaction with the leadership and succeeded only in creating chaos. It had no room for corruptionists like Frank Farrington or malcontents like Alex Howat. And, especially, it had no room for hypocrites like John Brophy, who made cynical alliances with communists and obstructionists and whose endless litany of complaints at national conventions both attested to the presence of free speech in the UMW and provided the union's enemies with all sorts of damaging ammunition.

Brophy's confrontation with Lewis reached a peak in 1926–27. Despairing of progress for the mine workers under Lewis's increasingly autocratic direction, the Pennsylvanian in August 1926 announced his candidacy for the UMW presidency. He could gain virtually no support from the Lewis-dominated hierarchy or from cowed district leaders. He did, however, enlist a group of gifted publicists and dissidents such as Adolph Germer, a socialist critic of the Lewis machine from Illinois; Oscar Ameringer, rebellious editor of the *Illinois Miner;* and Powers Hapgood, a Harvard graduate who had earned his spurs working in and attempting, often at great physical risk, to organize nonunion mines in Pennsylvania. Brophy also reached out to Lewis's traditional enemies in the UMW, accepting support from Farrington, despite his shadowy and opportunistic reputation, and from Howat, who had little interest in Brophy's positive program but who viewed the doughty Pennsylvanian as a means of attacking Lewis. Brophy, largely through Hapgood's contacts, also accepted support from American Communists, who shared the dissidents' criticism of the Lewis regime and who like them, had suffered continual verbal and physical abuse in their efforts to mount opposition.

In the election campaign, Brophy's program for the union received scant attention. His call for renewed efforts to organize the unorganized, to promote nationalization of the coal mines, and to purge the UMW of the corruption and autocracy that had followed Lewis's accession to power gained no coverage in the UMW *Journal,* whose Lewis-appointed editor confined himself to praise for the incumbent. Lewis ignored Brophy's substantive criticisms and focused largely on the pe-

41

ripheral issue of the presence of Communists among the challenger's supporters. At the October 1926 AFL convention, Lewis pointed to Communist trade union leader William Z. Foster, seated in the gallery, and linked Brophy's campaign to the efforts of this " 'arch priest of communism' " to gain control of the American labor movement.[22] With Lewis's forces firmly in control of the election machinery and the vote-tabulating apparatus, the UMW chief gained reelection by a count of 170,000 to 60,000.

Brophy continued to fight at the UMW's 1927 convention, pressing charges of vote fraud and pointing to the bankruptcy of Lewis's policies in view of the breakdown of the Jacksonville Agreement. Brophy's litany of UMW failures accurately depicted the plight of the union, whose dues-paying membership by 1927 had dipped below 200,000, a 60 percent falloff from 1920 tallies. Lewis ridiculed Brophy and charged that he was a tool of a sinister Communist conspiracy that aimed to wreck the UMW. To Brophy's reports of operators' contract violations and the increasing feebleness of the union even in its fields of traditional strength, Lewis replied with one of his favorite rhetorical devices, the portentous reference to antiquity: "In the days when people were besieged in a walled city and a soldier got upon the top of the wall and called to the enemy that the people were weak, they merely took his life and threw him off the wall to the dogs below." It was testament, Lewis argued, to the democratic nature of the UMW that even Brophy's vile attacks were permitted in convention, but, he added, "May the Lord save me from our alleged friend."[23]

Triumph—of a Sort

As the 1920s drew to a close, Lewis could claim a kind of triumph. True, the union's historic quest for regional and even national bargaining arrangements lay buried beneath the debris of the Jacksonville Agreement and the disastrous 1927–28 bituminous strike. True also that the UMW had retreated even deeper into the staunch union heartlands of the old CCF and that even here miners found less and less work for lower and lower tonnage and wage rates. Anthracite remained solidly UMW but both production and employment continued to erode. But at least, within the union itself, Lewis was now firmly ensconced. Between the UMW's founding in 1890 and his accession to power in 1919, it had had no fewer than ten presidents, with the sainted John

Mitchell enjoying the longest term in office—nine years. But defeat of Brophy and his allies removed the last substantial threat to Lewis's untrammeled power. At the tumultuous 1924 convention, with rebellious delegates shrieking their hostility and floor speakers assailing him and his policies from every quarter, the embattled leader had at times sounded defensive. "I don't expect to be treated any differently from my predecessors," he had declared. "Every one retired from office in a melancholy state of mind. . . . It will not be different with me." Though the dissident delegates applauded wildly, it was Lewis who had the final victory, however.[24]

In 1928, as befit his national stature as a mature and conservative trade union leader, Lewis was once again the Republican party's prized addition to the ranks of supporters of their presidential candidate, Herbert Hoover. Having mastered the convention loudspeaker, Lewis now went to the radio waves to broadcast his message. Hoover, he told his audience, was a true "revolutionary." An advocate of the gospel of high wages and mass consumer spending, a promoter of industrial rationalization through voluntary means, the secretary of commerce provided the kind of enlightened leadership modern America needed. Indeed, asserted the UMW chief, to Hoover's innovative policies was due much of the credit for the "present era of unprecedented prosperity" in which the nation basked.[25]

It is doubtful that many coal miners would have used this terminology. Low wages and repressive conditions dominated the nonunion fields to the south. Wage and tonnage rates in the union fields had tumbled to levels of 1917 or earlier. Sporadic employment yielded low annual income even where wage rates remained firm. Meanwhile, mechanization of the mines proceeded apace, eating into mine workers' employment and income, even as industrial, commercial, and even residential use of petroleum grew, keeping coal markets slack. By the fall of 1929, barely 85,000 of the nation's 500,000 soft coal miners were members of the UMW, and over 60 percent of these were in Illinois, the scene of bitter rivalry between UMW headquarters and district leaders. That year, citing financial difficulties, Lewis announced the cancelation of the union's scheduled international convention.

By then, few Lewis critics remained inside the UMW. His machine operated efficiently in its primary tasks—namely, supporting Lewis and eliminating his opponents. Brophy and others continued to hammer away, but now had to do so from outside, for Lewis systematically expelled dissidents from the union. "Judged by any standard," Brophy proclaimed in 1929, "the Lewis machine had failed."[26] But the usually astute Pennsylvanian was wrong. Mine workers' standards had collapsed and the union's efforts to stabilize the industry had unraveled, but the UMW machine provided Lewis with unchallenged control of the organization. For rank-and-file miners and for Lewis's vanquished opponents, this was a dubious achievement to be sure, but for Lewis it was a critical triumph indeed.

Studio portrait (ca. 1917). At age thirty-
seven Lewis is rapidly moving up the
UMW ladder. *State Historical Society
of Wisconsin*

Dressed for a White House reception, sometime in the early 1920s.
State Historical Society of Wisconsin

Anthracite strikes were chronic in the 1920s. The negotiators are (from left to right) operators' representative W. J. Brennan, Philip Murray, Lewis, operators' representative Thomas Golden, and Thomas Kennedy.
Archives of Labor and Urban Affairs, Wayne State University

Flanked by twelve-year-old daughter Kathryn and wife Myrta after visit with President Calvin Coolidge at the White House. *State Historical Society of Wisconsin*

Lewis's magnificent voice and Victorian rhetoric adapted marvelously to the radio (ca. 1925). *State Historical Society of Wisconsin*

The man who launched the CIO, 28 November 1935. *State Historical Society of Wisconsin*

With Socrates, daughter Kathryn's dog, in the summer of 1936.
State Historical Society of Wisconsin

Conferring with Michigan
Governor Frank Murphy during
the Flint sit-down strike,
January–February 1937. *Archives
of Labor and Urban Affairs,
Wayne State University*

With UAW leaders during the Chrysler sit-down strike, Detroit, March 1937.
Archives of Labor and Urban Affairs, Wayne State University

3

CAPTAIN OF A MIGHTY HOST: REBUILDING THE UMW, 1930–40

Lewis's second decade of stewardship was as spectacularly successful as his first had been dismal. The Great Depression, which blasted the hopes of so many Americans, eventually provided the opportunity to rebuild the union. To be sure, the UMW did not escape the effects of economic catastrophe. Wages, employment, and union membership plummeted dizzily. Collective bargaining became a dim memory in most soft coalfields while internal conflict ravaged the union. But Lewis survived the multiple disasters of the early 1930s. He suppressed his internal rivals and clamped an ever tighter personal grip on the organization. When the New Deal of Franklin Roosevelt came to power in 1933, he was well placed to help shape industrial recovery legislation and to secure federal support for organizing activities. The stunning rebirth of the union and resulting achievement of many of the collective bargaining goals for which it had struggled for so long catapulted Lewis to the center of national life. At fifty he seemed a grandiloquent failure, the increasingly dictatorial leader of a decaying organization. By age sixty Lewis had achieved power, prestige, and influence to match his taste for luxury and deference long before acquired.

Lewis at Fifty

On 12 February 1930, John L. Lewis turned fifty. Youthful heft had given way to a comfortable heaviness. Just under six feet tall, Lewis now weighed about 220 pounds. His naturally deep chest and his well-cut three-piece suits hid evidence of corpulence, although thickening jowls and a ring of flesh above the high collar of his tailored shirt provided a hint of acquired bulk. His full head of black hair was now flecked with gray. Although he took pains to project an image of robust good health, respiratory ailments sometimes sent him to bed for days at a time, on occasion in the midst of delicate negotiations.

The family still lived in Springfield, where Lewis now owned three houses, two of which were occupied by relatives. In 1934, the UMW abandoned Indianapolis for Washington, D.C. The Lewises followed, taking up residence first in the fashionable Wardman Park Hotel, and then in Alexandria, Virginia, where Lewis bought one of the city's oldest and most prestigious houses. Since the mid-1920s, his annual salary stood at $12,500 (at a time when three-fourths of American wage earners made less than $1,200 annually) and the union provided him with a virtually unlimited (and unscrutinized) expense account. In 1925 he bought his first Cadillac. During the 1930s, Washington became accustomed to seeing the UMW leader arriving at congressional hearings or elite banquets in his chauffeur-driven twelve-cylinder luxury car.

The tastes of Myrta Lewis ran more toward antiques and furniture. On their several trips to Europe in the 1920s, Mrs. Lewis paid top dollar for glassware, furnishings, and cutlery, and by the time they moved to Alexandria she had built an enviable collection. She added to it in Virginia. "The phrase 'Rich as John L. Lewis' was born in the antique shops of Alexandria, Virginia, during the past year," sniped a society columnist in 1937.[1] Claiming descent from the "First Families of Virginia," Myrta courted the Washington suburb's elite while remaining aloof from union affairs and politics. John had no quarrel with his wife's tastes and pretensions. He mixed easily with the Supreme Court justices, business notables, and Colonial Dames who gathered for Myrta's Sunday teas. Although perhaps not sharing the intensity of her hunger for acceptance by blue-blooded society, Lewis flourished amid the genteel surroundings.

Rarely did Lewis permit even the most pressing union matters to disrupt the Sunday gatherings. His own social life, however, revolved around business and politics. Belonging to several exclusive Washington clubs, a regular in the tasteful dining room of Washington's Carleton Hotel, a featured attraction at endless banquets and other gatherings of the business, journalistic, and political elite, the UMW leader conducted some of his most important bargaining and made some of his most significant alliances at the dinner table. Styling himself an executive rather than a labor leader, he rarely socialized with fellow unionists. Within the UMW, he preferred the role of all-powerful boss to that of good fellow, carefully keeping his subordinates at arm's length. Although he relied heavily on Philip Murray and Thomas Kennedy, UMW vice president and secretary-treasurer, respectively, neither was ever a guest at his home. Imperious and secretive, he carefully cultivated an image of himself as the all-knowing leader, dispensing largess or meting out punishment from behind his imposing desk.

He never made available, nor has any journalist or historian ever established, a detailed accounting of his personal finances. Apart from his handsome union salary, which was raised to $25,000 in 1938, and his generous expense account, he held stock in the United Labor Bank and Trust Company of Indianapolis and served as that institution's salaried president, thus adding at least $5,000 annually to his income. Other investments and sources of income remain unclear. In the world of coal mining, union leaders had on more than one occasion received bribes from coal operators. Although no evidence of personal peculation surfaced regarding Lewis, it was true that on many occasions he did use UMW funds to solicit information and to lend indirect support to operators who maintained their UMW contracts in times of business downturns. These transactions were rarely documented and only Lewis knew the real terms of exchange. Lewis was tempted at times to follow several of his predecessors as UMW president into the world of business, believing, no doubt accurately, that the financial rewards would far surpass those available in the union. But, although over the years his opponents in the union attacked him for every sort of chicanery and abuse of power, they rarely accused him of personal financial misdeeds, and when they did allude to such possiblities they were never able to offer substantive evidence.

If Lewis's income remains uncertain, his expenditures are amply documented. In addition to his expensive home and other real estate holdings in Illinois, his automobile, and Myrta's frequent purchases, the Lewis family enjoyed lush vacations in Florida, South Carolina, and Wyoming. Son John was sent to an exclusive (and expensive) prep school and eventually to Princeton. Daughter Kathryn spent two years at prestigious Bryn Mawr College. The Lewises employed three servants, including John L.'s chauffeur-valet, whose annual salaries came to about $4,600, or almost four times the annual wage of UMW coal diggers. At the 1936 convention, Lewis told the delegates that he and his fellow officers were "just as poor in this world's goods as any delegate to this convention,"[2] but no one familiar with his personal life took him seriously.

How, though, did he square his role as spokesman for the impoverished mine workers with such affluence? A man little given to self-reflection, Lewis never deigned to explain himself. In his mind there was no contradiction between his public role and his private life. If captains of industry and titans of finance stayed at the best hotels and commanded the most elegant automobiles, should the workers' representative settle for less? American labor leaders have been as subject as anyone else to a national ethos that celebrates upward mobility and defines individual success as the highest goal. Although Lewis could make the rafters ring with denunciations of greedy financiers, he always defined his goals (and hence, in his mind, the legitimate goals of the UMW and the labor movement) as the achievement of opportunity for the individual coal miner to earn a living, educate his children, and gain some of the good things of life. If, through his intelligence, energy, and personal qualities, Lewis had achieved some of this for himself, it was no cause for reproach or criticism.

Indeed, at times Lews seemed poised on the brink of abandoning the labor movement for business or politics. Besides serving as president of the United Labor Bank and Trust Company (a financial institution established in 1923 ostensibly to serve the needs of the several labor unions headquartered in the Indiana capital), he maintained close ties with wealthy coal operators and enjoyed a long-term and intimate association with the influential Harriman banking family of New York City. The Harrimans provided lines of credit to the UMW and invitations to its president to attend polo matches; Lewis used his influence in government (on one notable occasion) to deflect an investigation of the family's financial transactions. But it was the seductive call of political life that came closest to luring him from the UMW. In 1931, he lobbied openly for appointment as secretary of labor in Hoover's cabinet, only to lose out, seemingly at the last minute, to a railroad union functionary. Several previous UMW presidents had moved "up" out of the labor movement into corporate or public life, and it was natural that a man of Lewis's talents and ambitions should test these waters as well.

The reasons for President Hoover's rejection of the eager Lewis for the labor portfolio in 1931 remain unclear. The incumbent secretary of labor was James J. Davis, a bland functionary with only the most tenuous ties to the labor movement. Perhaps Hoover realized that a man of Lewis's ego and ambition could not serve with the necessary tact and discretion. Pehaps, as some observers believed, Lewis would not have taken the position but rather would have used the publicity his selection generated to aggrandize himself in the UMW and AFL. In any event, whether Lewis realized it or not, no corporate or political office could have provided what the UMW offered him: the power and influence that leadership of a half-million coal miners conferred. Although Lewis had by now little in common with the ordinary coal digger and although he cultivated the company of Virginia aristocrats and corporate captains, a man of his talent, ambition, and background had no realistic alternative but to stick with the union. In capitalist America, no middle-aged son of the working class could suddenly vault into the circle of corporate or even political influentials. As for the secretaryship of labor, in Hoover's own words (uttered with reference to Davis's role), its function lay primarily in "keeping labor quiet." For better or worse, despite the parlous state of the depression-racked UMW, Lewis's future lay with his union.

By 1930, this realization could offer little solace, for UMW membership and finances ebbed monthly. Impoverished mine workers hunkered down or lashed out in hopeless strikes. Rival organizations invaded UMW territory, often with considerable local success. Collective bargaining all but disappeared in the soft coal industry. Still, Lewis's almost-mystical belief that human events were governed by inexplicable cycles, that somehow the wheel of history had a way of lurching forward, may have helped him ride out the storm. Beset by enemies internal and external and leader of a union that had dwindled in ten years from militant army to corporal's guard, Lewis nonetheless told the 1930 convention that he would continue to speak out in behalf of working people and, he assured the delegates, "not in the quavering tones of a feeble mendicant asking alms, but in the thundering voice of the captain of a mighty host."[3]

The UMW in Crisis

These were brave and wishful words. The Great Depression turned disaster into catastrophe for the UMW. By the early 1930s the once-mighty union was all but extinct in the soft coalfields and was kept alive largely by the regular per capita tax paid by the fifty thousand or so working anthracite miners. Not only did the intensification of poverty, unemployment, and employer hostility slash membership totals. In addition, Lewis's shattered battalions faced serious rivals for the allegiance of mine workers. A Communist union, the National Miners' Union (NMU), established in 1928, challenged the UMW in Ohio, Pennsylvania, West Virginia, and Kentucky, embarking on desperate strikes, suffering piteous defeats, but often earning the loyalty of mine workers who felt betrayed or abandoned by the UMW. Even more serious was the situation in Illinois. There, in the most solidly organized of all the UMW's districts, dissident organizations of rank-and-file coal miners arose in 1930 and 1932 to combat Lewis's high-handed efforts to destroy District 12's autonomy and to impose unpopular contracts. As the impact of the depression worsened with each passing day through the early 1930s, Lewis and his aides expended most of their energy and much of the UMW's scarce financial resources in combating these so-called dual unions. Although eventually he did succeed in smashing or isolating these threats, UMW chronicler McAlister Coleman observed that the "victory" seemed to gain for him only the right "to preside . . . over the obsequies of the United Mine Workers of America."[4]

The tangled situation in Illinois laid bare both the desperate plight of the UMW and the ruthless methods of command to which Lewis increasingly resorted. In 1929, using charges of corruption leveled against District 12 officers by local unionists in the Prairie State as a pretext, Lewis suspended the district's elected leaders and imposed his own provisional functionaries. Since the proud Illinois miners constituted at least 60 percent of the UMW's total membership in bituminous (fifty-three thousand of eighty-five thousand) and since Illinois had historically been the UMW's most powerful, independent, and vigorous component, thousands of Illinois miners were outraged. When Lewis's emissaries reached Springfield to assume their duties, they found gun-toting District 12 loyalists barring access to the offices. Illinois leaders secured an injunction, preventing Lewis's men from taking over. Early in 1930, claiming that the UMW's failure to hold the constitutionally mandated convention in 1929 had in effect terminated Lewis's authority, Illinois dissidents called a convention. This gathering, which met in Springfield beginning 10 March 1930, launched the Reorganized

United Mine Workers of America (RUMW), a successor to the now legally defunct (in the dissidents' view) United Mine Workers of America. Joining forces in this challenge to the Lewis machine were his old foes. Alex Howat was chosen president, John Walker secretary-treasurer, and Adolph Germer vice-president. Participants also included John Brophy, Oscar Ameringer, editor of the Lewis-baiting *Illinois Miner*, current District 12 president Harry Fishwick, and longtime leader of Illinois mine workers Frank Farrington.

The RUMW had the support of perhaps half of Illinois' fifty-three-thousand miners. In addition, its leaders challenged the Lewis UMW in Ohio, Pennsylvania, and West Virginia, leading a strike of twenty thousand mine workers in the Mountaineer State in 1931. Brophy, Walker, Germer, and Ameringer were men of great integrity and their local supporters in Illinois included some of the most trustworthy and energetic rank-and-file unionists. The 1930 convention that had created the RUMW had rejected the old District 12 leadership of Frank Farrington and his successor, Harry Fishwick, both of whom were tainted with corruption, and at least to some labor journalists it seemed that the RUMW offered a refreshing contrast to the Lewis-dominated and increasingly enfeebled UMW.

But Lewis, though unable to coerce operators to the bargaining table or to outgun the deputy sheriffs who barred the UMW from the southern fields, acted ruthlessly and effectively to retain control of the UMW. Building on a core of Lewis UMW locals in Illinois, he poured money into the state, siphoning it from organizing campaigns and the anthracite districts. He used his influence in the AFL to brand the RUMW as an outlaw organization and his control over the UMW *Journal* and convention to keep up a drumbeat of vilification directed at Germer, Howat, and Walker. Of the RUMW's founding meeting, the *Journal* shrieked "TRAITORS CANNOT HARM THIS GREAT UNION BY HOLDING A SCAB CONVENTION."[5] In the coalfields, RUMW and UMW men squared off against each other. Attempting to speak in a UMW stronghold, Germer was beaten with brass knuckles. With his face bloodied, he nonetheless made his way to the meeting hall and held forth for an hour, hurling invectives at Lewis. Such beatings were common on both sides. "Soon," writes Coleman, "guns began to pop. Brother shot it out with brother, father with son. Through twisting alleyways of the small towns, out along the new hard roads, union man hunted union man."[6] Within a year, the UMW's superior financial and manpower resources had driven the RUMW out of the coalfields. Subsequent UMW conventions featured ritual recantations and "magnanimous" pardons of dissident Illinois miners.

In 1932, rebellion flared again in the Prairie State. This time, local unionists pulled out of the UMW entirely and created a separate organization, the Progressive Mine Workers (PMW). Though this rebel body did not have the support of such luminaries as Brophy, Germer, Ameringer, and Walker, it was able to secure contracts with a handful of operators and thus it managed to sustain a precarious presence in the Illinois fields. In both cases, however, dissident miners really had little to offer, other than outrage over the undemocratic methods and machine politics of the Lewis UMW. All the Illinois mine workers' unions, orthodox and rebel alike, had to accept wage reductions, and none, of course, could do anything about the lack of employment and mine closures that (in the words of two federal investigators) left "the countryside dotted with industrial tombstones—burnt out slack piles, rotting tipples, here and there a smokestack standing alone in the midst of a pasture—to mark the graveyard of almost 20,000 jobs."[7]

The Lewis Machine

Defeat of the rebellious Illinoisans left Lewis in undisputed control of the UMW. Over the years he built a machine that controlled the union's administrative, financial, and communications functions. He recruited a network of loyalists that reached down through the districts into the local unions. At the top were Secretary-Treasurer Thomas Kennedy and Vice President Philip Murray. Kennedy tailored his bookkeeping to Lewis's need for secrecy. Whereas his predecessor, William Green, had scrupulously observed the terms of the union's constitution and objected at times to Lewis's cavalier disbursal of funds to favorites and political allies, Kennedy mastered the art of hiding such payments and leaving his boss with a free hand. Kennedy's popularity also ensured the loyalty of Pennsylvania's anthracite miners, whose payment of the monthly per capita tax was the UMW's most reliable source of income in the grim depression months.

Vice President Murray was, like Kennedy, utterly loyal to his chief. He served as Lewis's link with rank-and-file soft coal miners, for in contrast to Lewis, Murray loved to tour the mines and visit with the ordinary coal diggers. Whereas Lewis derived pleasure from Myrta's

Sunday teas and his attendance at club functions and banquets, Murray liked nothing more than to drive out to a humble restaurant near Pittsburgh for Sunday chicken dinner and then repair to a nearby cousin's front porch, where he would visit with the coal miners and their families. For all his genuine humility, however, Murray was a canny operative, well versed in the economics and technology of the soft coal industry and—perhaps more important to his boss at this time—absolutely committed to Lewis in the union's internal conflicts.

Basic to the Lewis machine also was the control of information. His handpicked editors of the UMW *Journal,* first Ellis Searles and then K. C. ("Kacy") Adams, kept the paper free of criticism of the union leadership. They promoted the fortunes of Lewis-anointed district and local leaders and discredited rivals and rebels. Adams enjoyed a long-term and secretive relationship with Lewis. Publisher of influential mining and labor fact sheets before he joined the UMW payroll, Adams was (in the words of historians Melvyn Dubofsky and Warren Van Tine) "a purveyor par excellence of rumor and gossip, the more slanderous the better."[8] Always the inside dopester, Adams helped Lewis to plant rumors, leak information, float trial balloons, and defame enemies. Adams's intimate connections with influential coal operators facilitated off-the-record dealings that permitted Lewis to collaborate with cooperative operators in common battle against dissident miners.

Of a more savory character was Lewis's long-term association with W. Jett Lauck, an economist and public-spirited researcher and analyst. Holder of a Ph.D. in economics, Lauck was a storehouse of knowledge on economic, social, and political matters. In the years before World War I, he had served as an investigator on federal commissions looking into labor conflict, and in 1918–19 he had been secretary of the prestigious National War Labor Board. Sympathetic with the labor movement and convinced that a modern economy ultimately needed substantial governmental regulation and direction, Lauck began working for Lewis on a free-lance basis in the 1920s. He produced reports on the economics of the soft coal industry, changing patterns of energy use, and other technical and economic matters. Moreover, just as Adams's labyrinthine contacts with coal operators provided Lewis with information about and access to one set of opponents and bargaining partners, so Lauck's wide-ranging knowledge of labor activists, radicals, journalists, and reformers kept Lewis abreast of another coterie of potentially useful people. Indeed, in Lewis's world of limited intimacy and purely functional friendship, Lauck came to be perhaps closer to him than anyone else connected with the UMW, except perhaps (and even here only in certain contexts) Philip Murray.

Lewis also relied heavily on family members, rewarding their loyalty with union jobs and other favors. Until his death in 1931, brother George served as John's eyes and ears in Illinois. Another brother, Dennie, specialized in recruiting thugs and enforcers to keep order at UMW conventions and to punish critics. Brother-in-law Floyd C. Bell was made cashier of the United Labor Bank and Trust in Indianapolis and later in the 1930s became comptroller of the Congress of Industrial Organizations. Lewis gave the job of secretary at District 12 headquarters to brother George's widow, Hannah, thus fulfilling a family obligation and ensuring a steady flow of useful information from Springfield. While both Myrta and son John, Jr., remained pointedly aloof from UMW affairs, in the 1930s and 1940s daughter Kathryn became closely involved with her father's union activities, eventually serving as his private secretary and adviser.

Judicious handling of appointments to organizers' posts, carefully targeted loans to district officials, and the naming of officers in the expanding number of provisional districts extended the machine through the districts and subdistricts and into every local union. The Illinois rebellions of the early 1930s tended to discredit open dissent at UMW conventions, where any opposition to the Lewis regime could so easily be equated with sympathy for the "wreckers" and "betrayers" of the RUMW or PMW. Lewis was particularly adept at red-baiting, labeling oppositionists as communists and suggesting that criticism of his leadership played into the hands of scheming Bolsheviks.

By the early 1930s, virtually every district, whether it was provisional or not, bore the Lewis imprint. In West Virginia, Van A. Bittner sought to control the often rebellious miners, stamping out organizing efforts conducted by the NMU, the PMW, and an independent West Virginia Miners Union. In eastern Kentucky, William Turnblazer attempted to bring the UMW message to the impoverished miners of Harlan and Bell counties while at the same time beating back a vigorous NMU challenge. Silbey Barrett in Nova Scotia, William Mitch in Indiana, John Savage in Ohio, Patrick Fagan in western Pennsylvania, and a dozen other district leaders owed their jobs to Lewis and saw to it that local unions from their areas sent only Lewis supporters to UMW conventions. At the conventions themselves, these men and their retinue of delegates dominated the committees, controlled the floor debate, and when necessary, silenced dissidents who persisted in raising embarrassing questions.

Yet over and over at these same conventions, Lewis and his henchmen insisted that the UMW was a democratic body—indeed, Lewis told the 1936 gathering, it was "the most democratic . . . organization I know [of] . . . within the political confines of our country."[9] As was the case in the contrast between his life-style and his pleas of selfless poverty, there was for Lewis no contradiction between the highhanded governance of the UMW and his professions of democracy. The UMW was democratic in that it represented and spoke for mine workers; the fifteen hundred or so convention delegates had an equal voice and were chosen by their fellow workers in local unions around the country and in Canada. The convention proceedings down through the years were filled with attacks on Lewis and his fellow officers. Year after year, the delegates were treated to John Brophy's high-minded lectures, red mustachioed John Hindmarsh's vitriolic denunciations, and dissidents in local unions from Nova Scotia to New Mexico impugning the integrity of their leaders. If Lewis loyalists—the overwhelming majority of the convention—became impatient with these scurrilous attacks and the endless demands for time-consuming and expensive roll call votes, harsh words and fisticuffs were only to be expected in the tough world of coal mining. The UMW, after all, was no Ladies' Aid Society.

What "obstructionists" and "wreckers" really objected to, Lewis believed, were his efforts to create a modern, efficient, and effective union. Men such as Brophy and Walker, for all their progressive-sounding words, were rooted in the mine workers' past. District autonomy made no sense in an industry crying out for national standards and broad-scale collective bargaining. The days of the autonomous miner, the independent pit committee, and the sovereign district organization were over. The mechanization of mining, the entry of thousands of new, relatively unskilled mine workers, the expansion of the industry into the new southern fields, and the growth of a handful of large and influential producers such as Pittsburgh Consolidated and the Koppers Company had decisively shifted the locus of union power.

To the cries uttered at each convention for the restoration of the autonomous rights of provisional districts, Lewis replied with a mixture of scorn and condescension. The UMW, he asserted, took over "subordinate"[10] units only when members in a district complained of wrongdoing or ineptitude. The UMW had to act decisively, he lectured the delegates to the 1936 convention, for if anything went wrong in a district—if wildcat strikes broke out, violating contractual terms, for example—"it is the officers of your International Union who are pilloried in the public press and in the editorial columns of the great eastern newspapers."[11] Rank-and-file mine workers could be misled; they could, and often did, choose corrupt or inept leaders. In districts where employers had smashed the UMW, rebuilding the union required reliance on veteran organizers and administrators; rank-and-file activists were too green and inexperienced. In Ohio, Indiana, Illinois, West Virginia, and elsewhere, the story was repeated over and over. "A child of ten, twelve, fifteen, eighteen or twenty years of age might question the authority of the head of his household," Lewis told the delegates to the 1934 convention. "And yet there is none of us but what would say . . . that it is necessary to have order and discipline in the family."[12] In the UMW "family," it was the international officers who administered this "discipline"—and the district leaders, local unions, and rank-and-file miners who submitted to it.

Thus, in the same report UMW officers could call for "complete industrial democracy" while at the same time relegating the question of district autonomy to the status of a minor constitutional quibble. The executive board, the 1936 convention learned, "is apprehensive lest the granting of so-called 'autonomous rights' to these provisional districts may result in the creation of internal political turmoil." At the same convention Lewis asserted that district autonomy "is not a fundamental principle"; rather, he reassured his audience, "it is a question of business expediency and administrative policy." He posed what for him was the central question: did the delegates "prefer to sacrifice the efficiency of your organization . . . for a little more academic freedom in the selection of some local representatives?"[13]

Some critics stressed the strong-arm tactics that Lewis's supporters employed. For his part, Lewis publicly deplored violence. In a truly civilized world, when wealth had been made to serve humankind and when ruthless antilabor employers had been curbed, no doubt more peaceful means of resolving disputes would evolve. But just as the working lives of coal miners were harsh and often violent, so rival factions quickly resorted to the clenched fist or the barrel stave. Indeed, it was this very lack of discipline, this tendency of mine workers to resort too quickly to violence, that further justified the growth of responsible, centralized authority in the union.

For all their self-serving character, Lewis's rationalizations of provisional control and other limitations on mine workers' self-government did speak to some basic realities. Beyond the condescending rhetoric that depicted hard-working and often courageous miners as unruly children lay a central truth: in modern capitalist America bureaucratization and centralization proceeded apace, leaching power from local organizations and feeding centralized bodies. In businesses, educational and philanthropic institutions, fraternal orders, and government itself these trends accelerated with the pace of industrial change. It was a bureaucratic society, with the autonomous workman, the small farmer, and the independent businessman increasingly isolated and powerless. In an earlier day, autonomous workers could impose their will on the shop floor or at the mine face, needing only a loose national structure for occasional bargaining or political services. But vast changes in the modern economy and the crisis in the coal industry rendered such a conception of unionism anachronistic. "The primary interest of the International Union," declared the officers in 1936, "in all matters concerning the welfare of the membership is not necessarily the restoration of . . . 'autonomous rights,' but rather, is the establishing of an absolute recognition of the principle of collective bargaining." Indeed, it was the obligation of delegates, as responsible local leaders, "to sustain the hands of your officers" in the eyes of the rank-and-file miners back home "who are the beneficiaries of the accomplishments of this Union of ours."[14] The union, in short, could not afford the luxury of "an excess of democracy" and still function with the efficiency needed in the fast-paced world of the mid-twentieth century.

These were telling points. Certainly few labor unions, whatever their democratic aspirations, remained free from centralization and limitations on the autonomy of rank-and-file members. At the same time, however, Lewis's justifications for his constitution-bending actions clashed with his personal style of leadership. Far from re-creating the UMW as a streamlined, modern, efficient bureaucracy, he practiced rather the leadership style of the political boss or even the mafioso *cappa*. Modern bureaucracies, as an army of sociologists and management experts never tired of observing, were based on bureaucratic rules defining and rewarding merit. Leadership and promotion were based on explicit, concrete criteria; the organizational ladder had clearly defined rungs. An endless flow of paper directives, reports, and responses marched through clearly defined administrative channels. Rules and regulations proliferated. Financial records were kept meticulously. Expenditures were made only through clearly designated procedures. Yes, indeed, the economic and social changes of the twentieth century impelled virtually all organizations toward the adoption of rational, systematic modes of behavior and organization, and the traditional world of the coal miner and the traditional division of power in the UMW clearly did not fit this bureaucratic imperative.

But, as his critics pointed out, Lewis created no faceless, centralized, efficient bureaucracy in the UMW. Far from it. He permitted no rules or regulations to bind him. The UMW was no meritocracy, with objective criteria determining advancement, but rather a rabbit warren of nepotism and favoritism, with the only test that counted that of loyalty to the chief. In contrast to the efficient bureaucrat who felt uncomfortable without creating an elaborate paper trail to document his decisions, Lewis rarely committed anything significant to writing. Union officials, journalists, even businessmen trooped into his spacious office and marched across seemingly endless yards of thick carpet to Lewis's massive (but remarkably clear) desk. Favors, punishments, promises, and threats were handed down; no record of transactions remained to clutter the files. "Lewis," his modern biographers have observed, "operated more in the style of the big-city political boss than modern business executive. He dealt in power, not policy; patronage, not principles."[15]

And in the long run, the UMW suffered. With loyalty the only test of worth, Lewis eventually surrounded himself with sycophants and bully boys. Protracted provisional government killed grass-roots leadership. Secretive methods of administration and accounting invited corruption. While Lewis's freedom from ordinary constraints did permit him to recruit some able researchers, attorneys, and publicists, his highhanded and often personally demeaning treatment of subordinates—and he inevitably regarded everyone in the labor movement as his subordinate—alienated all but the most insensitive or obtuse. Far from creating a modern, efficient organization, fit for battle in the changing world of twentieth-century industrial relations, in the long run Lewis succeeded only in building a personal, almost feudal, fiefdom, held together with personal (and familial) loyalty, patronage, and, once the UMW's fortunes turned upward, the enormous charisma that a victorious Lewis projected. Such an organization filled Lewis's personal needs better than it did the long-range needs of the mine workers.

The crushing of the Illinois rebellions and the elaboration of his machine left Lewis firmly in control of the UMW. Although the UMW *Journal* was filled with reports of district revitalizations, new organizing campaigns, and a renewed spirit of growth, the winter of 1932–33 found the union, along with the rest of the country, in the doldrums. No amount of wishful thinking and public relations could change the facts: coal production was down disastrously; collective bargaining was virtually nonexistent in the bituminous fields except in the old midwestern mines; and even in this region, miners considered themselves lucky to get work at any wage.

In the South, coal operators' repressive responses to mine workers' protests intensified. In 1931, UMW organizers learned the difficulties of bringing the union message to the new fields when they sought to assist striking mine workers in Harlan County, Kentucky. Outraged over repeated wage cuts, brutalized by company guards and thugs deputized by compliant law enforcement agencies, and faced with eviction and eventual starvation, six thousand Harlan County miners left the pits in May. The UMW's efforts to organize the booming eastern Kentucky fields in the 1920s had failed repeatedly. Now organizers ventured back, only to find the strike virtually out of control. But UMW headquarters, preoccupied with defeating the rebel groups in Illinois, would not authorize funds for strikers' relief, believing that the spontaneous strike could not succeed. A pitched battle at the town of Evarts, Kentucky, brought in the National Guard. Eventually the rebellious miners, "impressed," in the words of historian John Hevener, "by the futility of the UMW's effort" and "disillusioned with the organization," drifted back to work.[16]

Communists moved in to fill the vacuum. The National Miners' Union sent in organizers, raised money from the eastern cities, and for a time gave hope to the desperate Harlan County miners. The NMU activists publicized the plight of the poor families of eastern Kentucky. By sponsoring visits to the coalfields by well-known writers and lawyers, by organizing large demonstrations of the impoverished, and by acting as a magnet for ever more vicious and provocative methods of repression, the Communists in the NMU brought the tribulations of the coal miners more forcefully to national attention than anything Lewis's UMW had been able to do. The Communist-supported strike of 1931–32 was hardly a strike in the normal sense of the term, for after the defeat of the UMW effort in May 1931 most employed miners continued in the pits. But the efforts of this "union of the damned" did trigger congressional interest and did lead to the publication of an influential volume, *Harlan Miners Speak*, which helped to put eastern Kentucky on the map of the national conscience. Thus even the documentation of the coal miners' misery owed less to the UMW than to the efforts of its rival, the hated Communist NMU.

Rebirth

Revival came with remarkable—indeed, it seemed, miraculous—suddenness. In the dismal winter of 1932–33, Lewis and his economic consultant W. Jett Lauck helped shape the industrial policy of the incoming Franklin Roosevelt administration. With Lewis delivering widely publicized testimony before the Senate Finance Committee in February and with Lauck part of the inner circle that drafted the eventual National Industrial Recovery Act (NIRA), the UMW's long-term views on industrial stabilization found expression in the sweeping new law. In particular, the union's insistence on government support for collective bargaining through independent unions survived the attacks of employer groups and was contained as Section 7(a) of the legislation. Even before the actual industrial recovery bill gained passage in June of 1933, however, coal miners throughout the Appalachian fields had begun to organize. Lewis, his internal enemies now subdued, committed the UMW's resources to the organizing crusade, and scores of organizers quickly tapped into the rekindled enthusiasm. By July, tens of thousands of bituminous coal miners had signed up. By September, Lewis had an agreement that covered virtually all the Appalachian fields, from Pennsylvania to Tennessee.

In the 1932 presidential election, Lewis had renewed his personal support for Hoover. At the same time, however, other UMW leaders, notably Kennedy and Murray, had openly backed Franklin Roosevelt. Lewis in fact may have quietly encouraged support for the Democrat, playing both sides of the fence. In any event, although Roosevelt had gained election without committing himself to any specific plan, the desperate economic plight of the nation demanded energetic action. Fully a quarter of the labor force was unemployed. Tens of thousands of farmers faced foreclosure. Episodes of social violence—strikes, farm protests, hunger marches, antieviction demonstrations—multiplied. Clearly, Roosevelt would have to act vigorously.

It was in this crisis atmosphere that Lewis's boldness and intelligence paid dividends. He perceived a vacuum in Washington. The public demanded action and the incoming administration promised relief. But its plans remained inchoate, with rival groups of advisers and special interests attempting to shape the adminstration's basic policies for agricultural and industrial recovery. In this struggle of diverse interests to gain access to Roosevelt, Lewis had some decided advantages. True, he had not been a vocal supporter of the president-elect, but Murray and other UMW officials had been. The UMW languished with fewer than 100,000 members but it had been a powerful organization and might once again become one. Articulate businessmen and corporate officials had access to the president-elect, and his advisers worked closely with men such as financier Barnard Baruch and General Electric chairman Gerard Swope. Still, millions of Americans blamed big business for the country's plight. Any plan of industrial recovery would have to carry the approval—and hence, to some extent, the imprint— of noncorporate bodies, notably the labor movement. And in the labor movement, no one had devoted more time and energy to problems of governmentally supported stabilization than John L. Lewis.

Lewis's public opportunity to influence recovery legislation came in February, two weeks before the new administration took office. Senator Hugo Black of Alabama and Congressman William Connery of Massachusetts had introduced legislation to mandate the cutting of hours of employment to thirty per week without commensurate wage reductions. A controversial effort to expand employment and increase consumer purchasing power, the "Black thirty-hours bill" as it was known challenged partisans of the incoming administration to develop their own version of a coherent industrial policy. When Roosevelt himself promised that he would present a full-scale recovery bill to Congress, even greater attention focused on the Finance Committee hearings.

Lewis rose brilliantly to the occasion. Drawing upon the arguments put forth in his 1925 book, *The Miners' Fight for American Standards*, he spoke eloquently in behalf of working people and their families. The revival of mass purchasing power, he argued, was the key to economic recovery. Handouts to corporations, subsidies for banks, economies in government expenditures—none of these gestures would put money in the pockets of the farmers, workers, and housewives whose spending generated economic growth. In 1925, Lewis had painted a picture of victimized miners and their families, impoverished islands in a sea of prosperity; now, however, the catastrophe of the depression had victimized almost everyone. The miners' fight for American standards had become the American people's fight.

How could government act to bolster purchasing power? Certainly, Lewis believed, Congress should enact emergency measures providing federal relief for the destitute, perhaps even government-financed employment for jobless workers. But the single most important measure to boost purchasing power was the protection of workers' rights to join labor unions. Here was a reform that would require minimal governmental action—really, government had only to see to it that the Constitution applied to Kentucky coal mines and that employers could no longer victimize workers with impunity. Moreover, here was a reform that not only encouraged immediate expansion of purchasing power as strong unions gained higher wages for their members but also erected a permanent structure for maintaining American standards. For years, reformers and government officials had paid lip service to protecting labor's right to organize; on the railroads, federal legislation in fact explicitly recognized the desirability of unions. During the last great national emergency, World War I, federal authorities had encouraged union growth as part of the industrial mobilization effort. Clearly, Lewis asserted, now was the time for government to provide working people not with handouts or subsidies but with protection of their basic rights as free citizens.

Lewis's testimony also drew on the UMW's fruitless efforts to gain congressional legislation for regulation of the soft coal industry. Ever since 1927, the union had pressed for governmentally regulated stabilization in the industry, for the chaos of unregulated competition was plain for all to see. Its victims were coal consumers and impoverished miners. The UMW proposals did not call for governmental ownership or operation of the mines. But the bills introduced in every session of Congress did envision federal standards of safety, conservation, marketing, and labor conditions. And, of course, they threw the mantle of federal protection around the right to organize. As Lewis and Lauck thought of coal legislation, it would have enlisted both the soft coal operators and the UMW in a program of federally overseen self-regulation. Restrictive antitrust laws would be set aside. Coal operators would be encouraged to apportion markets, adopt common standards of land use, and share technologies and equipment. Unionization would drive wages from the competitive calculus and would bring enhanced purchasing power to the coalfields. Suppression of antiunion activities would remove the goons and thugs from the mining communities, bringing peace to the troubled valleys. Regular collective bargaining would ensure that well-compensated workers would not need to resort to the strike weapon, thus benefiting coal consumers.

Congress, of course, had not had the wisdom to adopt these proposals. But, Lewis argued, the national demand for industrial recovery now gave it an opportunity to adopt similar legislation not only for the soft coal industry but for the entire economy. This was not socialism or fascism. Lewis had nothing but scorn for the authoritarian state-controlled economies of the Soviet Union and Italy. It was just sensible modern progressive Americanism. The details of such legislation, of course, would have to be worked out, but for Lewis the central feature, the engine that would make the whole enterprise go, was the guarantee of the rights of union organizing and collective bargaining.

Lewis's presentation was powerful and effective. He combined an eloquent appeal in behalf of the toiling masses with detailed knowledge of economic affairs and legislative mechanics. The debate over the thirty-hours bill and the circulation of innumerable industry-sponsored proposals for governmentally sanctioned cooperation provided fertile ground for Lewis's ideas. Key Roosevelt advisers such as Raymond Moley and Rexford G. Tugwell, charged with developing legislation in behalf of industrial recovery, found much in Lewis's testimony with which to agree. Clearly, any program to be presented to the public and steered through Congress would need organized labor's support, and with his powerful testimony Lewis had put himself in the front ranks of labor's spokesmen.

Thus, in March, as the new administration set about to draft recovery legislation, Lewis quickly became a key figure. He delegated Lauck, his confidant, adviser, and general factotum, to work with the administration officials charged with framing legislation. Lauck joined a select group of lawyers, business leaders, and government officials who met daily to give shape to the recovery program. In Lauck, Lewis had a first-rate spokesman. Because the economist had been active on the Washington scene for over twenty years, few people knew as much as he about public finance, employment, and overall economic trends. He shared with the New Dealers delegated to produce legislative proposals a conviction that a strong governmental presence could right the economy, expand purchasing power, and eliminate the cutthroat competition that was widely believed responsible for the current crisis. Lauck's role in drafting the earlier UMW proposals for bituminous stabilization added to his reputation, and he quickly became part of the inner circle that met daily.

Throughout the spring of 1933, Lauck kept in close touch with Lewis. Lewis in turn used his years of association with businessmen and members of Congress to lobby for the forthcoming legislation. Business groups favored recovery legislation, but for the most part they envisioned a law that would suspend antitrust laws while permitting business-run trade associations, with little governmental scrutiny, to exercise self-regulation. Although business spokesmen were resigned to some sort of acknowledgment of labor's rights of organizing and collective bargaining, they hoped—and worked assiduously to ensure—that any such declaration would be toothless and would permit them to continue to avoid organization by unions such as those affiliated with the AFL. On 5 May, however, Lauck reported optimistically to Lewis that the new industrial recovery bill closely reflected the UMW approach and was all but ready for the president's signature. As currently framed, the economist reported, the law "will suit our purposes."[17]

On 16 June 1933, Roosevelt signed the National Industrial Recovery Act. An omnibus law, it allocated $3.3 billion for government employment projects. At its heart, however, lay the creation of the National Recovery Administration (NRA), empowered to establish codes of fair competition in each industry. Although no employer would be forced to operate under the code in his industry, the law suspended certain antitrust laws and provided tempting tax advantages for those who did participate. The codes of fair competition, each to be developed through consultation among industry leaders, government officials, and labor and consumer representatives, would embrace standards of production, marketing arrangements, business practices generally, and minimum wage–maximum hours stipulations. Section 7(a) endorsed workers' right to organize, seemingly putting the power and authority of the federal government at the disposal of organized labor. As the bill neared passage, Lauck assured the UMW chief that "it will be all right as a basis for organizing the [soft coal] industry."[18]

Lauck's assessment was an understatement. Anticipating favorable action on the bill, Lewis in the spring began husbanding the UMW's financial resources and assembling a corps of organizers. On 1 June, the UMW launched its campaign, with organizers moving through the Appalachian fields, defying the company guards and deputy sheriffs, invoking the authority of the federal government and the personal charisma of Franklin Roosevelt in behalf of their cause. "The president wants you to join the union," miners were told. Mine workers responded massively. In dozens of coal camps and towns, miners organized themselves, with UMW representatives doing little more than handing out membership cards by the hundreds. Organizers and local unionists in

West Virginia, Pennsylvania, Tennessee, Kentucky, and even Alabama reported thousands of new members and dozens of new locals. "The men flocked into the union so fast," reported an organizer in West Virginia, "it took away their [the companies'] breath." From War Eagle, West Virginia, a local unionist declared that now "these mountains belong to us."[19]

The surge of mine workers into the UMW astonished organizers. The union, seemingly moribund just weeks earlier, now glowed with life. In reality, however, reports of the UMW's death in the southern Appalachians had always been exaggerated. True, since the mid-1920s card-carrying union members had been hard to find and organizers rarely ventured into the coal camps. Still, memories of the last successful organizing drives of the World War I years and early 1920s remained vivid. Union traditions ran strong, even where the union presence had been expunged. Moreover, even in the depths of the depression Appalachian miners had risen in sporadic rebellion. Early in 1931, for example, twenty thousand West Virginians had struck, and the Harlan miners' 1931 walkout had at least for a time hurled defiance at the most solidly antiunion mining interests on the continent. The NMU strikes had sown seeds of rebellion as well. Thus, despite the years of repression and the long record of UMW defeat, Appalachian miners were primed to respond to Lewis's organizers and did so with a vengeance.

It was not always easy. Some employers fought back as they always had, with thuggery, firings, and evictions. Organizer Jesse Aquino's mid-June mass meetings in West Virginia's McDowell County drew thousands of mine workers—and dozens of Baldwin-Felts company guards. "At the first meeting I held in the county," Aquino told investigator Edward Wieck, "one of them put a gun to my back." But now Aquino had some weapons of his own. "I kept talking about the Recovery Act and the President and finally he moved away." Later, machine-gun bullets riddled his car as he drove along the winding mountain roads to another mass meeting.[20]

On the whole, however, the mining companies were too uncertain and too cautious about the meaning of the NIRA to respond with their customary vigor. The law's intrusion of federal authority in labor relations caught them off guard. Wanting to take advantage of the enactment's provisions, company officials had not had a chance as yet to devise new antiunion strategies. Lewis's blitzkrieg tactics were designed to exploit this uncertainty, to organize the coalfields (in the words of one organizer) "before the employers wake up to the fact that there were ways of getting around the law."[21] Observed one local unionist, who had rebuilt his local after almost a decade of operating nonunion, "Without the help given us by the NRA and the Administration we could not have done it. The men would not have dared and the company would have fought back in the same old way."[22] It was not that federal marshals or U.S. troops patrolled the coal camps, protecting organizers and working men. There were none. It was rather the sense that joining the union was a way of participating in Roosevelt's recovery program and that FDR, already a figure of intense popular adoration, stood beside the organizers and union men. And right along with Franklin Roosevelt stood John L. Lewis, the miners' leader. "John L. Lewis was having beer and sauerkraut with President Roosevelt every night," went the folk imagery of the mine fields, "and to hell with the company guards."[23]

Collective Bargaining, 1933–39

Coal miners expected great things of their rebuilt union. For Lewis, the transformation of the UMW from a defeated and declining organization into a rich and powerful mass movement held out the promise of his achieving goals that since 1890 had eluded him and his predecessors. With replenished ranks came a bulging treasury. In 1937, despite heavy expenditures for political campaigns, support of other labor organizations, and a lavish new headquarters building, Secretary-Treasurer Kennedy reported over $2.5 million in cash. Armed with this newfound financial and organizational strength and enjoying the support of the Roosevelt administration, Lewis resolved to improve miners' standards while at the same time creating a permanent structure of collective bargaining in the bituminous fields. Throughout the rest of the 1930s, backed by the militancy of rank-and-file miners, he used the overlapping devices of collective bargaining, NRA codes, congressional legislation, and, perhaps his greatest asset, intervention by the executive branch of government to achieve these ends.

The first test of the UMW's strength came in the late summer and fall of 1933. Simultaneously conducting collective bargaining with Appalachian coal operators' associations and trying to shape the NRA code for the industry, Lewis and his aides exploited their advantages in membership and governmental support. In both the code, which was made public on 7 September, and the agreement signed with the operators two weeks later, Lewis was determined to increase wages, reduce hours, require operators to accept union checkweighmen, curb abuses in payment schemes and company store operations, and secure strong grievance procedures. Equally important was the UMW determination to eliminate—or at least to reduce—wage differentials that favored southern coal operators over their unionized northern counterparts.

Throughout this complex dual bargaining, impatient mine workers kept up the pressure. Strikes rippled throughout western Pennsylvania and West Virginia and threatened to spread through the entire soft coal area. Impatient with bureaucratic delays, expecting quick progress now that the union had been rebuilt, militant miners defied coal operators. Repeatedly, Lewis persuaded the restive miners to go back to work, warning them that the whole nation relied on them not to sabotage the Roosevelt recovery program. At the same time, the UMW chief played upon the fears of government officials, justifying the mine workers' militancy in view of operators' intransigence. In a masterful performance as a "manager of discontent," Lewis used the leverage that his marching miners provided to pry concession after concession from the operators' associations and NRA code authorities.

Coal operators had no real plan with which to confront Lewis's agenda. Northern producers, many with long records of dealing with the union, tacitly endorsed the UMW program. Some southern operators continued to resist union demands, opting out of the regional association established to conduct the bargaining for bituminous producers. Even so, basic wage, union recognition, and work rules provisions were to be included in the bituminous coal code, giving them the force of law. Though southern operators were able to retain wage differentials that paid southern miners less than their northern counterparts, the eventual code and collective bargaining agreement of September 1933 reduced differentials sharply and boosted wages in the southern fields. Miners in Tennessee, Virginia, Kentucky, and Alabama who had been paid as little as $1.50 a day now were to earn the code minimum, $4.20 a day, only 40 cents less than miners in Pennsylvania and Ohio. The relative uniformity of the code and the companion agreement, Lewis believed, would eliminate wage competition and compel the operators toward cooperation in marketing, pricing, and business practices generally. At the very least, the agreement and the code firmly established the UMW's status as a major partner—indeed, in view of its accumulating wealth and singleness of purpose, *the* major partner—in the industry. Reflecting on the sweeping union victory in writing the terms of the coal code, one journalist remarked that "the defeated mine-owners agreed to all things that deputy sheriffs usually shoot people for demanding."[24]

A revision of the code in 1934 added to the UMW's achievements. In a bravura performance at the April 1934 hearings, Lewis humiliated Alabama mining spokesmen, overwhelming them with his detailed factual knowledge of the economics and demography of the industry and charging them with defiance of the federal government in view of their threats to ignore the coal code's labor provisions. Perhaps, Lewis suggested to NRA authorities, the Alabama operators were contemplating a declaration of war against the United States. If so, he pledged, "the United Mine Workers of America is ready . . . to furnish the president . . . with 20 army divisions to help make the Alabama operators comply with the law."[25] A renewal of the 1933 collective bargaining agreement in March of 1934, along with favorable revisions in the code, gained the UMW important union security and dues checkoff advantages, solidifying the union's position and extending its coverage to include over 95 percent of working bituminous miners.

In May of 1935, the Supreme Court struck down the NIRA and, of course, along with it the bituminous coal code. In reality, by the fall of 1934 enforcement of the code's provisions had become so uncertain that, in Jett Lauck's words, "The N.R.A. is more or less of a flat tire."[26] Increasingly, Lewis looked toward permanent federal coal legislation to establish the basic principles of bituminous stabilization. With the powerful UMW lobbying machine, aided by cooperative operators, functioning at full tilt, Congress enacted stabilization laws in 1935 and again in 1937 (after the Supreme Court had struck down the earlier measure). Both of these cumbersome enactments sought to mandate basic labor standards and to use federal authority to induce operators to develop cooperative marketing and pricing policies. Swift court disapproval of the 1935 law aborted it before it had a chance to function, and the complex provisions of the 1937 enactment led to endless bureaucratic entanglements before its ineffectual mandate expired in 1942. Lewis's fifteen-year effort to attain bituminous stabilization through legislation ended in a bureaucratic whimper. Indeed, his unsuccessful pre-1935 efforts in this project were more important than his later successes in securing passage of legislation, for advocacy of coal stabilization laws in the 1920s and early 1930s had permitted him to speak with authority in the crucial debates over the eventual NIRA, whereas the actual coal stabilization laws soon proved unworkable and irrelevant.

With the demise of the NRA and the disappointments of legislation, only collective bargaining remained as a means of entrenching the union and stabilizing the industry. Despite the heroic performance of the UMW in 1933–34 and despite Lewis's soon-legendary negotiating performance over the remainder of the decade, mine workers emerged from this turbulent period with rather limited gains. Despite the union's new power, basic economic facts continued to bedevil soft coal mining. True, union contracts by the late 1930s made coal miners virtually the highest paid blue-collar workers in the country. On the other hand, the miners' old nemesis, irregularity of employment, remained. In 1939, for example, for all the high daily rates contained in UMW agreements, the average miner brought home only $22.99 a week, a meager 17 cents a week more than the average unskilled male factory worker.

The agreements negotiated with the bituminous operators' associations in 1934, 1935, 1937, and 1939 could do little to change these circumstances. Soft coal strikes erupted in 1935 and again in 1939, but the issues in dispute focused on tightening union security rather than on achieving drastic increases in compensation. For in the coalfields, as in much of the rest of the country, deprivation and unemployment lingered through the 1930s, despite flurries of recovery in 1933–34 and 1935–37. Coal operators continued to lose money, and the basic problems of the industry—too many mines, too much tonnage, and too many miners—remained in force.

Union gains were nonetheless real. The breaking of the arbitrary power of the mining companies, the creation of local grievance committees, the presence of union checkweighmen, and higher union rates providing a living wage even for irregularly employed miners solidified the UMW in the hearts of its members. The extension of the union into the most obdurate and antiunion bastions—first the so-called captive mines, operated by the powerful utilities and steel companies, and later places such as Harlan County, a synonym for poverty and repression— helped to secure these gains and to ease the fear and civic helplessness that had so long characterized so many mining communities.

At the same time, UMW contracts, both explicitly and implicitly, helped to intensify some of the miners' problems. The mandating of high wages and union work rules encouraged operators to turn to mechanization as a means of reducing costs. In the 1930s, use of cutting machines and, especially, mechanical loaders mushroomed. Periodically, miners protested, pointing out that mechanization exacerbated the underemployment in the mine fields. Moreover, greater reliance on machinery eroded the miner's traditional skills, making him more and more like any other industrial worker, simply a small cog in a vast machine.

Lewis had little sympathy for such views. His brief career underground had been spent in a mine known for its pioneering and extensive use of machinery. Lewis applauded when the diesel engine replaced the mule and the mechanical cutter did away with laborious pick work. No UMW contract contained any prohibition or discouragement of mechanical innovation. Indeed, beginning with the 1934 contract, the union insisted on exercising the right to discipline wildcat strikers, men who sometimes rebelled against the introduction of new machinery by employing the miner's time-honored (but now punishable) practice of throwing up a picket line until issues relating to safety, compensation, and job assignments were resolved. "We think," Lewis told the UMW convention that year, "the machine will make possible greater wages, shorter working hours and improved conditions." In China, he noted, "it is cheaper to take the motor out of a ten-ton truck and hire fifty men to pull that truck with ropes . . . than to buy gasoline." God forbid that Americans should ever agree to work this cheaply. No, Lewis's UMW would never be a party to a policy of machine breaking or technological retrogression.[27]

Actually, as Lewis well knew, the problem of technological replacement was not really this simple. Miners did not protest the introduction of machinery in the abstract. It was rather helter-skelter, heedless technological experimentation that drew their anger. American mines were notorious for their poor safety performance, and operators rarely paid scrupulous attention to mine safety when attempting to get maximum use of an expensive new piece of equipment. Indeed, technological innovation proceeded so rapidly that rarely could state safety laws keep pace. Thus, introduction of a new drilling or cutting machine in a particular mine with distinctive atmospheric or geological features might or might not be dangerous, but, given the language in which state mine safety laws were typically written, it would not be illegal. What recourse did miners have, then, but to call in the pit committee, refuse to work with the new machinery, and perhaps call a wildcat strike? To the Lewis-led UMW, however, such spontaneous stoppages were anathema. For if mine workers were to enjoy the benefits of a stabilized, high-wage industry, they would have to regard the collective bargaining agreement as a sacred trust. The contract was the worker's protection. At the same time, it was his pledge to his employer and to the consuming public that he would work faithfully and follow instructions. Lewis's whole campaign of centralizing control over the union, fighting for broad-scale bargaining arrangements, and tightening discipline over rank-and-file miners was based on this premise.

To be sure, Lewis recognized the dilemmas that the industry's poor safety record and the unemployment caused by technological change created. Toward the end of the 1930s, he lashed out at the appalling record of American mines and demanded tough federal safety legislation to replace patchwork state enactments. The 1937 contract created a UMW-operator committee to study the effects of mechanization of mining with a view to recommending policies to help displaced workers. Lewis followed this innovation up with calls for publicly sponsored retraining initiatives. Moreover, coal miners, even in the classic days of traditional mining, had always cared more about the fatness of the pay packet than about questions of safety. Many prided themselves on their fearlessness and willingness to take risks. Newer mine workers— and the bulk of the union's membership in the 1930s consisted of men with little or no direct experience with the union—cared less than their fathers about erosion of the traditional skills and more about the implications of the mechanization on their own take-home pay. It was, in short, a complex series of questions.

To Lewis, the inevitability of mechanical intrusion was a given. The replacement of men by machines was all to the good. He refused to romanticize the filthy and dangerous work. If high wages compelled operators to bring in machines to replace vulnerable human beings, Lewis believed that UMW goals were being achieved. Strong federal safety legislation, contractual provisions designed to protect veteran miners from layoff, and well-financed programs, perhaps underwritten by the mining companies, perhaps publicly funded, to retrain miners and provide alternative employment constituted Lewis's response to the dilemmas of an industry rapidly mechanizing under the impetus of high-wage UMW contracts.

In the 1930s, the UMW rose from the ashes of defeat to reclaim its status as American's largest, most powerful, and most vigorous labor union. The contrast between the union's desperate condition of 1932 and the robust health it enjoyed only a few years later could not have been greater. The upgrading of wage standards and working conditions, the achievement of broad and stable regional bargaining arrangements, and the extension of the union presence into virtually every coalfield in the country signaled the UMW's remarkable transformation. The delegates who gathered in Columbus, Ohio, in January 1940 to mark the organization's fiftieth anniversary, represented a half million UMW members. "The work of a half century has borne fruit," the officers reported, pointing to the union's "splendid condition" and "magnificent structure."[28]

Lewis was now nearly sixty years old. In the past seven years he had demonstrated a remarkable ability to dominate both debate over federal labor policy and the collective bargaining process. His booming voice now reached mass radio audiences on a regular basis. His skillful use of the press, his combination of intimidation and sweet reasonableness in bargaining, and his shrewd manipulation of government kept the mine workers at the center of public attention. The miners' self-organization in 1933–34 and their staunch militancy strengthened his hand with anxious federal conciliators and cabinet members. The strikes of 1933, 1935, and 1939 convinced even the most powerful coal barons of the UMW's power and of the mine workers' determination to prevent any renewal of the union-busting tactics of the past.

No one knew better than Lewis that his power rested on this militancy and steadfastness. Nor did he fail to realize how crucial the role of the federal government had been in the rebuilding of the union. At the same time, however, even his bitter enemies of the 1920s admitted that his boldness, intelligence, and uncanny ability to dramatize the miners' demands were likewise central to the UMW's renewal. Declared John Brophy in 1935, "I am sold on him today. . . . He is a genius on timing."[29] Powers Hapgood, whose vocal criticism of Lewis had gotten him regularly ejected from UMW conventions throughout the 1920s, hailed "The New John L. Lewis."[30] The man and the moment, it seemed, had met.

Old critics did not entirely forget the earlier Lewis record. Thus, for journalist-investigator Edward Wieck, he remained "the same old Lewis, . . . keen, intelligent, quick to grasp opportunities," to be sure, "but ruthless, unscrupulous, dictatorial" at heart.[31] For most, however, the rebuilding of the union and the improvement in miners' standards pushed aside memories of earlier transgressions. In addition, believed men such as John Brophy and Adolph Germer, Lewis and his revitalized UMW held the key to energizing and expanding the entire labor movement. Here indeed was a project worthy of even the most skeptical UMW dissident.

4

LEWIS AND THE CIO

Even as the UMW rose from the ashes, Lewis fought to expand organization of the American working class and to broaden the labor movement's power and influence. First within the AFL and then, after 1935, through a new industrial union committee, he exploited the resentment and desire for organization among workers in mass production industries to create a new and dynamic force in the labor movement, the CIO.[1] Revealing now a boldness and eloquence hitherto reserved for his rivals in the pre-NRA United Mine Workers, Lewis stood at the forefront of the single most significant development in American labor history, the expansion of organized labor from a handful of protected enclaves to the vast steel, auto, rubber, electrical, and other manufacturing centers. Whether dominating tense negotiations with corporate leaders, defying the AFL's established leadership, supporting Roosevelt's reelection bid in 1936, or speaking to mass meetings and huge radio audiences, Lewis captured public attention while adding a new dimension to the American labor movement.

Breaking with the AFL, 1933–35

Between 1933 and 1935, Lewis urged the AFL to exploit the opportunity the NRA offered to organize mass production workers. Convinced that laborites had to modify or abandon traditional policies and to respond to the new dynamics within the working class, he prodded the federation to embrace industrial unionism. Equally convinced that only the vast expansion and transformation of the labor movement could save the country from the rule of a cabal of destructive financial and corporate interests, Lewis aligned himself with the thousands of new unionists from the auto, rubber, steel, and other mass production industries. By late 1935 Lewis had concluded that the federation was in fact wasting a unique opportunity to expand. In October, he used the forum of the AFL's annual convention to dramatize his determination to wage an aggressive campaign for industrial unionism, even without AFL sanction.

The surge of organizing that accompanied the NRA was not confined to coal miners. Workers in every trade seized the opportunity, rebuilding old unions and forming organizations for the first time in many occupations. Garment and clothing workers revived once-strong unions that had fallen on hard times. Building tradesmen, truck drivers, and cargo handlers used Section 7(a) to revitalize unions brought low by the depression. But the most dramatic growth came in the vast nonunion mass production sectors. Thousands of auto, steel, rubber, textile, and other manufacturing workers joined existing AFL organizations or created entirely new unions. Tens of thousands of these workers in basic industry had never before belonged to unions. The labor movement, whose membership had slipped below 3 million from a World War I high of nearly 5 million, gained new life. Between June 1933 and August 1934, over 2 million new recruits poured into labor's ranks. "I have so many calls for organizers," declared one veteran unionist in July 1933, "that I have neither the men nor the money to take care of all of them."[2]

John L. Lewis played little direct role in this initial surge. The rebirth of his own union and the tense negotiations that solidified the spectacular gains of 1933 absorbed most of his time and energy. Quickly, however, he saw that this upheaval represented a once-in-a-lifetime opportunity for the labor movement to move from the margins to the center of American life. Having seen his own union plunge from strength to crisis fifteen years before, he knew how precarious and tentative this rebirth was. Now, for a golden moment, and no longer, organized labor had the opportunity to reach out to thousands of new recruits and to enhance the political and economic power of labor unions and labor leaders. As the UMW's position in the coalfields solidified, Lewis pressed his colleagues in the AFL to exploit this great, but, he was convinced, fleeting opportunity.

When Lewis spoke on these matters, he spoke with authority. The brilliant revival of the UMW made it once again the largest American union. Lewis's bold reorganizing tactics, his skillful manipulation of governmental authorities, and his stunning successes in collective bargaining and code writing under the NRA pushed him to the forefront of the labor movement. Moreover, the UMW's historic role gave its leader unique standing in the matter of mass organizing and industrial unionism. Unlike most AFL affiliates, the UMW embraced in one organization all workers at the job site; whether they were skilled miners, craftsmen who repaired electrical or mechanical equipment, or draymen and laborers, all mine workers belonged to the UMW. The AFL historically reflected the interests and priorities of the craft unions, organizations such as the Carpenters, Electricians, and Machinists that were confined to relatively skilled practitioners of particular trades. But the UMW, in part because of the remote locales of so many coal mines, was an outpost of mass organization, an industrial union in a federation primarily composed of craft unions.

Not only that, coal mining was integrated into the very structure of mass production industry. The great steel mills of Pennsylvania, Ohio, Indiana, and Illinois were often directly adjacent to the mines that fed their furnaces. Indeed, large steel corporations and utilities owned and operated mining properties, the so-called captive mines. Would UMW locals in these vulnerable enclaves be safe without organization of the mills themselves? Throughout the industrial heartland of the country, former UMW members now toiled in the mills and factories that made steel, automobiles, rubber, garments, and other mass-produced goods. The expansion of industrial UMW-style unionism into these sectors, with their hundreds of thousands of potential recruits, was a natural and necessary next step for the ambitious leader of the mine workers. Repeatedly, Lewis reminded his coal miners of their heritage and their destiny: they were, he asserted, the shock troops of the labor movement.

Indeed, Lewis believed, organizing mass production workers was crucial, and not only for the workers and the labor movement. On organized labor's success in the months following the passage of the NIRA, he warned, lay the fate of the country as a free society. Although Lewis had no explicit ideology with which to analyze the cataclysmic events of the 1920s and early 1930s, he did perceive a sinister trend toward corporate control, monopolistic domination, and eventual destruction of all but the most formal attributes of a free society. The concurrent destruction of workers' movements in Germany and Italy and the rise of European fascism provided dark omens for the American working class.

With Jett Lauck supplying the academic analysis, Lewis pointed to the vast concentration of wealth and financial power in the United States, a trend that had accelerated in the 1920s. A small circle of corporate leaders and their banking associates had poured money into the expansion of production. Lauck's detailed accounts of the mechanization of coal mining, the development of ever more efficient turbines, and the vast growth of power-generating and power-using machinery filled the pages of the UMW *Journal*. In the mines, innovations were redefining the traditional role of the miner. "Ford methods," declared one influential observer in the 1920s, had begun to transform mining into another mass production industry, entailing the "greater regimentation of work."[3] Increasingly, coal miners were, like the vast majority of their counterparts in the urban working class, semiskilled operatives.

Mechanization, however, was only part of the story. In addition, Lewis warned of the sociopolitical implications of corporate and financial control. Lauck directed his chief's attention to the effects of the concentration of economic decision making into the hands of this small group of banking, investment, and financial potentates. Frenetic technological innovation with its attendant surge in productivity per manhour had overwhelmed the ability of American workers to consume the products of their labor. Absent strong unions or governmental regulation, corporate decision makers followed only the short-term lust for profit. In 1929, they had plunged the country into economic chaos, just as Germany's leaders had plunged that now-Nazified country into chaos. Could American democratic traditions survive such a crisis?

Reflecting Lauck's views, Lewis's speeches depicted a plutocratic cabal "working out its objectives silently, invisibly, and without official recognition." Mindlessly, "this small inner group of New York bankers and financiers" had cast the country into depression. Only the organization of the masses of industrial workers offered salvation, for an aroused working class could force the increased wages that would provide the consumer spending to refloat the economy. More than that, however, seizing this brief opportunity to turn the AFL from an elitist organization into a mass movement would put democracy on the offensive and rescue the country from the "stupid financial leadership" that had brought it to the brink of ruin.[4]

Throughout the NRA period, Lewis preached this almost apocalyptic warning. He tried to persuade the leadership of the AFL to seize the opportunity that Section 7(a) offered to transform the labor movement. In the 1920s, the federation had sunk into lethargy, a state that the onset of the depression had done little to cure. Its unions were driven from large-scale industrial enterprise, where for a brief spell during and just after World War I they had gained shaky footholds. Dominated by a band of complacent union bosses, the AFL pursued cautious policies, rarely venturing to challenge powerful corporations that employed thousands and kept unions at bay. Nor had Lewis, despite his mine workers' deserved reputation for militancy, opposed this tide of inertia. Content with exercising power within the parochial world of the AFL executive council, where he occupied a prominent seat, Lewis seemed to typify the bombastic and cynical "labor statesman." "He is the grand walking delegate, the glorified organizer, the perfect boss," sneered one socialist critic.[5]

But the events of 1933 and after opened new vistas. As an AFL organizer in the pre–World War I years, Lewis had gained valuable knowledge of the increasingly mechanized nature of American industry. The steel, rubber, and electrical workers he had sought to organize included relatively few skilled craftsmen and vast numbers of operatives— men and women who tended machines, performing repetitive tasks. He had seen these workers wage courageous battles in the effort to build unions. He knew at firsthand that in the mass production mills and factories there toiled vast numbers of potential recruits for the labor movement. But powerful craft unions, with theoretical jurisdiction over mass production operatives, were nonetheless reluctant to invest the time and money to recruit them. Unwilling to abandon their claims, they actually impeded drives to organize nonskilled workers. In Akron, Pittsburgh, and elsewhere in the industrial heartland, young organizer John Lewis had seen the AFL's structural setup and internal power relations repeatedly torpedo his efforts. In Pittsburgh, he once recalled, "We organized 12,000 of the 16,000 employees at the Westinghouse plant." But, he added, "we lost out—because the crafts said the workers must be segregated."[6]

As a fledgling organizer at that time, however, Lewis was in no position to criticize the AFL openly. But he did not forget the lessons learned, and in the electric atmosphere of the 1930s, he lost few opportunities to drive them home. In 1935, recalling his experience as an organizer, he boasted to his fellow unionists that "I have had perhaps as much experience in organizing workers in the various industries as any member of the Executive Council." He recalled his frustration, as mass production workers formed unions only to watch the AFL split them apart to satisfy the jurisdictional claims of the craft unions. "Practically every attempt to organize those workers broke upon the same rock that it breaks upon today," he charged. "For twenty-five years or more the American Federation of Labor has been following this precise policy" and has compiled "a record of twenty-five years of constant, unbroken failure."[7]

Beginning in late 1933, with his UMW firmly back on its feet, Lewis began speaking out. As a federation vice president he championed the new industrial unions struggling for life under the federation's clumsy and often inept nurture. As the wave of unionizing enthusiasm began to ebb in mid-1934, he attacked his fellow AFL leaders for their lack of daring and their insensitivity to the needs of workers in mass production industries. In 1933 and early 1934, the AFL achieved a beachhead in such antiunion industries as rubber, autos, and steel, but increasingly it seemed that AFL president Green and the federation's other leaders did not know what to do with the hundreds of new local unions. Aging federation chieftains fretted endlessly over jurisdictional wrangles. Powerful unions such as the Carpenters and Teamsters forced the newly created locals in manufacturing plants to turn over their skilled cadres—often the most active and effective members—to the established craft unions. Impatient workers, now facing harsh employer counterattacks in the form of firings, harassment, espionage, and even beatings at the hands of thugs and "security" personnel, found the AFL leadership wedded to formal procedures and chary of workers' militancy. Counsels of restraint greeted outraged accounts of victimization. To energetic young workers trying to unionize the gas and coke byproducts field, Green offered the AFL's standard homilies. The Bible-quoting labor leader reminded the enthusiastic activists that "'he who keepeth his head is stronger than he that taketh a City.' Remember gentlemen keep your head and respect jurisdictional rights."[8] Hundreds of "NRA babies," new unions formed in the flush of enthusiasm for the Blue Eagle, collapsed, and the clink of discarded union buttons could be heard on the streets of industrial America. Given the AFL's record, could the federation—the only substantial labor movement the country had—find the strength to fight the corporate cliques and financial octopi?

Initially, Lewis hoped that the AFL leadership would share his sense of urgency. At the October 1934 convention, he had authored resolutions directing the executive council to issue charters to create separate industrial unions in the major mass production industries. Despite the opposition of traditionalists, he did gain passage of a statement requiring the council to issue such charters after ironing out possible jurisdictional conflicts with established unions. Moreover, Lewis and his allies pressed successfully for expansion of the executive council. Since other leaders with a bias toward industrial unionism, notably David Dubinsky of the Ladies' Garment Workers, Sidney Hillman of the Clothing Workers, and Charles Howard of the Typographical Union, had begun to play a larger role in federation affairs, industrial union advocates were initially optimistic. Alas, however, the charters eventually issued to the automobile workers and the rubber workers sharply restricted their potential membership and forced them to surrender many of their members to the craft unions. Nor did President Green move effectively to tap organizing enthusiasm among hundreds of thousands of steelworkers, a matter of particular concern to the UMW, which had about forty thousand members in the captive mines. So, successful in rebuilding his own union, Lewis grew ever more impatient with the federation's ineptitude.

By the time of the October 1935 AFL convention in Atlantic City, the UMW chief was ready to force the issue. Marshaling behind him a strong minority of delegates critical of the AFL's lack of responsiveness to the opportunity to organize industrial workers, Lewis put on a dazzling display. Voicing openly his contempt for his fellow council members, on 16 October he held the floor for half an hour, pleading for action in behalf of the AFL's fledgling industrial unionists while heaping scorn on the federation's leaders.

At the 1934 AFL convention, he reminded his audience, President Green had spoken glowingly of the imminent organization of 25 million workers. "Where are those twenty-five million?" Lewis challenged. Instead, hundreds of unions created in the flush of NRA enthusiasm were folding, "dying like the grass withering before the Autumn sun." The 1934 convention, Lewis asserted, had pledged the AFL to issue industrial union charters and to mount organizing campaigns in steel, automobiles, and rubber. But the charters issued were frauds, and no campaigns were launched. The behavior of the AFL leaders, he proclaimed, "was a breach of faith and a travesty of good conscience."[9]

As he began his oration, delegates, journalists, and onlookers perked up their ears. The imposing Lewis had earned an unmatched reputation for convention oratory. With his bushy eyebrows, his perfectly cut three-piece suit, and his booming voice, he stood out vividly from the dry-as-dust functionaries who normally occupied the floor at AFL gatherings. In prose salted with biblical, Shakespearean, and classical allusions, Lewis gained a ready audience among the scores of newspapermen covering the proceedings. Here indeed was quotable copy. Nor did Lewis always observe the federation's polite protocols, for his pointed barbs and scathing asides named names, leaving dignified fellow chieftains squirming in their chairs. Master of the high-sounding phrase and the proverbial meat cleaver, Lewis in full voice turned a dreary convention into exciting theater.

The theme of betrayal punctuated the speech. A year earlier, Lewis confided, he had believed the honeyed words of the leadership's pledges to step up organizing. "At San Francisco they seduced me," but "now . . . having learned that I was seduced, I am enraged and I am ready to rend my seducers limb from limb."[10] And he identified one prominent council member as his chief seducer and as the first candidate for this dreadful vengeance.

He pointed with particular exasperation to the AFL's failure to launch a campaign to organize the steel industry. Thousands of steelworkers had joined local AFL unions in the wake of the NRA, but the leaders of the ancient and decaying affiliate with jurisdiction over them had been so fearful of this new breed of aggressive rank-and-file unionist that they spent all their time and resources hamstringing the new locals and the energetic young recruits. But now, when pressed by the United Mine Workers to bring organization to steel, federation leaders meekly deferred to this discredited union, the Amalgamated Association of Iron, Steel, and Tin Workers (AA). Lewis scornfully assured the convention that the AA could not organize the industry. "The officers of the American Federation of Labor might as well sit down in their easy chairs and twiddle their thumbs and take a nap as to conclude that any results will come from that kind of organization." He warned the traditionalists: "If you go in there with your craft unions they [the employers] will mow you down like the Italian machine guns will mow down the Ethiopians in the war now going on in that country." Not only that, "they will mow you down and laugh while they are doing it."[11]

The speech dripped with contempt. By implication, and occasionally by name, Lewis charged the leadership of the AFL from William Green on through the executive council with cowardice, lack of vision, complacency, and deceit. The owners of the steel industry's captive mines, emboldened by the AFL's failure to organize steelworkers, were "trying to starve my people to death." Alabama coal operators, taking their cue from steel corporations with captive mines in that state, now refused to abide by NRA codes and had locked out twenty-one thousand UMW members. "Our people are suffering," Lewis warned, "and they are suffering . . . by the fact that the American Federation of Labor . . . has failed . . . to organize the iron and steel workers. . . . How long," he continued ominously, "does any one think the United Mine Workers of America will be satisfied with that policy?"[12]

It was well known among the delegates that various groupings of dissidents had been caucusing, planning strategy. Knots of youngish industrial union advocates gathered in Atlantic City's bars and hotel lobbies. One group of feisty electrical workers drew crowds of admiring reporters and onlookers by putting on a skit in which they mimicked the hoary rhetoric and pretentious do-nothingism of well-known federation leaders. Lewis's right-hand men, Philip Murray, Pat Fagan, and Thomas Kennedy, had been seen at some of these gatherings. Something was in the air. But Lewis's mesmerizing speech outlined no plan of action or issued no direct threat. Instead, it closed with a final plea for the leadership to "heed this cry from Macedonia that comes from the hearts of men. Organize the unorganized and in so doing you make the American Federation of Labor the greatest instrumentality that has ever been forged in the history of modern civilization to befriend the cause of humanity and champion human rights."[13]

As Lewis anticipated, his biting words changed few votes. In the showdown over the wisdom of the federation's policies, the convention endorsed the Old Guard by a weighted vote of 18,000 to 10,000. Moreover, as the convention wound down, triumphant traditionalists lost few opportunities to embarrass and isolate their industrial union critics, many of them young men and women attending their first AFL convention. Never one to suffer defeat silently, Lewis bided his time over the next three days as his opponents cheerfully steamrollered the dissidents.

At last, on the nineteenth, Lewis created an opportunity for a dramatic gesture. Ohio rubber workers sought the floor in an effort to keep alive the debate over industrial unionism. William ("Big Bill") Hutcheson, the powerful, beefy boss of the Carpenters union, objected on a technicality. Lewis spoke out, defending the rubber workers. He called Hutcheson's repeated calls for points of order on minor matters "rather small potatoes." Stunned delegates and reporters watched as the two burly men—Indianapolis poker-playing cronies not so long before—exchanged insults. Bystanders heard Hutcheson call Lewis a "bastard." Lewis, who surely had been called worse in his trade union life, sprang into action. Now on his feet, he vaulted a row of chairs and delivered a right jab to Hutcheson's jaw. Moments later, Big Bill's friends assisted the blood-streaked unionist from the hall while Lewis, relighting his cigar, strolled casually to the rostrum.[14]

Creating the CIO

Between 1935 and 1937, Lewis presided over the creation of a great new flowering of the labor movement. The birth and rise of the CIO represent his most outstanding and enduring contribution to American life. For two years he was constantly front-page copy in the nation's press as he put himself at the head of the thousands of mass production workers struggling to bring collective bargaining to the auto, steel, rubber, electrical, and other central core manufacturing sectors. More than any other single person, Lewis determined the basic institutional patterns into which the industrial union surge flowed. At the same time, he was the key figure in the increasingly acrimonious debate between the established AFL leadership and the upstart unionists in the CIO. He oversaw the establishment of collective bargaining in the auto and steel industries, and in 1936 he broke with tradition by pouring vast sums into President Roosevelt's reelection campaign, thus bringing the labor movement forcefully into the national political arena for the first time. "John L. Lewis," declared one admiring journalist, "is the Babe Ruth of the labor movement."[15]

Lewis undertook these innovations without any master plan in mind. Although he later intimated that he had been plotting for months, if not years, to build a national labor federation rival to the AFL, in reality—and characteristically—he was responding to immediate circumstances in the fall of 1935. If the ineptitude of the AFL stood in the way of organizing mass production workers, Lewis would create a new vehicle. If restless and angry workers felt betrayed by the AFL's timid response to their efforts to organize, Lewis would provide a new start. Through 1934 and into 1935, he had tried to work within the AFL; now he would have to strike out on his own.

The CIO was actually born the day after the AFL's 1935 convention. On Sunday, 20 October, Lewis, accompanied by his UMW associates, met at his suite in the President Hotel with friends of industrial unionism such as David Dubinsky of the Ladies Garment Workers, Sidney Hillman of the Clothing Workers, and Typographical Union president Charles Howard. At his elbow sat John Brophy, rescued from exile and now installed as Lewis's chief functionary in the industrial union crusade. Three weeks later, on 9 November, these same men, along with several other presidents of smaller AFL affiliates sympathetic to industrial unionism, met at UMW headquarters. The UMW, the Amalgamated Clothing Workers (ACWA), and the International Ladies Garment Workers (ILGWU) each pledged five thousand dollars to meet expenses. Brophy was named director of organization and the group designated itself the Committee for Industrial Organization (CIO), a body created to function within the AFL to encourage industrial forms of organization among mass production workers. Since the AFL had in principle endorsed organization of auto, steel, rubber, and other manufacturing workers, this new CIO could claim loyalty to the old federation even while it encouraged new forms of organization. The CIO committee authorized the printing of pamphlets, provided for a skeletal headquarters staff, and laid plans for a CIO newspaper. Nine days later, Brophy began operations in the Rust Building, directly across the street from UMW headquarters.

That this CIO was Lewis's creature was never in doubt. He had handpicked Brophy, his one-time enemy, as director and the UMW paid his salary, as it paid the salaries of the CIO's small office staff and publicity director, Len De Caux. Throughout the late fall and winter of 1935–36, representatives who circulated throughout the industrial heartland in behalf of the CIO were on the payroll of the UMW. Hillman and Dubinsky provided some money and a few organizers, but Lewis and the UMW dominated the CIO's financial and organizational affairs.

The CIO launched no immediate new organizing campaign. Despite his willingness to part with tradition, Lewis was not eager initially for an irrevocable break with the AFL, and some of his associates, notably Dubinsky, urged restraint. Around the country, industrial workers greeted the formation of the CIO enthusiastically, reveling in Lewis's assault on craft union stalwart Hutcheson and hailing the new committee as the cutting edge of mass activism. But at first, Lewis merely had Brophy and other former Mine Workers Union dissidents such as Powers Hapgood and Adolph Germer travel through the auto, steel, and rubber cities of the Middle West, assessing prospects.

It is likely that Lewis would have preferred avoiding an open break with the AFL. Certainly, although he did part with some venerable traditions of the labor movement, he intended no thoroughgoing revolution in the way in which unions did business. Brophy and other CIO functionaries followed standard institutional forms in nourishing CIO sentiment. Some enthusiasts urged the CIO to abandon organized labor's commitment to collective bargaining in favor of various schemes of worker control or anticapitalist politics. Activists among agricultural workers begged Lewis and his associates to waive organized labor's bureaucratic methods of dues collection and accounting so that ill-educated and poverty-stricken farm workers could become part of the labor upsurge. At times it seemed that labor organizations that embraced all workers in a given locale, rather than merely those in a given industry or trade, made the most sense in the crackling atmosphere of the mid-1930s. The CIO, claimed some laborites, should revert to the promiscuous organizing of the old Knights of Labor of the 1880s and abandon—or at least modify—the practice of organizing by plant or industry.

Lewis paid no heed to these notions. The CIO would, to be sure, jettison the AFL's crippling thralldom to the craft unions in its recruitment of mass production workers. It would create new unions to provide centrally directed organization of steel, meat-packing, and other key sectors. It would eliminate the high initiation fees and steep dues structures of the craft unions and would back its organizers with hundreds of thousands of UMW dollars. But the CIO remained at all times, despite these departures from the AFL's norms, firmly within the basic structures and traditions of the mainstream American labor movement as embodied originally in the AFL. If for no other reason, Lewis preferred originally avoiding an open break with the AFL because he believed that the mass organization of industrial workers was inevitable. Hundreds of thousands of new members would shift the balance within the federation, and Lewis, as the sponsor and champion of the new recruits, would emerge as the leader of a vastly strengthened AFL.

The federation's blank refusal to recognize the CIO as a legitimate grouping within its ranks and Green's unwillingness to cooperate in organizing steelworkers convinced the CIO chief, however, that progress within the existing structure was impossible. In January 1936, as the AFL executive council met in sunny Florida to denounce the CIO, Lewis addressed mass meetings of rubber and other industrial workers in frigid Cleveland and Akron. Enthusiastic workers filled the halls and two weeks later thousands of Akron rubber workers were on strike. Such corporate giants as Goodyear and Firestone refused to modify their arbitrary disciplinary, layoff, and wage payment practices. They would not meet with union representatives, who in turn led rolling waves of strikes, sit-downs, and slowdowns in the plants.

Throughout the bitterly cold winter of 1936 and into the spring, turmoil gripped Akron. Rubber workers resurrected the device of the sit-down strike, simply occupying a building or department until an obnoxious foreman was removed or a fired union activist was reinstated. On 17 February, fifteen hundred workers shut down the giant Goodyear factory, establishing a picket line eleven miles long around the sprawling facility. Three hundred shanties, hastily constructed from tarpaper and old tires, provided strong points. When a 150-man sheriff's contingent massed to enforce an injunction aimed at the pickets, ten thousand rubber workers, many armed with baseball bats, lead pipes, and bowling pins began forming up to head it off. The sheriff backed away, the pickets remained huddled around their fires, and the plant remained silent, with 5000 Goodyear workers eventually on strike.

Akron's rubber workers had a long history of activism. In 1913, Lewis himself had served as an AFL organizer during a massive strike. In 1933–34, AFL federal unions had sprung up in the tire factories in response to Section 7(a). But this time, the AFL was nowhere to be seen. Rubber workers looked not to William Green and his representatives, as in 1933–34 they had so futilely done. They looked now to John L. Lewis and the CIO. Brophy came in to address a mass meeting. Germer spent weeks in Akron, advising and cautioning the sometimes-impetuous rubber workers. Rose Pesotta of the Garment Workers and Leo Krzycki of the ACWA provided negotiating advice and moral support, and CIO dollars (really, UMW dollars) flowed in. When a compromise settlement was reached in March, the United Rubber Workers (URW) was firmly entrenched in the great tire factories, and the CIO had passed its first major test.

Steel, however, was the key. Lewis watched impatiently as the AA frittered away the gains in membership that had come in the NRA period. Convinced by April of 1936 that the AFL would not mount a steel campaign and that the AA was simply too weak and irresolute to do the job, Lewis now acted swiftly. He hammered together a Steel Workers Organizing Committee (SWOC) to be headed by Murray. Financed largely by the UMW, it would mount a centralized campaign, ignoring the jurisdictional claims of AFL affiliates such as the Machinists, Sheet Metal Workers, and Electrical Workers. All steelworkers, like all mine workers, would be recruited into the same union. To the officials of the AA he offered an ultimatum: cast in your lot with SWOC and retain your positions or be crushed by the CIO juggernaut. After feeble protests, the AA, an AFL affiliate for fifty years, agreed to enlist in the SWOC campaign and thus had to bear the wrath of Green and his cohorts. On 19 June 1936, the CIO announced the formal creation of the Steel Workers Organizing Committee and pledged $1.5 million to underwrite a massive campaign to bring unionism and collective bargaining to the nation's half million steelworkers.

The creation of SWOC made a final break with the AFL certain. Despite his many provocative statements and his defiance of AFL leadership, Lewis had sought to maintain at least a semblance of "legality" in launching the CIO. He always insisted that the CIO wanted merely to encourage the growth of industrial unions within the AFL and that it posed no threat to existing AFL affiliates. Green and his associates on the executive council had refused to acknowledge Lewis's concern with these niceties. So far as they were concerned, SWOC revealed the UMW president in his true colors as a destructive megalomaniac, running roughshod over the legitimate rights of a dozen AFL unions, bullying the AA into cooperation, and ignoring a half-century of AFL tradition and practice. After June 1936 the American labor movement clearly was split into two rival federations, although for two more years the CIO continued to maintain the fiction that it was not a separate organization.

Through the spring of 1936, Green and Lewis had engaged in a sharp public debate over the activities of the CIO. In January, the executive council ordered Lewis and his associates to disband the CIO, and in response Lewis abruptly resigned from the council. As Lewis browbeat the AA into joining with SWOC, Green issued public statements charging his one-time associate with betrayal while dissociating himself and the AFL from Lewis's grandiose project. Always the master of invective, and always careful to see to it that the reporters had prompt access to the correspondence, Lewis heaped disdain on Green. Green's objections to CIO plans to organize steel, sneered Lewis, were characterized by "inane ineptitude." If the AFL did not follow the CIO lead, Green would have "to sit with the women under an awning on the hilltop, while the steel workers in the valley struggle in the dust and agony of industrial warfare." After Green's final ultimatum in June, Lewis again ridiculed Green's and the AFL's do-nothing approach to organizing workers: "Candidly," he wrote in a widely publicized letter, "I am temperamentally incapable of sitting with you in sackcloth and ashes, endlessly intoning 'O tempora! O mores!'" Formal recommendation in

August by the executive council to suspend the CIO unions and the suspension itself, accomplished at the October 1936 convention, came as anticlimaxes.[16]

Thus, by the summer of 1936 the CIO seemed ready for action. Lewis had committed the UMW's vast resources to the CIO project. After the August suspension, the renegade unions, now joined by the embryonic United Automobile Workers (UAW) and United Rubber Workers (URW), stopped paying their monthly per capita tax (dues) to the AFL and sent the money instead to Brophy at CIO headquarters, thus helping to build the war chest for mass organizing. By the time of suspension, the CIO contained international unions embracing approximately 1.2 million workers, or about 30 percent of the AFL's total membership. With auto, rubber, steel, and other mass production workers reviving their NRA unions and looking expectantly to Lewis, the CIO, and SWOC for help, the test of Lewis's rebellion seemed at hand.

But one item remained on Lewis's agenda before the CIO could devote full energies to organizing industrial workers. It was 1936, a presidential year, and Lewis was convinced that labor's continued gains depended on the reelection of Franklin Roosevelt. A long-term Republican and deeply skeptical of the ultimate intentions of the Democratic president, Lewis nonetheless believed his reelection imperative for labor. Throughout the spring and summer of 1936, he hammered away at the theme of financial and corporate domination of American life, linking it to the reactionary elements that he believed had gained control of the Republican party. As early as the UMW convention in February, Lewis sounded the clarion: predatory Wall Street interests were out to defeat Roosevelt, boasting that they "can raise enough money to elect a Chinaman" in Roosevelt's place if they chose to. But the UMW would thwart these plans by "allying itself with a virtuous statesman who is giving to the fullest degree of his great strength, his marvelous ability, and his brilliant courage to protect the common people of this country." Since millions of workers would vote for FDR, declared the quondam Republican, "me thinks that there isn't any doubt how the election will go."[17]

During the campaign, Lewis's voice aroused working people in scores of campaign rallies and radio broadcasts. He urged them to defeat the designs of the conspiracy of wealth that had taken over the GOP and nominated Alfred M. Landon. The Kansas governor, however, was only the errand boy, declared Lewis. In reality, the opposition to Roosevelt consisted of Rockefeller, Morgan, and Du Pont. During World

War I, these same wealthy conspirators had fastened their monopolistic tentacles on American industry. In the 1920s, they had gobbled up much of the country's basic productive capacity, hurling the nation into depression in the process. Now this "sinister, reactionary, selfish"[18] combine had leeched onto the Republican party and was out to destroy Franklin Roosevelt, "the champion of industrial democracy."[19]

Nor did Lewis limit himself to oratory. In April, in conjunction with CIO associate Sidney Hillman and George Berry, president of the AFL Printing Pressman's union, he launched Labor's Non-Partisan League (LNPL), an independent body created to provide organizational and financial support to Roosevelt and other prolabor candidates. In the past, labor leaders had supported candidates and parties. Some laborites had even worked actively as part of the Republican and Democratic campaign organizations to channel funds to their candidates. Indeed, in 1924 and 1928 Lewis had been a prominent member of the Republican apparatus. The LNPL, however, was established as an entirely separate body, staffed and run entirely by men and women named by participating unions. It collected money and directed the activities of field workers in behalf of favored candidates independent of party organizations. This was an autonomous voice for labor, a declaration that organized labor, spearheaded by Lewis and the CIO, would play a central role in this election and, by implication, in all subsequent ones.

Lewis's UMW contributed the staggering sum of $600,000 to the Roosevelt campaign, an amount that dwarfed all previous laborite political contributions. In September and October, UMW and CIO field representatives suspended organizing work to throw themselves into the Roosevelt campaign, another unprecedented move. Lewis himself toured the familiar industrial towns of Pennsylvania, West Virginia, Ohio, Indiana, and New York. On 27 October, he addressed a monster rally at Madison Square Garden in New York City. He devoted little attention to Landon—"just as empty, as inane, as innocuous as a watermelon that had been boiled in a washtub"—and drove home to his working-class audiences the lesson that trade unionism and politics were inextricably linked. A Roosevelt defeat meant domination by plutocratic dictators, stillbirth for the resurgent labor movement, and, he sometimes implied, curtains for American democracy.[20]

Of course, Roosevelt swept to victory, carrying all but two states and piling up massive majorities in the industrial heartland. Unionists rejoiced at the outcome. Even the normally restrained Lewis grew exultant in the light of the huge margins for Roosevelt coming out of the steel towns, the coal camps, and the working-class precincts of Detroit, Pittsburgh, Akron, and the other industrial centers. "We . . . must capitalize on the election," he told the CIO executive board. "The CIO was out fighting for Roosevelt, and every steel town showed a smashing victory for him." Now the CIO must launch its organizing campaigns— now, while it had "a President who would hold the light for us."[21]

1937: Industrial Unionism Victorious

Lewis and the other industrial union advocates were brilliantly vindicated in the six months following FDR's reelection. In February 1937 automobile workers in Flint, Michigan, wrested a path-breaking contract from the titan of the auto industry, General Motors. Six weeks later, Chrysler succumbed to a wave of sit-down strikes. The SWOC made rapid headway organizing steelworkers, and the signing of a contract between SWOC and U.S. Steel in early March was a stunning triumph. Together with the ongoing successes of the Rubber Workers in Akron, important gains in the electrical appliances industry, and other industrial union strides, the victories in auto and steel proclaimed eloquently the wisdom of Lewis's break with the AFL and the determination of workers in mass production sectors to have their own unions. Through all the marching, picketing, and negotiating in this remarkable year of labor's rebirth, Lewis stood at the center of the CIO. "Lewis," declared journalist James Wechsler, "was its founding father, its emotional symbol, its commander-in-chief. And nearly all of the rollicking recruits who signed CIO cards identified the movement with the name and person of John L. Lewis."[22]

Even so, it was thousands of auto, steel, rubber, electrical, and other industrial workers who were at the heart of the CIO. Lewis negotiated in their behalf and his speeches articulated their demands and concerns. The frenzied enthusiasm that greeted him in his appearances at strike rallies and mass meetings caused conservatives to deplore his mesmerizing presence. But as Lewis never forgot, industrial unionism was the product of no one man. As a shrewd and skillful leader he knew that he who led best first saw where his troops were headed and then hurried to put himself in their van.

Nowhere was this more evident than in the automobile industry. The November elections of Roosevelt and liberal Democrat Frank Murphy as governor of Michigan encouraged restive autoworkers throughout southeast Michigan. Earlier attempts at building permanent unions among the largely semiskilled autoworkers had failed, first in the wake of World War I and then during the period of the NRA. But the grievances of the half-million or so men and women who produced the country's automobiles, trucks, and components remained. Arbitrary personnel policies, frequent layoffs, favoritism in job retention and rehiring, chronic speedup of the pace of work on the endless assembly lines, harsh and punitive disciplinary actions—these and other complaints festered in the plants of Detroit, Pontiac, Flint, and other auto centers. With business picking up and with corporations such as General Motors having contributed heavily to the ill-fated Landon campaign, militants in the auto plants began truculent confrontations with supervisors and plant managers. Strikes broke out in key plants in and around Detroit as a gifted cadre of young leaders exploited the unwillingness of manufacturers to risk work stoppages at a time of rising sales and brightening economic prospects. Workers in several Detroit plants learned that the sit-down strike, in which workers simply shut off the machinery and occupied the work site, gained decisive leverage for them in prying concessions from management.

Lewis and his aides did not consider autoworkers sufficiently well organized to take on the major corporations. Certainly, there were hardly any UAW members in Ford, which specialized in the use of thugs and ex-convicts to brutalize union-minded workers. General Motors, the world's largest corporation, also fought organization, devoting hundreds of thousands of dollars annually to infiltrating the weak UAW locals and to stockpiling tear gas and other weapons for use by its security forces and compliant local law enforcement agencies in the event of labor trouble. Leaders of the CIO believed that the auto industry could not be organized until SWOC made major breakthroughs in steel. Throughout December, however, activists staged one sit-down after another until finally on 30 December, UAW members pulled the switches and occupied key plants in General Motors' huge and strategic Flint complex.

Lewis did not hesitate for a moment. Despite his belief that steel should be the first priority, he pledged full CIO support to the sit-downers and dispatched Brophy and CIO legal counsel Lee Pressman to assist the UAW. With hundreds of auto workers occupying the affected plants, the UAW had to devise a complex system of support and supply. The Flint police assaulted the strikers, but a fusillade of door hinges and other auto parts hurled from second-story windows drove them back.

Governor Murphy brought in the Michigan National Guard to preserve order, refusing for the time being to use it to drive the sit-downers out.

As the strike drama unfolded in the bitterly cold Michigan winter, Lewis came forcefully into the picture. Public officials, GM executives, and newspapermen saw in him the key to the strike. Workers, they believed, would obey their majestic leader. When he arrived in Detroit on 3 February and began meeting first with Governor Murphy and then with GM executives, accounts of the strike focused increasingly on this charismatic figure. Yet better than anyone, Lewis knew that the key to the strike lay in the occupied plants and in the working-class neighborhoods of Flint. Throughout weeks of complex negotiations, he remained steadfast in his determination that the strikers would not leave the plants until GM had concluded a settlement with the UAW. Through good fortune and skillful legal maneuvering, Lewis and his aides were able to sidetrack GM's efforts to force the courts to enjoin the sit-down. Finally, in the second week in February, GM capitulated, signing a contract with the UAW and ending the six-week-old strike.

For those familiar with the elaborate UMW contracts, the UAW-GM accord of 11 February 1937 seemed a pretty flimsy affair. It made no reference to substantive issues, such as wages and working conditions. It granted the UAW only partial and temporary recognition as bargaining agent for its members in twenty or so of the company's fifty-odd facilities nationwide. It did pledge the company not to discriminate against UAW members and to foreswear bargaining with any other employee organization, but only for a period of six months. In the coal mines, Lewis would have disdained such an agreement, but in Flint the document was a glorious victory for the UAW. At last, GM had been forced to sign a contract. The very fact of victory gave the UAW enormous prestige. No sooner had its terms been released than thousands of new recruits in Flint and other auto centers flocked into the triumphant organization. Union grievance men began operating in GM plants, boldly asserting workers' rights and battling hard-nosed foremen and supervisors. Whatever the limitations of the contract, the judgment of historians Melvyn Dubofsky and Warren Van Tine is on target: "The UAW victory over General Motors legitimized the CIO as a national trade union center competitive with the A.F. of L. and magnified Lewis's role and influence as a labor leader."[23]

The dynamics of CIO victory in the steel industry were different from those in the auto plants. Steelworkers, with a long history of defeat and failure, proved initially less militant than the feisty auto and rubber workers. Moreover, the campaign to organize steel was a thoroughgoing UMW operation, with Lewis himself and his chief lieutenant Philip Murray playing the key roles. Whereas company unionism, for example, played little role in the auto factories, these employer-controlled bodies had gained at least tentative acceptance among steelworkers in many mills. The SWOC campaign, into which the CIO poured over a million dollars (most of it from the United Mine Workers), was an orderly, well-coordinated affair in contrast to the decentralized grassroots nature of organizing in the auto industry. Employing hundreds of organizers, many of them recruited from the UMW and from the various radical organizations such as the Communist party that shared the commitment to industrial unionism, SWOC made headway through 1936 and into 1937. Membership reached perhaps 150,000 by the end of the year—nowhere near a majority and too few in any given steel center to risk an open confrontation, but impressive in light of the corporations' bitter opposition to SWOC.

Of equal importance to the growth in membership was SWOC's increasing ability to control the company unions. By 1936–37, many of these employer-sponsored bodies had developed adversarial relations with plant management. Members of SWOC, not confident of openly challenging the company unions, would offer themselves for election to the company unions' leadership. There they would press militant demands, taking credit for SWOC when successful, using setbacks as a means of educating workers as to the need to establish a "real" union, namely a SWOC local. Through the key 1936–37 period, tensions mounted in the mills of U.S. Steel, by far the industry leader, as company union after company union seethed with rebellion and SWOC recruited ever larger numbers of new members.

Aside from some brief work stoppages in the Pittsburgh area, the CIO's breakthrough in steel was relatively peaceful. In January 1937, Lewis began meeting with U.S. Steel's board chairman Myron Taylor. These discussions grew out of a chance encounter in the dining room of Washington's Mayflower Hotel when the two men exchanged pleasantries and briefly visited each other's table as noonday diners craned their necks and strained to hear, hoping to observe history in the making. Over the next seven weeks, they met privately in Taylor's hotel and at his home in New York, working out an agreement between SWOC and U.S. Steel. Thus, even as he skillfully steered the UAW negotiations in Detroit toward a successful outcome, Lewis was preparing an equally impressive coup, an agreement with the country's most notoriously antilabor corporation.

To the luncheon observers, nothing seemed more incongruous than the sight of Lewis and Taylor head-to-head. In actuality, the two men had a common interest in curbing the turmoil in the steel mills. For Lewis, of course, an agreement with U.S. Steel would vindicate his entire course of action and transform SWOC into a labor organization of the first rank. The pattern of worker activism in the mills, moreover, was troubling and uncertain. If the company unions did retain credibility and become established as independent worker organizations, perhaps SWOC would die on the vine, and Lewis and the CIO would remain outsiders in the steel industry.

For Taylor, recognition of SWOC would end the labor troubles and workplace disruptions that had become chronic since the passage of the NIRA in 1933. An agreement with Lewis would settle things once and for all; Taylor could not help but be aware of Lewis's strong record of contract compliance in the UMW. With Lewis and Murray in charge, Taylor could be sure of having a "responsible" union in his mills, but if militants and hotheads gained control of the company unions, who knew where the turbulence would lead? With steel production rising, peaceful labor relations could make it possible for U.S. Steel to capture new markets and perhaps reclaim the position of industry dominance it had once enjoyed but from which it had been slipping for a quarter of a century.

Taylor was not a steelmaker per se. He was a financier, with little of the taste for industrial combat and less of the gut-level hostility toward unions that had shaped his predecessors' labor policies. Taylor and Lewis were both executives—substantial, calculating, rule-breaking men who could put aside the industry's ancient bloodletting and its grim record of labor struggle to work out a sensible agreement and restore order in the mills.

And so they did. On 2 March, just nineteen days after the GM-UAW settlement, the public learned of an agreement between SWOC and U.S. Steel. Like the automobile agreement, this one was a modest affair. As eventually concluded in more detailed negotiations, it provided for modest wage increases and reductions in hours of employment, changes that U.S. Steel would likely have made in any event. More significant was its provision for a detailed grievance procedure which gave the union de facto recognition as the sole workers' agent in day-to-day operations of mills covered by the agreement. It withheld formal recognition of swoc as exclusive bargaining agent but pledged the company and its affected subsidiaries to cease support for other workers' organizations (the company unions) and to deal only with swoc. The contract was to run for one year.

Taken together, the steel and auto agreements vindicated Lewis's course. Both CIO victories had immediate repercussions. In Detroit, autoworkers stormed into UAW locals, boosting the fledgling union's membership to over 300,000 by August. Organizing fever swept the Motor City, embracing cigar makers, store clerks, office workers, and restaurant employees as well as all sorts of industrial workers. An epidemic of sit-downs brought aggressive industrial unionism into a city long a citadel of the open shop. In March, a mass sit-down strike brought an agreement from Chrysler, giving the union firm footholds in two of the big three automakers. Meanwhile, UAW activists began mobilizing for an assault on the holdout, Ford Motor Company, convinced that an irresistible tide of unionism would soon sweep over even that antiunion bastion.

In the steel industry, swoc also mushroomed. By early June, the steelworkers' union had concluded over one hundred collective bargaining agreements. The U.S. Steel settlement served as a signal to workers to sign up with the union. In one week in May, it tallied over 37,000 recruits. Before it was a year old, swoc claimed over 300,000 members, more than all but a handful of venerable AFL affiliates had. Regional Director Clinton Golden reported an interesting dilemma: victory in the steel mills was triggering organizing fervor throughout the shops and plants producing all kinds of metal goods. Throughout Pennsylvania, organizers were chartering local unions for workers who made toys, locomotives, diesel engines, turbines, tin cans, bedsprings, enamelware, stoves, cutlery, air compressors, metal signs, and a dozen other items. Indeed, Golden worried about the new organization's ability "to properly direct and guide this huge army of the rawest kind of Union recruit."[24]

Initially also, it appeared that swoc would translate the U.S. Steel victory into success among the so-called Little Steel companies. These corporations, such as Jones & Laughlin, Inland Steel, Republic Steel, and Youngstown Sheet & Tube, were all large concerns in their own right, each employing over 30,000 workers. But they were small in comparison with the industry leader, U.S. Steel, with its 100,000 employees. In the past, they had followed the industry giant's lead in most respects, including labor relations. When Jones & Laughlin, a major Pittsburgh-area producer, sought to test SWOC in May, the suddenly potent new union shut down the company's key Aliquippa, Pennsylvania, facilities, recruiting thousands of new members. Aroused steelworkers, many nursing decades of resentment against the company's autocratic rule and the city's antiunion police, seized virtual control of the area around the Aliquippa Works. Known scabs and harsh foremen were singled out for beatings. "All Aliquippa was there," reported one observer. Although SWOC had called this work stoppage, the strike was "now a rank-and-file affair." Even after SWOC official Joe Timko addressed the crowd and announced the terms of a favorable settlement J & L had signed, crowds of workers and supporters continued to fill the streets around the mills. Wanting to avoid ugly incidents that might stain this great victory, he recruited a marching band. Waving an American flag, he put himself at the head of a procession that soon numbered twenty thousand. Steelworkers and family members quickly fell in behind him and marched out along the Ohio River, at last clearing the streets around the Aliquippa Works.[25]

The CIO's success was not limited to autos and steel. Organizing fervor rolled through virtually every industry and occupation. Glass workers, hard rock miners, longshoremen, merchant seamen, agricultural workers—even actors, newspaper reporters, and government employees surged into unions in the aftermath of the CIO's stunning victories. At the beginning of the year, the CIO was a small committee of dissident unionists, still hoping to avoid complete alienation of the AFL. By December, it was a mass movement embracing at least 2.5 million workers and holding collective bargaining agreements with General Motors, U.S. Steel, and other powerful corporations. And CIO growth boosted the AFL. In 1937, total union membership rose by 3 million. By the end of that eventful year, almost one-quarter of all non-agricultural workers were enrolled in unions, triple the proportion of 1932–33.

The Man and the Movement

Lewis celebrated his fifty-seventh birthday the day after the announcement of the Flint settlement. As the CIO tide rolled on into the spring and summer he stood at the apex of his labor union career. Newspaper reporters, government officials, and business executives looked automatically to the charismatic Lewis as the instigator of the industrial union crusade, simplifying the process of union growth by personalizing it. And Lewis's adept negotiations in Detroit, his high-level conferences with Taylor, and his rousing speeches did nothing to dispel this equation of man and movement. "The masses," grumbled a conservative writer, ". . . are invading the domains of sovereignty: and . . . John L. Lewis is their special representative."[26]

In the hectic days of organizing, strikes, and negotiations, few observers and fewer participants attempted to define the precise relationship between Lewis the man and the entity called the CIO. Organizationally and institutionally, of course, the issue was clear: Lewis, with support from other industrial unionists such as Hillman, Howard, and Dubinsky, had created the body called the CIO. Under his direct supervision, the UMW had staffed and financed the CIO. Also, SWOC was really a creature of Lewis's ambitions and was both conceived and run as a direct extension of the UMW, with its chairman, Philip Murray, still retaining his position as vice president of the mine workers' union. Lewis's personal role in all the activities of the CIO during its first two years—his politicking for Roosevelt; his conduct of negotiations with GM; his agreement with Taylor; his general presence in the newspapers, in the union halls, and on the picket lines—was enormous. At every turn in the CIO's remarkable string of successes, observed James Wechsler, "it was his name that workers scrawled on the walls of corporate tyrannies" and "his poetry [that] lifted the CIO from the prosaic terms of another union drive to the level of a great crusade."[27]

And yet the CIO that emerged in the heat of 1937's battles was both more and less than Lewis ever intended or envisioned. He was, by his own frequent admission, responding to events, attempting to revitalize the labor movement by exploiting the momentary opportunities that the current political and economic circumstances presented. In 1936 and 1937 a unique constellation of forces had coalesced to permit a drive to bring unionism to America's mass production industries. A friendly administration in Washington, an upturn of uncertain duration in the economy, the availability of a cadre of battle-hardened organizers, and the smoldering resentment of ill-used mass production workers combined to offer to those bold enough to take the risk the chance to build a new labor movement. No one could direct this juxaposition of disparate forces. There were too many variables. For every corporation executive suddenly converted to the virtues of collective bargaining—

Myron Taylor—there were others—Henry Ford, Republic Steel's Tom Girdler—resolved to renew the bloody battle against unions. In 1936, the inscrutable FDR had been the champion of the working class, resolving to drive the money changers out of the temple of the Republic, but how long would it take for the president to shift his affections and to forget his laborite friends? Most unpredictable of all were the workers themselves, militant unionists one day, indifferent and preoccupied the next.

No phenomenon was more associated with the rise of the CIO than the sit-down strike. It played a crucial role in the Rubber Workers' victories in Akron, and the Flint sit-down more than any other single event legitimized the CIO. One observer calculated that in the nine-month period beginning in September 1936, almost half a million workers were involved in sit-downs. Wrote *Time* magazine, "Sitting down has replaced baseball as a national pastime."[28] Yet the sit-down strike, that critical lever of union recognition, did not derive from some master plan devised by Jett Lauck and ordered by John L. Lewis. Indeed, in normal times, union boss Lewis would have frowned on these spontaneous, often ill-planned, and almost universally unsanctioned work stoppages. Even as he bargained with corporate leaders and government officials in behalf of auto and rubber workers engaged in sit-downs, he toughened the language of UMW contracts to penalize any sort of spontaneous or unauthorized work stoppages in the coal mines. While some advocates of the sit-down strikes saw them as liberating episodes of worker power, with the capability of transforming the repressive nature of the workplace, Lewis viewed them as fortuitous (and no doubt short-lived) tactical thrusts. While the auto and rubber workers were sitting down and galvanizing their coworkers into mass action, he defended them, playing upon the fears of his bargaining adversaries to gain recognition for their unions. But the aim was no radical restructuring of power relations in industry. "The CIO," he said, "stands for punctilious observance of its contracts. . . . A CIO contract is adequate protection for any employer against sit-downs, lie-downs, or any other kind of strikes." If employers refused to meet with their workers' representatives or to recognize their unions, "we are not losing any sleep" over workers' resort to unorthodox tactics. But the aim—always—was a formal signed agreement, regulating the workplace and as binding on workers as upon employers.[29]

Nor was the grass-roots democratic unionism that surfaced in key CIO affiliates in tune with Lewis's bedrock values as a union leader. In swoc, it was the centralized organization that created the local unions and that controlled their internal activities. In fact, swoc incorporated the changes that Lewis had been engineering in the umw for fifteen years, for its central officers were appointed by Lewis, its regional districts were purely administrative conveniences, and its local unions were tightly controlled from headquarters in Pittsburgh. In short, swoc was the quintessential international union in the Lewis tradition in terms of its structure and governance.

But swoc was only part of the cio. Other key affiliates could not be poured into its mold. The Amalgamated Clothing Workers, for example, dated back to 1914 and served as the power base for Lewis's associate—and often rival—Sidney Hillman. While the umw's financial stake and Lewis's enormous personal contributions ensured that the cio would not move far from his orbit, the participations of unions such as the acwa and leaders such as Hillman prevented it from being merely an adjunct to Lewis and the umw.

Even more problematic were the new affiliates in autos, rubber, and electrical appliances. The uaw and the urw were products of no centralized organizing committee. Both had grown up from disparate local unions, initially brought to life after the passage of Section 7(a). Little bound by traditional trade union rules, these local unions quickly became cockpits of disputation and contention, often serving as vehicles for anticapitalist radicals seeking entry into the labor movement and for ambitious young men and women eager to climb out of the shops and serve their fellow auto, rubber, or electrical workers. Under Lewis's direction, the cio could and did support these workers and these new unions, both financially and organizationally. And Lewis's prestige was so great that grass-roots activists and aggressive new leaders paid respectful attention to the advice and counsel of Lewis and his aides. But in the end, these new unions were simply too democratic, too immersed in their own internal politics, and in the case of auto and electrical workers, they had too much capacity for growth and vigor ever to be frozen in the umw-swoc mold. Although loyal members of the cio, and deeply grateful to Lewis, the auto, rubber, and electrical workers nonetheless soon went their own way.

In so many ways, the new cio both partook of and transcended the kind of labor unionism brought to it by Lewis and his umw stalwarts. The umw, for example, had long enjoyed a reputation for relative racial equality. Black and white mine workers could be found in the same local unions and the dynamics of coal mining dictated that segregation and discrimination at the job site translated into weakness in confrontations with coal operators. Almost alone among AFL affiliates, the mine workers' union could boast of a tradition of egalitarianism.

In the CIO, however, this de facto commitment to racial justice quickly expanded beyond the often provincial perspective of the UMW. In many mass production plants, black workers toiled in strategically located jobs. In the meat-packing plants, the metal foundries, and the steel mills, CIO organizers found that black workers were suspicious of organized labor. Some had been hired as strikebreakers, replacing AFL workers whose unions barred blacks from membership. Moreover, CIO organizers often came from backgrounds in socialist and other radical parties and unions, organizations in which belief in racial justice was often a litmus test of one's political seriousness. Thus, before long the CIO's identification with the rights of black workers—and black citizens—went beyond the relatively practical egalitarianism that characterized the UMW tradition—and far beyond the often-discriminatory practices of AFL unions.

The CIO's openness to political radicals also distinguished it from the traditional labor movement. Lewis used experienced socialist and communist organizers to build the CIO even while he continued to keep them out of the UMW. In the 1920s, Lewis had been among the foremost red-baiters in the labor movement. Under his direction, the UMW had barred Communists from membership. He lost few opportunities to discredit his critics by calling them Communists or Communist dupes and drove out the UMW's most prominent socialists, notably Brophy, Germer, and Powers Hapgood. Throughout the 1930s, he kept tight control of the UMW, stifling any hint of radical dissent even as his public speeches lashed out at the minions of capitalistic greed.

At the same time, Lewis knew that to build a steelworkers' union, he needed shrewd, intelligent, and experienced organizers. The ranks of the UMW provided some, of course, but many of the best organizers available were socialists, communists, and veterans of the Industrial Workers of the World (IWW). Lewis did not hesitate to sign them on. Here were men (Lewis and his UMW cohorts regarded the hard and dangerous work of organizing to be a male preserve) steeled in the fires of industrial combat. America in the 1920s and 1930s possessed a yeasty radical subculture. Many young people combined formal education with serious membership in various radical parties and organizations. The Communist party, the Socialist party, the IWW, and other anticapitalist groups provided a rich education in organizing, public speaking, edito-

rial and publicity work, and the other skills needed by a union representative. One estimate held that of the 250 or so organizers recruited
by SWOC, nearly 100 came out of these parties and groups. In the various new unions, notably the UAW and the United Electrical, Radio,
and Machine Workers (UE), left-wing activists quickly came to play
major roles. Moreover, in 1936 Lewis appointed as the CIO's general legal counsel and publicity director, respectively, two talented young
men, both with backgrounds in the Communist party. Fired with a vision of a better world and utterly committed to the cause of industrial
unionism as a means of achieving it, radical organizers and union activists often proved among the most dedicated, articulate, and effective of
the CIO's cadres.

Lewis, however, had not suddenly become converted to the cause
of world revolution. His employment of Communists and other radicals
was, as usual, opportunistic. When asked if he did not fear that Communists would take over the CIO, he replied dismissively, "Who gets the
bird, the hunter or the dog?" Yet the left-wing influence in the CIO
quickly went beyond Lewis's sanguine expectations and soon came to
have a life of its own, both in some of the new federation's key affiliates
and in the CIO itself.

Nineteen-thirty-seven was not completely a year of triumph. The
CIO suffered sharp setbacks as well. Late in the year, the economy
turned sour once again, and soon layoffs and rising inventories curbed
some of the militancy that had punctuated the spring. Early projections
by Lewis and Murray based on the auto and steel victories of 8 or 10
million CIO members began to seem wildly unrealistic, especially since
the AFL began responding to the challenge of the new organization with
stepped-up organizing and vigorous rivalry in key industries.

Still, Lewis's achievement was remarkable. By some reckonings,
the CIO could count 3.4 million members.[30] As CIO delegates gathered
in October for the federation's first national meeting—in Atlantic City,
naturally—the spirit of success and optimism pervaded. The CIO conference, exalted Germer, "was an educational treat. There was as much
difference between that meeting and the A.F. of L. conventions I have
attended as there is between night and day." Despite the successes in
building the new unions, the CIO was still dependent on the largess of
the UMW and the leadership of Lewis. The organizing campaigns had
been costly: in the period June 1936–September 1937, the CIO had
spent $1,745,968 and had collected in dues a mere $308,388. The
UMW had provided the CIO almost $1.25 million. "There can be no

doubt," Lewis's biographers remind us, "that Lewis created the CIO" and that "without Lewis's generosity, . . . there would have been no CIO."[31]

Critics on both the Right and the Left raised questions about this new organization and its patron. Conservatives worried about the extent of Communist influence and the CIO's potential for promoting class war. Liberals and radicals worried that Lewis seemed to lack a broad vision, that (in the words of one friendly chronicler of the CIO's growth) "still he [does] . . . not put forth any program for basic organization of the economic process."[32] Lewis refused to answer his critics or reassure his sympathizers. Ill with the flu, he appeared only briefly at the conference. No stem-winding speech proclaimed the next phase of his agenda; his remarks merely repeated his determination to establish industrial unionism and bring the blessings of collective bargaining and industrial democracy to American workers. He paid no attention to the threats of AFL leaders, gathering simultaneously in Denver for their annual convention, and refused to speculate on reports of factory closings and expanding unemployment in the CIO's industrial heartland. This was a year of triumph, as the extension of collective bargaining into auto, steel, and other core manufacturing sectors testified. Only a fool would predict the future or dare to anticipate the next lurch in the wheel of history. Flushed with achievement but alert to the ever-shifting possibilities, Lewis awaited events.

The "Babe Ruth of the Labor Movement": Labor Day parade, Toledo, Ohio, 5 September 1938. *Archives of Labor and Urban Affairs, Wayne State University*

By 1938, more than an aisle separated Lewis and his erstwhile colleague, bespectacled AFL President William Green.
Archives of Labor and Urban Affairs, Wayne State University

The man who defied Roosevelt (ca. 1940). *State Historical Society of Wisconsin*

The fedora, the cane, the high-gloss shine, the three-piece suit—Lewis projected a high profile in Washington, D.C., March 1941. *State Historical Society of Wisconsin*

Lewis after Federal Judge T. Alan Goldsborough issued him a $20,000 fine and the UMW one of $1.5 million for continuing their strike in defiance of a federal injunction, 20 April 1948. *Archives of Labor and Urban Affairs, Wayne State University*

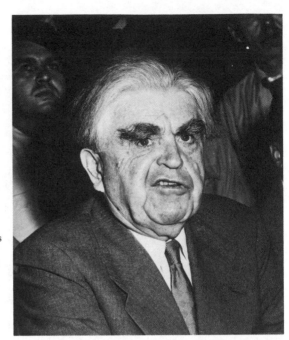

The face of contention: Lewis in Detroit, June 1951. *State Historical Society of Wisconsin;* Detroit Free Press

The visage is stern but the big battles are over, 18 January 1951. *State Historical Society of Wisconsin; Capitol Photo Service, Washington, D.C.*

The face of tragedy: at the scene of the West Frankfurt, Illinois, mine disaster, 21 December 1951, in which 119 miners died. *Archives of Labor and Urban Affairs, Wayne State University*

At home, but at ease? 12 September 1953. *State Historical Society of Wisconsin*

With daughter Kathryn at the dinner marking Lewis's fortieth anniversary as UMW head and his retirement from the union's presidency, January 1960. *State Historical Society of Wisconsin; Chase Studios, Washington, D.C.*

5

BREAKING RANKS, 1938–42

Lewis's hour of triumph <u>was short-lived</u>. The return of depression-like conditions in 1938 and the country's drift toward war soon pitted him against both his erstwhile allies in the labor movement and the president. By 1940, Lewis had broken irrevocably with FDR, first attempting to patch together an antiadministration progressive political bloc and then in the fall issuing a stunning endorsement of Roosevelt's Republican rival, Wendell Willkie. By the end of 1941, he was cutting loose from the CIO, having stepped down from its presidency in November 1940. Soon Lewis was on his own, and UMW organizers challenged both the AFL and the CIO for the allegiance of workers in war-engorged industries. Early in 1942 the mine workers' union severed its ties completely with the industrial union federation Lewis had launched six years before.

As in his triumphant creation of the CIO, Lewis again captured headlines, aroused fierce passions, and stirred endless speculation about his motives and intentions. His pre–Pearl Harbor opposition to the Roosevelt administration's foreign and defense policies led to charges of disloyalty and to alienation from the great majority of labor leaders who feared the rise of Axis power and who supported the president. His mounting attacks on those who helped him build the CIO led critics to denounce him as a megalomaniacal wrecker. His support for Willkie, his angry departure from the CIO, and his grandiose organizing campaigns seemed to his former allies bizarre and quixotic.

Yet Lewis's dramatic actions in 1940 and 1941 did raise important questions about the relationship of organized labor to the emerging national security state. His appeals for a progressive coalition to complete the unfinished work of the New Deal and his attacks on FDR for slighting his liberal and labor allies while embracing southern racists and corporate conservatives were sharp reminders of the price the nation was paying for building military power. His critique of the administration's moderation of its support for the CIO underscored the tenuous and insecure nature of the gains industrial workers had made in the 1930s. Finally, Lewis's warnings—often difficult to grasp amid the bluster, showmanship, and venom with which they were delivered—about the dangers to organized labor in becoming an appendage to the military-political machine were shrewd and even prescient.

At no time during his long and controversial career was Lewis's combination of qualities so dramatically evident as during this somber and exciting period. He combined keen insight with insufferable bluster, high-minded defense of the American worker with mean-spirited humiliation of loyal associates, provocative criticism of militarization with head-in-the-sand isolationism, impassioned pleas for organizing the masses with half-baked plans for achieving this goal. To those who attempted to put Lewis into some ideological framework, his companion and confidant of these years, CIO legal counsel Lee Pressman, replied with impatience. Lewis, he remarked in 1957, was "just one of those strange creatures that God throws up every now and then."[1]

Lewis and Roosevelt

Even amid the triumphs of 1937, conflict between the CIO president and FDR rumbled beneath the surface. Both chary and needful of administration support for expanding the CIO, Lewis at once recognized and deplored the fact that Roosevelt's great popularity among workers bore little relationship to the president's specific policies. As Roosevelt backed off from public support for the CIO surge, embarked on recession-producing economic policies, and began to bargain away progressive initiatives to secure conservative support for his defense buildup and foreign policy, Lewis escalated his criticisms. By the end of 1939, the union leader had begun to cast about for alternatives to FDR.

At first, however, Lewis supported the domestic policies and political maneuvers of the early second Roosevelt administration. The CIO chief applauded FDR's controversial plan to expand the Supreme Court as a means of overcoming a conservative majority that had disallowed key New Deal measures. Similarly, he hailed the president's effort in the 1938 congressional elections to purge conservative Democrats. Indeed, he used UMW funds to back some of the president's men. In 1937 the UMW joined other industrial unions to help the administration pass the Walsh-Healey Act, a measure that sought to improve compensation and conditions of work on federally financed projects. The UMW also joined CIO lobbyists in support of the Fair Labor Standards Act of 1938, which regulated wage rates and hours of employment in private industry. Lewis regarded these administration enactments as weak and limited, but he accepted the need for compromise and settled for partial measures in hopes that subsequent congresses would expand upon these modest beginnings. This cooperation with the New Deal's political and legislative initiatives hardly suggested that Lewis had suddenly become a hell-raising madman, determined to impose his will at any cost.

Lewis's skepticism about the depth of FDR's support for labor had justification. In the spring of 1937, for example, the president's glib response to the killing of ten striking steelworkers in Chicago shocked even his most ardent adherents. Seemingly disregarding the fact that the peaceful strikers had been gunned down by a Chicago police contingent, FDR told a press conference that the nation had had enough of industrial unrest. It was time, he said, for labor and management to resolve their disputes peacefully. If incidents such as the Memorial Day shootings continued to occur, he remarked, the public—and by extension, the president himself—would repudiate both sides. "A curse on both your houses" was how the president put it. In view of the massive violations of workers' civil liberties being almost daily uncovered during the steel strike and the shocking brutality of the Chicago police— whose weapons and facilities were partly paid for by the Republic Steel Corporation—Roosevelt's words angered those who considered him a friend of organized labor and who remembered the unions' tremendous efforts in the president's behalf in the election only seven months before.

A few months later, Lewis had some choice words of rejoinder for the president. Speaking to a Labor Day radio audience numbering perhaps 25 million, he reminded his listeners that the dead in Chicago were but the latest in a long roll of victims of corporate greed and governmental indifference. "Labor, like Israel," he intoned, "has many sorrows. Its women weep for their fallen, and they lament for the future of the children of the race." Then in an electrifying example of Lewisian oratory, he bore down directly on the president: "It ill behooves one who has supped at labor's table and who has been sheltered in labor's house to curse with equal fervor and fine impartiality both labor and its adversaries when they become locked in deadly embrace."[2]

These scathing words were delivered as part of a message that sought to remind FDR of how loyally laborites had supported him and how critical labor was to his legislative and electoral chances. Increasingly, however, it seemed to Lewis that FDR listened not to labor's men or other liberals but to southern Democrats and conservative advisers from the worlds of finance, business, and academia. In late 1937, concerned about unprecedented budgetary deficits, the president slashed relief and government emergency employment expenditures, throwing tens of thousands of poor people off the assistance rolls and expanding the army of the unemployed. A sharp recession—the "Roosevelt Recession"—reversed many of the economic gains of 1935–37, bringing economic indicators back down near the levels prevailing when FDR took office in 1933. The downturn stopped the CIO drive in its tracks. Employers laid off workers, forced unionists to make contract concessions, and grew bolder in their resistance to the industrial union surge. Far more than the president's insensitive words about the steel workers, his regressive economic policies embittered Lewis.

But it was the administration's foreign and defense policies that drove him into open opposition. The rise of Hitler and of Japanese militarism convinced FDR that the country faced imminent global crisis. Yet a powerful tide of isolationism led Congress to adopt strict prohibitions against American involvement in the international arms trade. Roosevelt could act only with extreme caution to use American influence to bolster the foes of Hitler, Mussolini, and the Japanese war party. Japanese invasion of China in July 1937 and Anglo-French capitulation to German demands in Czechoslovakia in September of the next year deepened the international crisis. An alliance of the aggressor powers, the Berlin-Rome-Tokyo Axis signed in September 1940, spurred the administration's determination to find ways to aid their enemies.

Lewis spoke out against each administration initiative to build military defenses and channel support to Great Britain and its allies. As early as March 1937, in the midst of the decisive negotiations involving swoc and U.S. Steel, Lewis cautioned against foreign involvements. Addressing a mass antiwar rally in New York City, he warned that "Europe is on the brink of disaster and it must be our care that she does not drag us into the abyss after her."[3] Two and a half years later, as Hitler's divisions rolled across Poland and England and France declared war on Germany, he told a Labor Day audience that "war has always been the device of the despairing and intellectually sterile statesman. Labor in America wants no war or any part of war. Labor wants the right to work and live—not the privilege of dying by gunshot or poison gas to sustain the mental errors of current statesmen."[4]

As detestable as he found Hitler and the Japanese warlords, Lewis simply did not believe that they posed a threat to the United States. Roosevelt's warlike policies, he thought, advanced no vital U.S. interests. Rather, they tied American foreign policy to the tail of British imperialism and threatened a reenactment of the futile bloodshed of 1917–18. Moreover, the president's misguided interventionism forced him to rely on conservative political and economic interests that held no love for the New Deal. Wall Street financiers, Lewis believed, were eager to use American power to back up their international investments and now counseled the president, as did racist and antilabor politicians from the southern wing of the Democratic party. The appointments in 1940 of Republicans Frank Knox and Henry L. Stimson as secretaries of the navy and war, respectively, drove home this point.

Conservative support for Roosevelt's foreign and defense policies did not come cheap. Now the president spoke little of the uncompleted agenda of the New Deal and abandoned his earlier suggestions of forging a liberal realignment of American politics by purging conservative Democrats from the party. The Fair Labor Standards Act, passed in June 1938, was the last important piece of domestic reform legislation. The president stopped his attacks on corporate greed and the concentration of wealth, stressing now the need for national sacrifice and worker discipline. He bowed to conservative criticism of the National Labor Relations Board (NLRB), established by Congress in 1935 to curb employer abuses of workers' rights to form unions, and initiated changes in the board that complicated the CIO's efforts to organize the industrial core.

Particularly galling was the route that FDR chose in attempting to gain the cooperation of industrial unionists for defense mobilization. On 28 May 1940, the president created a National Defense Advisory Commission (NDAC); seven months later, he upgraded that body by forming the Office of Production Management (OPM). Lewis was not surprised that the president appointed prominent industrialists to the two agencies' key posts. But Roosevelt made no effort to consult him, the head of the industrial union federation, in matters affecting labor. Instead, Roosevelt named Sidney Hillman, president of the Amalgamated Clothing Workers of America (ACWA), first as labor representative on the NDAC and, in December 1940, as codirector of the OPM. In the guise of "consulting" labor, it seemed, Roosevelt was going over Lewis's head and awarding Hillman a privileged position in the administration.

Nor was this a skirmish over prestige or recognition. Lewis and Hillman had become rivals within the CIO, with the Clothing Workers' head increasingly critical of Lewis's antiadministration views. At CIO gatherings, UMW and ACWA delegates sniped endlessly at each other over a wide range of issues, from CIO internal finances to political differences and attitudes toward foreign policy. In effect, Lewis believed, by appointing Hillman the president was reaching into the CIO ranks to sow dissension and to attempt to undercut Lewis's authority and strength.

Nor did the manner in which the administration conducted the military buildup during the period of defense mobilization (1939–41) please Lewis. The government let out bids totaling hundreds of millions of dollars to corporations notorious for their repressive labor policies. Lewis insisted that Roosevelt issue an executive order denying defense contracts to corporate abusers, but the president evaded this demand, eventually turning the matter over to the faithful Hillman in his capacity as labor adviser to the government in defense production. Hillman in turn rejected Lewis's call for immediate action, relying instead on cautious prodding by NDAC and OPM functionaries to change corporate behavior.

Lewis fumed. "A great number of corporations," he declared in 1940, ". . . are inflating their pockets by manufacturing guns and ammunition and military supplies and armor plates and warships. . . . These corporations are breakers of the law." Bethlehem Steel, a major beneficiary of defense contracts, continued to flaunt its open support for its company unions; reported SWOC chairman Philip Murray, "its plants are running amuck with a thousand and one systems of espionage" aimed at throttling the Steel Workers Organizing Committee. The NLRB had cited Bethlehem for innumerable labor law violations, yet the giant company, showered as it was by lucrative defense contracts, was "laughing at the law."[5]

By early 1940, Lewis had given up on Roosevelt. Hitler's attacks on Poland in September 1939 and a string of Nazi successes in Europe accelerated administration efforts to find ways to aid England and France. Defense production soared. Appeals to patriotism and sacrifice recalled the atmosphere of 1917–18. Determined to thwart the administration's war-bent course and convinced of labor's need to assert an independent voice, the UMW chief now attempted to create a new progressive coalition. Throughout the late winter and early spring of 1940, he cultivated liberal groups, speaking before conventions of Negro, youth, peace, farm, and labor organizations, always with the same message: the rush toward war must be reversed; Roosevelt must be repudiated; the liberal beginnings of the mid-1930s must be fulfilled. "The United States," he told the National Association for the Advancement of Colored People in June, ". . . went backward after the election of Franklin D. Roosevelt" in 1936. "If it is our mission to save Western Civilization," he declared to the National Negro Congress convention, "then let us begin by saving it right here in our own country."[6] The nation, he told a youth organization, had a lengthy, unfinished agenda. The unemployed needed jobs. Young people needed schools. Black Americans needed protection in the basic rights of citizenship. A Roosevelt-inspired foreign war would destroy this agenda even as it created lush profits for law-breaking corporations and for the same arrogant financial interests that had led the country into the Great Depression.

Yet, whatever the eloquence of these appeals, Lewis faced limited practical options in implementing his anti-Roosevelt crusade. Initially, he declared that Roosevelt stood little chance of renomination for an unprecedented third term and less chance of victory in the November election. If indeed Democrats "could be coerced or dragooned into nominating him," he told the UMW convention in January, "I am convinced that . . . his candidacy would result in ignominious defeat."[7]

Lewis attempted to promote Montana Senator Burton K. Wheeler, a veteran progressive with strong isolationist views, as an alternative to Roosevelt. But Wheeler aroused little enthusiasm, even among Lewis's UMW ranks.

For a time, the embattled unionist hinted at the creation of a new political structure, uniting all progressive groups—labor, farmers' organizations, youth, minorities, and the elderly—into a grand coalition.

There would be, he told an audience in West Virginia, "the assembling of a great delegate convention"[8] to confront the established parties and to arouse citizen activism, using the still extant but virtually defunct Labor's Non-Partisan League as the nucleus. Toward the summer, Lewis switched strategies once again, now reverting to an earlier enthusiasm. "I believe," he told a Philadelphia audience in a speech that flew in the face of every informed analysis of the political scene, "that the working people of the United States need and want the leadership of Herbert Hoover,"[9] a man whose name was synonymous with depression and failure throughout working-class America.

Such maneuvering bordered on the bizarre, adding substance to his critics' charges that he had allowed his ego to distort his view of reality. True, his antiwar speeches touched a responsive chord; public opinion polls regularly showed overwhelming opposition to involvement in another conflict. Even as the ruthlessness of Hitler's regime and the desperate plight of Britain and its allies became apparent, Americans remained determined to avoid a repetition of 1917. At the same time, however, Roosevelt's appeal to working-class voters remained enormous. Resolutions at the UMW's convention in January urged a third term on the president, defying the Lewis machine. Whatever the limitations of the administration's policies and whatever the fear of global involvement, working-class support for FDR was a basic fact of political life which no amount of Lewisian eloquence or maneuvering could change.

By the fall, Lewis had only one further possibility: support for FDR's Republican rival. On the evening of 25 October he addressed a multi-network national radio audience and announced his preference. He wasted little time in extolling the virtues of GOP candidate Wendell Willkie, a lawyer for large utility companies. Roosevelt was the issue. The president, he declared, wanted war. Only American belligerency would rescue him from the failures of his presidency. His reelection "would be a national evil of the first magnitude." His return to office "may create a dictatorship in this land," for FDR had a "personal craving for power." True, Willkie was a lawyer who had made his fortune representing large utility interests. "But America needs no superman." Lewis spoke directly to his working-class constituency: "Sustain me now, or repudiate me," he told the CIO members in his audience, pledging to step down from the presidency of the organization he had done so much to create if indeed industrial workers cast their ballots for the war-mongering Roosevelt.[10]

Lewis's announcement for Willkie stunned laborites. In union halls and workers' homes, unionists sat speechless. In Austin, Minnesota, a group of CIO meat packers had gathered to hear their chief. As Lewis's words hit home, they grew silent. At the end of the broadcast, no one spoke. At last, one woman strode to the front of the meeting room, yanked from the wall the portrait of the CIO president that glowered over the assemblage and heaved it out a nearby window. Only then did the workers begin to express the sense of betrayal they felt.

A few CIO leaders close to the federation's influential and temporarily antiwar Communist faction supported the leader, but most others were outraged or distraught. A New Jersey leader charged that Lewis had "betrayed organized labor . . . for Wall Street," and New York City CIO activists branded him a "Benedict Arnold." The president of the CIO textile workers' union intoned "May heaven help John L. Lewis." Even among the mine workers, only Lewis's most sycophantic followers went along. Both Philip Murray and Thomas Kennedy, his ablest lieutenants, reaffirmed their commitment to Roosevelt. In the larger world of organized labor, William Green gloated at the CIO's disarray. The only major labor leader to declare himself for Willkie was the Carpenters' William Hutcheson, Lewis's victim in the 1935 fistfight that had launched the CIO.[11]

Standing Apart, 1939–41

The endorsement of Willkie proved a turning point in Lewis's relationship with the CIO. For the next year, he led the UMW on a course increasingly antagonistic toward it and its new leadership. His isolationism became more intense; among the new allies he embraced in the crusade to keep America out of war were notorious antilabor figures. Meanwhile, the CIO's new president, Philip Murray, along with most other prominent industrial union leaders, drew closer to the administration, welcoming its efforts to aid Great Britain and its stepped-up military spending. By the time the Japanese attacked Pearl Harbor on 7 December 1941, Lewis was on the verge of an open break with his former allies.

Large Roosevelt majorities throughout the industrial heartland on 5 November fueled speculation about Lewis's course. He had, of course, pledged to leave the CIO's presidency were workers to ignore his advice and give FDR their support again. Clearly, he had received a stinging

*Will he
just play
A good?*

rebuke at the hands of those for whom he claimed to speak. At the same time, however, few in the world of labor could envision the UMW chief actually abandoning a position of power and influence, nor could they envision a CIO without Lewis at its helm. The denouement came at the CIO's annual convention, which opened two weeks after the election.

Lewis's name still held magic for rank-and-file unionists. Sporting "Draft Lewis" buttons, United Mine Workers delegates mounted lengthy demonstrations in behalf of their chief. The CIO's Communists and their sympathizers urged that the convention ignore Lewis's pledge to step down and insist that he continue in power. At the same time, however, Lewis's recent neglect of CIO affairs and his odd political thrusts had taken their toll. True, Lewis was the great organizer and the father of the CIO, but the industrial union federation depended on harmonious relationships with government. Could it afford to have at its head a man who so openly scorned the president of the United States?

Hillman, smarting under the lash of Lewis's criticisms for his conduct on the NDAC, shrewdly encouraged Lewis's departure from CIO leadership. He gave the devil his due. He cherished his association with Lewis, the articulate New Yorker told the convention. Lewis was such an able debater that "when I am in disagreement with him I am scared of his effectiveness." Alas, Hillman assured the audience, he regretted Lewis's decision to leave the CIO presidency. Still, he said, he respected Lewis's courage and, he added, he knew that however much misguided delegates sought to dissuade him, Lewis was a man of his word and would stick to his decision.[12]

Whether Lewis wanted or expected a draft, none materialized. His selection of Murray as his successor, ratified unanimously by the delegates, reassured those for whom John L. Lewis was the heart and soul of the CIO. For a generation, Murray had been his closest aide: although an able and intelligent functionary in the UMW and as head of SWOC, he scarcely seemed the man to make the hard decisions and to lead labor's mighty hosts. Lewis, many observers believed, would continue to give the CIO its marching orders while Murray, suitably close to the Roosevelt administration, would supply the political and public relations facade. Murray's bathetic acceptance speech encouraged this sort of thinking. Racked with doubts about his ability to lead the federation and with feelings of inadequacy about stepping into his chief's shoes,

Murray fed the worst fears of Lewis's critics. After emotional pledges of fealty to his boss, Murray admitted that some thought him weak and dependent on Lewis. But, he declared, "I think I am a man. I think I have convictions." Veteran labor observers, reflecting on Murray's twenty years' service as a Lewis satellite, were not so sure.[13]

Lewis now grew more unrestrained in his criticisms of the administration and laborites who supported it. He hammered away at the awarding of defense contracts to labor law violators. By implication, and at times more directly, he attacked those such as Hillman and Murray whose criticisms of the administration were less vehement than his own. As military spending drove employment figures upward, workers became more aggressive, determined now to complete the unionization of the industrial core and to translate defense-generated profits into healthy wage gains. Lewis served as tribune of this rekindled militancy, aligning himself with strikers in the shipyards, aircraft factories, and munitions plants. In the period before 22 June 1941 his call for militant action was echoed among the CIO's Communist faction, strong in the defense-sensitive auto, electrical, and heavy machinery sectors. This de facto alliance between Lewis and the Communists—which ended abruptly when Hitler attacked the Soviet Union and the Communist party swung immediately behind the U.S. military buildup—further distanced him from the likes of Murray and Hillman, who were apprehensive over the Communist presence in the CIO.

Lewis's condemnation of the Roosevelt administration and his championing of striking workers sometimes pitted him directly against others in the CIO. Hillman especially drew his wrath, as the codirector of the OPM on several occasions sanctioned the use of federal troops to end strikes in defense industries. In April 1941, for example, the Clothing Workers' president endorsed FDR's dispatch of soldiers to end a walkout of UAW aviation workers in California. Hillman and other CIO leaders attempted to balance the interests of their members and organizations with the country's defense needs; after all, the California aircraft workers emerged from the episode in question with their union intact and with wage gains. To a growing body of labor officials, Lewis's categorical endorsement of militant activism amounted to hypocritical grandstanding, especially in view of the suppression of rank-and-file activism he continued to practice in the UMW.

And by the middle of 1941, Lewis's critics had a good case. A triumphant Hitler stood astride Europe, his racist fulminations now translated into swaggering hegemony over most of the Continent. Allied with fascist Italy, expansion-bent Japan and, tacitly, the Soviet Union, the Nazi führer imperiled the most basic values of the American people. As Britain stood alone amid German air assaults in the fall of 1940 and spring of 1941, leaders of both the AFL and the CIO put aside labor's traditional antiwar instincts and their quarrels with specific administration actions to support aid to Britain and massive military expenditures. To be sure, union leaders chafed at Roosevelt's reliance on prominent businessmen and his unwillingness to shut out labor law violators from juicy defense contracts. But, said CIO official John Brophy, when all was said and done, "we recognized the war danger, [and] with Hitler on the loose . . . we could not ignore the war in Europe."[14]

Moreover, the support that most laborites awarded FDR in defense and foreign policy paid dividends. One by one, the Little Steel companies, which had beaten back SWOC in 1937, capitulated. Militant steelworkers and smoothly functioning NLRB proceedings brought union recognition and contract gains to tens of thousands of workers. A UAW victory over Ford in the spring of 1941 completed organization of the automobile industry, with an NLRB election sealing the defeat of the once-impregnable antiunion automaker. True, on occasion union leaders might have to dampen rank-and-file enthusiasm, and in principle few disagreed that defense contractors should be held to strict conformity with the country's labor laws. Still, genuine gains through the summer of 1941, combined with the terrifying international situation— Japan was poised for a strike into Southeast Asia and Germany was now rolling into the Soviet Union—convinced laborites of almost every stripe of the foolishness of Lewis's lonely defiance. Indeed, despite his championing of militant activism, the United Mine Workers' chief commanded only sporadic support among working people. A poll of factory workers conducted in the spring revealed that more of them viewed Lewis as a negative factor in labor relations than they did Henry Ford, whose hired thugs were even then assaulting UAW organizers.

The captive mines dispute of the fall of 1941 also underlined Lewis's isolated position in the labor movement. By 1941, the UMW represented virtually everyone who dug coal in the United States. In the commercial mines—those mines, accounting for over 90 percent of all production, that produced coal for general markets—the UMW had negotiated union shop contracts. The union shop was a form of union security; it stipulated that anyone working at a given mine had to become a member of the union (and, of course, pay his dues to the union) soon after beginning work. Opposed by many mine owners on the grounds that it was an infringement on the freedom to work and because it strengthened the union in dealings with management, the union shop was nonetheless popular among the vast majority of working miners. Together with the checkoff of union dues, wherein the employer deducted and turned over to the UMW the miners' monthly per capita tax, the union shop ensured that everyone who benefited from the union's presence would support it financially. There would be no free riders. By ensuring a steady flow of income to the union, the union shop and the checkoff freed the union from the expensive and time-consuming tasks of constant recruitment and dues collection, allowing it to concentrate on collective bargaining and grievance handling. For years a controversial feature of negotiations in both soft and hard coal bargaining, the union shop by 1940 had become standard in UMW contracts in the commercial fields.

By 1941 also the UMW had successfully organized the captive mines, enjoying over 95 percent membership in these facilities, which were operated by large steel, railroad, and utilities corporations. But Lewis's demand for the union shop in the 1941 contract talks met with blank refusal. Determined to bring the captive mines into conformity with other UMW contracts and to solidify beyond doubt the union's hold in these corporate-run mines, the UMW leader took his miners out of the pits on 27 October.

Through the tense autumn of 1941, the captive mines dispute smoldered. Operators objected less to the union shop per se than to the means by which the UMW might achieve it. If miners employed by U.S. Steel, for example, gained this demand through collective bargaining, no doubt the huge corporation's steelworkers would also demand it, a concession the industry giant was determined not to make. If, however, the captive mine operators were forced by direct governmental intervention to compromise on the union shop, U.S. Steel could better resist the steelworkers' demand.

The dispute then was something of a symbolic show of force. In the 1920s, these same powerful corporations had smashed the UMW; now they attempted to keep industrial unionism from becoming irrevocably entrenched in their factories. For Lewis and the mine workers, nothing less than the union shop would do. To be sure, with 95 percent of the captive miners enrolled in the union already, the union shop would not materially affect work relations in the pits and shafts. On the other hand, Lewis understood better than anyone how quickly union power could be sapped. He had only to reflect back on the grim days after World War I to be reminded.

Who could tell what the impending war would bring? If the union shop changed little, why was it so fiercely resisted? Why should the giant steel, railroad, and utilities concerns that operated the captive mines not conform to the legitimate demands of the UMW? As the captive mine operators appealed endlessly to government to find a way for them out of their dilemma, Lewis grew ever more incensed. Without the meddling of the OPM and the newly created National Defense Mediation Board, he was certain, the UMW's strike would quickly force the devious operators to grant the union shop. Government officials—including Sidney Hillman in his capacity as OPM codirector—cajoled, threatened, and harangued him. Lewis wondered aloud why the same pressures that were used to force the coal miners back to work were not imposed on the rich Wall Street financiers who, he asserted, in reality controlled the captive mines. With a mere nod of the head these plutocrats could cause their underlings to grant the UMW's demand and end the dispute. To a presidential hint of direct federal intervention, Lewis replied, "If you would use the power of the State to restrain me, as an agent of labor, then, Sir, I submit that you should use the same power to restrain my adversary in this issue." His "adversary," the UMW leader reminded Roosevelt, was not the government or the American people. His adversary was "a rich man named Morgan, who lives in New York."[15]

After several work stoppages, repeated presidential interventions, and hundreds of anti-Lewis newspaper editorials, the captive mines dispute flickered to a halt in December. The elaborate ritual ended in a presidentially arranged scheme of arbitration, with Lewis approving the plan because he knew that the arbitrator would favor the UMW's position. "A controversy that involved only 53,000 workers in a nation of over 100-million . . . had kept Congress, the presidency, and the general public in heated agitation," note Lewis's biographers.[16] And once again, Lewis emerged victorious.

The captive mines dispute proved awakward for Lewis's colleagues in the CIO. From within the Roosevelt administration, Hillman proposed solutions that fell short of Lewis's demands and thus earned the renewed hostility of the UMW chief. Murray loyally supported his mentor, resigning on 10 November from the National Defense Mediation Board when that body ruled against UMW claims. Still, Lewis's insistence on so militant a course on an issue that many even in the labor movement believed marginal soured relations between Lewis and the CIO leadership. With the plunge into world war only a matter of time and with so many labor battles to be fought, was it wise for the CIO to expend its political capital on a matter of this kind? Lewis consulted no one in planning or conducting the strike, but he expected total support. Thus, despite the CIO's formal endorsement of his position, the dispute strained the already-weakening bonds that bound the UMW and the CIO.

Despite the attention the captive mines attracted, its settlement went largely unnoticed. For the arbitration board did not hand down its ruling favoring the UMW until 7 December, hours after Japanese planes had attacked Pearl Harbor and brought the United States into World War II. Ten days later, AFL and CIO leaders, meeting in Washington with the president and management representatives, pledged to forgo the strike weapon for the duration of the war and to cooperate with the government in the development of dispute resolution machinery, production goals, and manpower programs.

Alone among the labor figures attending this conference in December, Lewis arrived with a detailed plan for government-labor cooperation. Merely to pledge loyal support of the war effort, he believed, would make labor captive to whatever programs Roosevelt and his advisers—increasingly drawn from the corporate boardrooms—cooked up. Without concrete proposals for a basis on which to build labor's support for the war effort, the labor movement become a cat's-paw, hostage to business and military priorities. His proposal received little response, in good part because government officials, corporate leaders, and labor representatives alike did not relish having Lewis anywhere near the heart of wartime decision making. Thereafter, he lapsed into uncharacteristic silence. He never again sought to supply general leadership for organized labor's wartime course. "Partly out of patriotism and partly out of the realization that his motives were always suspect," observe his recent biographers, "he imposed on his union a strictly formal and proper posture toward the war."[17] The union's officialdom pledged unstinting effort to reach production records. War bonds were oversubscribed. Thousands of miners marched off to fight. Possibly because of the controversial nature of so many of his prewar utterances, Lewis confined his attentions to the specific concerns of the coal miners, rarely venturing to speak more broadly for the duration of the conflict.

Pulling Away, 1941–42

By the end of 1941, Lewis was on the offensive. Even as his estrangement from the Roosevelt administration froze into permanent alienation he chopped his remaining ties with the CIO, taking the UMW out of the industrial union body early in 1942. Most alarming to leaders in both the CIO and the AFL, the United Mine Workers' chief launched seemingly bold new organizing campaigns, designed to challenge both existing federations and to expand the UMW's base of power into construction, general industry, and even agriculture.

Lewis took on the AFL through a body he created while still presiding over the CIO, the United Construction Workers (UCW). Since the building trades unions were at the heart of the older federation's strength, a well-financed campaign, conducted with Lewis's élan and UMW resources, potentially posed a serious challenge to the AFL. This construction workers' initiative attacked the AFL craft unions at their weakest points: its opening manifesto pledged the new union to eliminate the racial discrimination that the AFL unions exhibted and to abolish the anachronistic work rules, arbitrary demarcations between trades, and jurisdictional conflicts that made the American construction industry inefficient and strife-torn. The UCW, in short, would bring industrial unionism into the very heart of AFL territory.

To challenge the CIO, Lewis revitalized and reorganized a small UMW unit, District 50, created in 1936 to organize workers in the chemical, cosmetics, and utility fields whose work brought them into contact with by-products and derivatives of coal. It had struggled along, a poor stepchild of the powerful UMW. Now, in August 1941, Lewis regrouped District 50, naming his daughter, Kathryn, secretary-treasurer and assigning to it UMW organizers hitherto on the staff of the CIO. By the fall of 1942, Lewis reported, District 50 had launched organizing campaigns among a wide variety of industrial workers, many of them clearly falling under the jurisdiction of AFL or CIO unions, in thirty-nine states and over three hundred communities. Attached to District 50 was a new division, created early in 1942 to organize the nation's 2.5 million dairy farmers.

Laborites and journalists alike regarded these initiatives with a mixture of amusement and apprehension. The Construction Workers campaigns, actually begun in retaliation for the AFL's granting a charter to a group of dissident mine workers in Illinois, was in theory the most legitimate and coherent of these schemes to recast the labor movement under Lewis's leadership. The AFL unions were indeed resistant to new construction methods; often their arcane jurisdictional rivalries tied up building sites. Several were tainted with corruption and charges of collusion with contractors; most pursued racially discriminatory policies of recruitment and membership, particularly harmful to black workers because construction unions often enjoyed closed shop arrangements with employers. The Construction Workers' opening manifesto addressed itself to these problems, projecting an attractive alternative to business-as-usual. With defense-related construction booming, the creation of an industrial union of construction workers seemed Lewis's bid for expansion into a key sector of the economy.

Despite its impressive beginnings, however, Lewis's Construction Workers initiative never had a chance of fruition. The powerful AFL building trades effectively boycotted work performed by their rivals. Contractors knew that agreements with Lewis's outfit would turn job sites into battlegrounds. Nor did it seem that the UMW leader was serious in making this move. Appointment of his brother Dennie as Construction Workers head ensured utter loyalty but saddled the new organization with inept and unimaginative leadership. The organization straggled along for several years, hardly even a thorn in the side of the AFL. Lewis never channeled significant resources to it and in 1942 it was quietly absorbed into District 50.

This catchall unit originally seemed to have greater plausibility. It soon began to receive lavish funding. Unlike Dennie Lewis, daughter Kathryn was an able and intelligent administrator who had by 1941 logged five years as her father's assistant in the UMW and CIO. For a time in 1941 and 1942, as UMW District 50 organizers fanned into industrial America, both CIO and AFL leaders became jittery. Probing into paper mills, farm equipment plants, munitions factories, metal working shops, food processing facilities, and a score of other diverse sectors, Lewis's organizers seemed at times to recreate the magic of 1936–37. Similarly, Lewis's bid to organize dairy farmers and forge a farmer-labor bloc under his leadership gained some initial success and created concern among his rivals. Cartoonists, noted journalist Dale Kramer, might have a field day with their depictions of the bushy-browed Lewis squatting on the milk stool, but "in many circles the proposal was greeted with anything but amusement."[18] However controversial in public, Lewis had a reputation for tough bargaining, and thousands of dairy farmers in New York State, whatever their distaste for organized labor in the abstract, signed up with Lewis's United Dairy Farmers' Division. And, remarked

Kramer, "if successful in fitting the trade union key to the milk industry, Lewis would be certain to expand in other directions," no doubt seeking alliances with wheat, cotton, and livestock producers.[19]

In the end, however, both initiatives fizzled. A CIO report concluded that by 1945, District 50, despite the fanfare with which its campaigns were conducted, had absorbed over $3.5 million in Mine Workers' resources but had gained only fifty thousand members in four years. The dairy farmers campaign ended almost as quickly as it had started. With its demise went any plans Lewis might have had to outflank union rivals by creating a farm-labor combine. In all this maneuvering, years of Lewis's authoritarian control of the UMW had taken their toll. His more astute and effective henchmen and organizers stayed with Murray and the CIO, while only those who could demonstrate total loyalty to the chief remained with the UMW. In the heyday of CIO success in 1936–37, Lewis could supplement his UMW cadres with energetic radicals, but after June 1941 the Communists were utterly committed to American participation in the war and reviled their former ally in the harshest terms for his antiwar views. Other gifted organizers had found homes in the new CIO unions. To challenge the established unions and the conservative farm organizations, journalist Kramer observed, Lewis had to "largely depend on old retainers who after a thousand battles could prefer to live out their lives in peace."[20]

Even as he launched these organizing initiatives, Lewis drew ever more tightly into the world of the UMW, distancing himself from Murray and the CIO, indulging in dramatic public gestures seemingly designed to embarrass—perhaps to wreck—the industrial union federation. Lewis did not attend the CIO's 1941 convention in Detroit, delegating Dennie to lead the UMW contingent. Murray loyally supported Lewis in the then-raging captive mines controversy, but otherwise the convention brimmed with pro-Roosevelt sentiments and supported the government's foreign and defense policies. The UMW sponsored resolutions criticizing Hillman and Roosevelt, but they failed, triggering fistfights and beatings in the hotel lobbies and taverns. *New York Times* reporter A. H. Raskin laid the violence directly at the door of Dennie Lewis, noting that members of his bodyguard were seen assaulting UAW activists. The next day, with squadrons of burly autoworkers protecting their leaders, Dennie Lewis left the hall, flanked by fourteen tough-looking assistants. Reported Raskin, "The group walked in platoon fashion to the hotel."[21]

Early in 1942, Lewis repeatedly provoked and embarrassed Murray and the CIO. On 17 January, front-page stories reported that Lewis had floated a dramatic new plan to unify the AFL and CIO. This "accouplement" (Lewis's widely publicized term) would facilitate the war effort and eliminate the regrettable rancor and divisiveness that had plagued the labor movement for the past six years. In Lewis's scenario, William Green would retire, Murray would become secretary-treasurer of the new organization, and current AFL secretary George Meany would assume the top position. When queried about the timing and provenance of this plan, Lewis responded by noting that for several years now he had been chair of a CIO committee charged with negotiating with a similar AFL body about reunification of the labor movement. He was merely seeking to carry out his responsibilities.

Talk of the Lewis initiative dominated the labor world. Perhaps the UMW chief had patched things up with Roosevelt and was acting on the president's behalf, hoping for labor unity in time for the 1942 congressional elections. But then again, perhaps Lewis was attempting to unify the labor movement under his indirect aegis as a means of keeping organized labor from growing too dependent on the administration. Perhaps, still another line of speculation ran, Lewis was merely attempting to remind Green and Murray that whatever their formal positions of leadership, he was still the kingpin in the labor world and could, at will, command immediate national attention with even the most outlandish proposal. For the AFL, Green issued a disdainful dismissal of Lewis's plan. Murray, whose whole career had been spent as an appendage to Lewis, was hurt and humiliated. Lewis did not deign to attend the next CIO executive board meeting, once again dispatching brother Dennie. "All that I wanted . . . Denny [sic]," Murray remarked plaintively, "was a little bit of conversation, . . . a telephone call—that's all." The CIO president felt that Lewis's failure to consult him indicated that his long-time mentor now regarded him with the same contempt he assigned to AFL chief William Green. What "I have at stake here," Murray observed in a poignant reminder of his 1940 acceptance speech, "is the question of manhood."[22]

Simultaneously, Lewis dropped another bombshell on the CIO. The UMW secretary-treasurer, Lewis's long-time aide Thomas Kennedy, informed the CIO comptroller, Lewis's brother-in-law Floyd C. Bell, that the books showed that the CIO owed the UMW over $1.6 million. In all, Kennedy declared, the miners' union had supplied almost 90 percent of the CIO's financial needs during its first two years of existence; total UMW contributions to the industrial union federation were calculated at more than $7 million.

Kennedy's letter was preceded by no informal notice or quiet discussion of UMW-CIO finances. Like the "accouplement" scheme, it stunned CIO people. To be sure, Kennedy reassured the CIO that the miners' union did not demand immediate payment, or even actual cash recovery. The UMW, the letter announced, would simply stop paying its monthly dues of thirty thousand dollars to the CIO for the next couple of months, the amount to be credited against the $1.6 million balance. It did not take long for Murray and CIO secretary-treasurer James B. Carey to realize that if Lewis chose, the UMW could hold back its monthly dues for five years. Since the UMW payment represented about 25 percent of the CIO's income, Kennedy's letter seemed clearly an attempt to cripple and embarrass the federation.

Throughout his tenure as CIO president, Lewis had kept CIO finances off the record, running the organization with his customary lack of accountability. Indeed, when Murray assumed control in November 1940, he found that the industrial union body was virtually bankrupt and that its central office staff could barely function. Only comptroller Bell, Lewis's brother-in-law, had any records of the organizaton's financial history. Murray, Carey, and Director of Organization Allan S. Haywood worked ably over the next year to put the CIO on a self-sustaining basis. By the beginning of 1942, they could point to a surplus of over $300,000 and an efficient system of dues collection and accounting. Lewis's sudden announcement of the CIO's indebtedness exploded in the face of an executive council eagerly contemplating the opportunities for expansion of membership that war production was then presenting. Said UAW president R. J. Thomas, "If this is the way unions operate, I'm beginning to learn something that I didn't know before."[23]

As in the labor unity controversy, Murray took this new reminder of Lewis's determination to put the CIO on the defensive as a personal affront. Murray and Kennedy had been Lewis's stalwart aides for twenty years, yet Kennedy never contacted him about these financial matters, choosing to communicate through Lewis's lackey, Bell. When Bell gave him the letter, Murray "damned near went down through the floor." He and others in the CIO had assumed that the UMW contributions were fraternal gifts, part of the obligation of the strong to help the weak. "I have never known of any time in the history of the labor movement,"

Murray grumbled, "of one organization dunning another." Confessed the CIO chief, "it hit me pretty hard. . . . I felt like a lost soul, that is how I felt."[24]

Soon after, the UMW simply stopped paying its monthly dues. In May, Lewis drummed Murray out of the Mine Workers' union, where he had remained a vice president, in a humiliating proceeding that exploited Murray's loyalty to the UMW and his deep personal attachment to Lewis. Dominating the "trial" and citing a long list of Murray's "betrayals" of the UMW, Lewis now referred to his associate of nearly a quarter century as "a former friend."[25] At the UMW's October convention, Lewis lashed out at the CIO leaders, many of whom, such as Van Bittner, Allan Haywood, and Murray himself, had spent their careers in Lewis's shadow and whose attachment to the UMW verged on the religious.

In his assault on his once-trusted henchmen Lewis exhibited again the ruthlessness and disdain for ordinary human sentiment that had marked his career. Since Murray and his associates had over the past year pursued policies in behalf of the CIO that conflicted with Lewis's new plans to expand the UMW through District 50 and the Construction Workers unit, they were worthy only of contempt. Despite Murray's public support for the UMW in the captive mines controversy, Lewis charged that "the leadership in the CIO . . . were attempting to sell the United Mine Workers of America down the river in the captive mines dispute."[26] "I gave five years of my life and work in organizing the unorganized workers" for the CIO, he told the 1942 UMW convention. What thanks did he get? Accusations and innuendos, apostasy and betrayal. But, he told his miners, "life is too short for me to answer the yappings of every cur that follows at my heels." Let the "lap dogs and the kept dogs and the yellow dogs" bed down with their governmental and corporate keepers. He had only contempt for the "miserable mediocrities of the CIO."[27] One by one, he read his old associates out of the UMW, shedding all association with a CIO that he now believed had abandoned its militant origins in favor of cozy dependency on the scheming Roosevelt.

He had failed to stop the rush to war. His warnings about FDR's program of co-optation of the labor movement fell on deaf ears. His efforts to find an alternative candidate had fizzled, as had his attempt to build a progressive coalition. Workers had ignored his plea to elect Willkie. The CIO, which under his leadership had been on the verge of achieving for labor a degree of power and public influence unmatched in the history of American labor, was now, he believed, tame and fat, an appendage to Roosevelt's machine. But the UMW had no need of any of this. With 600,000 members and ironclad contracts with virtually every mine in the country, it could defend itself alone. Astride the most critical of all defense industries, Lewis and his legions would lead by example, demonstrating that American workers could support their country while at the same time resisting the claims of the pervasive national security state. Waste no tears on the CIO, he counseled his miners. As in the past, the UMW would stand alone.

The Lewis Enigma

The complex controversies of the late 1930s and early 1940s revealed a John L. Lewis at the height of his powers and in the middle of insoluble dilemmas. Many contemporary observers saw in his machinations evidence of megalomania and cynicism. To account for his growing hostility toward President Roosevelt and his deepening estrangement from his erstwhile allies in the CIO, critics stressed his egotism and personal ambition. Liberal journalists and presidential supporters insisted that Lewis had become unbalanced by the success of the UMW and the rise of the CIO. He had begun to see himself as a rival to the president. Rumors persisted about the labor leader's lust for political office, this time centering on his alleged determination to join Roosevelt on the 1940 ticket ("as a candidate for which office?" FDR allegedly asked). When it became clear that Roosevelt regarded him as merely a powerful labor leader and as only one element in a complex political equation, Lewis broke loose and sought both to punish the president and to demonstrate his (and labor's) centrality. The growing knowledge, in journalist Benjamin Stolberg's words, that in a showdown "Gentleman Jim Corbett Roosevelt could knock out John L. Sullivan Lewis, the tough boy from Iowa," drove the Mine Workers' leader to escalate his attacks on the administration,[28] culminating in his bewildering endorsement of Wall Street insider Willkie.

The stress on personal factors to account for his treatment of fellow laborites also dominated contemporary commentary. The emergence of the CIO as a vital force in American life apart from Lewis's leadership offended his self-image. The rise of labor leaders such as Sidney Hillman, Philip Murray, and Walter Reuther of the UAW to national stature could not be tolerated by a man who insisted on primacy in all matters. Perhaps even the awareness that, in the long run, the new CIO affiliates in steel, autos, electrical goods, and related fields were bound to surpass the rapidly mechanizing coal-mining sector in membership and, no doubt, in influence drove him to ever more abusive attacks on former allies and to ever more grandiose if misconceived organizing campaigns. Journalist James Wechsler, a bitter critic of Lewis in those years, thought that a cartoon in a UMW newspaper provided an answer to the riddle of Lewis's behavior. It depicted the heroic leader of the Mine Workers union descending from the clouds "to rescue the oppressed." Noted Wechsler, "the same newspaper linked attacks on him to the persecution suffered by Christ. All this," he concluded referring to the past several years of Lewis's seemingly inexplicable behavior, "is presumably a build-up for the Second Coming of John L. Lewis."[29]

Apart from his retinue in the UMW, Lewis had few public defenders in those years. For a time, it is true, the CIO's active and influential Communist component aligned with him, ignoring his long record of red-baiting. From the time of the Soviet pact with Germany in August of 1939 to Hitler's sudden assault on the Soviet Union twenty-two months later, the American Communist party pursued a strident anti-war line. As Lewis castigated the administration for its warlike policies, Communists awarded him their allegiance. When Congress passed the nation's first peacetime military conscription bill in September 1940, Lewis denounced it as the first stop in the road to the enslavement of the American people. The pro-Soviet Almanac Singers echoed his warning, although in a jauntier idiom: the lyric to the "Ballad of October 16" had a peace-loving worker pledging to his dying mother that he would never go to war. But Wall Street had gotten the president "and his boys on Capitol Hill" to begin the draft. The worker now found himself in uniform, lamenting that "I'm wearing khaki jeans and eatin' army beans and I'm told that J. P. Morgan loves me so."

But Communist support proved as transitory as it had been passionate. Hitler's attack on 22 June 1941 imperiled the Soviet motherland. American Communists turned, literally in mid-speech in some instances, into enthusiastic advocates of military preparation and U.S. intervention. By the fall of 1941, Lewis, once hailed as the defender of American democracy, had become public enemy number one, as Communists vilified him for shutting down the captive mines and criticizing the military buildup.

Despite the near unanimity of his critics, however, Lewis's course

125

was neither as quixotic nor as headstrong as his many opponents depicted it. His break with FDR grew from rival conceptions about the nature of the labor movement and its relationship to political power and governmental patronage. Coming out of the solidaristic traditions of coal mining, Lewis had a deep, if nonideological, sense of group loyalty. In his view, steel, auto, textile, and other mass production workers were to be thought of as having the same sense of solidarity and loyalty to the union and the union's leadership that the coal miners exhibited. But industrial workers were not coal miners. They were, to an extent impossible in the remote and self-contained locales in which mining flourished, integrated into a sophisticated complex of competing ethnic, political, and cultural loyalties. The fact that they had a free-standing attachment to FDR, that loyalty to union and union leader was qualified and contingent, confused and provoked Lewis.

In reality, of course, even the fabled solidarity of his coal-mining legions had limits. Increasingly, in all but the most primordial conflicts with management, it was loyalty that owed as much to the patronage and bullying of the Lewis machine as it did to affection for the leader. Nor could Lewis, for all his control of the UMW, persuade even his own membership to abandon FDR, either in the 1940 UMW convention or the November election. Whether Lewis's bitterness over FDR's continued appeal flowed essentially from his wounded ego or from his vision of an autonomous labor movement free from compromising constraints, it dramatized the extent to which the revived labor movement of the 1930s departed from the tribal cohesiveness of a bygone era.

Moreover, of course, Lewis had been a Republican throughout the 1920s. Support for FDR in 1936, not endorsement of Willkie in 1940, was the aberration. The president's party was honeycombed with representatives of corrupt (and often antilabor) urban machines and racist southern warlords. The aggrandizement of the national state, the expansion of military production, the conscription of young men, the onward rush toward war—Lewis was not alone in deploring these developments, even if his fellow labor leaders thought it politic to support the president and reap the temporary benefit of increased employment. Harking back to World War I, Lewis sought to remind his associates that a wartime government, however prolabor in the short run, would not tolerate dissent or opposition.

As for his isolationism, it grew naturally from his background and experience. He had grown up in the heart of the country, and on his travels around the United States he had seen its great wealth and plenty. The county had such an enormous domestic market, he believed, that it had no need for extensive foreign trade. It was only the greedy financial interests, with surplus profits looted from the ill-paid American workers and overcharged American consumers, that had an interest in overseas markets. Along with millions of his countrymen, Lewis believed that the crusade of 1917–1918 had been a mistake, that the American people had been duped by Wall Street and munitions manufacturers. To be sure Hitler was a ruthless dictator. Since 1933, Lewis had pointed to the Nazi führer's destruction of the German labor movement as a warning to free people everywhere. But foreign adventure in alliance with cynical British imperialism and, eventually, the despotic Soviet state would lead only to regimentation and suffering.

Ultimately, Lewis's rupture with FDR and his intense isolationism cut him off from the labor movement itself. The specific issues around which controversy swirled—the captive mines dispute, the accouplement scheme, UMW-CIO financial problems, even the endorsement of Willkie—could have been compromised. Lewis might have used his enormous influence and charm to have insinuated his views. But anything approaching political compromise within the house of labor was not his style. Philip Murray was, ultimately, a satellite so far as Lewis was concerned, regardless of the formal position he held as head of the Steel Workers and the CIO. Men such as Brophy, Hillman, and young Walter Reuther of the Autoworkers who spoke frankly and independently in opposition to Lewis in CIO circles aroused in him enmity, contempt, and ridicule. Lewis elevated his differences with CIO leaders to matters of highest principle. That he had relied on government to succor the UMW in the 1920s and again in the early 1930s was forgotten, that Murray and Hillman derived strength from association with FDR put them beyond the pale.

Lewis never explained his motives. In 1957, Lee Pressman, whom Lewis had appointed in 1936 as the CIO's legal counsel, spoke at length about his years with the Mine Workers' leader. Closely associated with Lewis throughout the 1930s, assisting him in the General Motors and Chrysler bargaining of 1937, and beneficiary of many hours of discursive conversation dispensed in moments of relaxation, Pressman insisted that principle, and not mere questions of prestige and preferment, dictated Lewis's course in those years. Lewis, Pressman believed, was impatient to build a powerful, independent labor movement that could play a decisive role in all areas of American life. He had no ideological agenda; indeed, he was a provincial man, little aware of developments in the labor movements of other countries. Whereas men such as Hillman and Murray transcended their provincial backgrounds and seemed to enjoy contact with intellectuals and politicians, Lewis focused all his energies on the aggrandizement of organized labor. Of course, Pressman went on, to Lewis labor's rise in power was inconceivable without his being in the vanguard. He had seen the labor leaders, politicians, and savants come and go over the years. Who was as able, as shrewd, and as forceful as he was? There was, Pressman admitted, an arrogance about Lewis, but is was an arrogance born of experience and success.

By 1939, Lewis had become convinced that the president was merely toying with the labor movement. Men of immigrant backgrounds such as David Dubinsky, Philip Murray, and Sidney Hillman had a respect verging on awe for the presidency, but for himself, a son of Iowa and a frequent visitor to the White House in the days of Coolidge and Hoover, presidential flattery had no impact. He began to see his creation, the CIO, drift toward absorption by Roosevelt into the vast governmental-political machine that the New Deal had spawned. Lewis, Pressman believed, rarely planned his moves out systematically. Chacteristically, he probed, tested, experimented, launched trial balloons, trying to find the combination of circumstances that would open up opportunities for him to exploit.

Perhaps, he believed, his dramatic endorsement of Willkie would alert the labor movement to the depths of the peril it faced in becoming an appendage to FDR's ambitions. Just possibly leadership in a coalition of progressive groups would encourage laborites to question their dependency on the government. Maybe new organizing campaigns would revive the élan of the mid-1930s and prove to workers that they did not need the government to build unions. Perhaps his provocations of the CIO would somehow force Murray to understand that labor's integrity was in the balance and that a labor movement dependent on government was doomed to eventual failure. In everything that Lewis did, Pressman concluded, "All the time he was thinking how to enhance the voice of labor."[30] From Pressman's viewpoint, actions that to others seemed arbitrary, quixotic, or cynical reflected rather Lewis's belief that bold gestures and dramatic gambles sometimes paid off. Whereas Hillman and Murray sought predictability and incremental growth, Lewis tried "capturing the imagination of people and leaping forward." After Lewis stepped down from the CIO presidency, "No one knew just where the c.i.o. was heading for. . . . It was just a complete new era of the American labor movement"—a time, Lewis believed, for boldness and daring, not calculation and caution.[31]

Pressman, the brilliant legal counsel for the CIO, presented a lawyer's brief in behalf of his benefactor. Clearly, Lewis's magnetism and drive toward power continued to captivate him years after the events he described. Another long-term Lewis associate and observer, John Brophy, assessed Lewis's behavior in the early 1940s from a sharply different perspective. Principled opponent of Lewis in the 1920s, Brophy had been appointed CIO director of organization in 1935. By the time of Lewis's break with the industrial union body, however, Brophy had been shunted aside, put in charge of secondary matters in the CIO bureaucracy. Yet, as with everyone in and around the labor movement, Brophy remained fascinated with the transfixing Lewis.

Lewis, in Brophy's view, was simply perplexed by the domestic and international events of the late 1930s. As the CIO surge came to a halt, he groped for solutions. He feared that Roosevelt recession would do to the UMW and the CIO what the depressions of 1921–22 and 1929–33 had done to the UMW; he looked to Roosevelt to bail him out and when the president proved unresponsive, the Mine Workers' leader turned against him. Lewis's newfound hostility toward government sponsorship of labor organizations did not impress Brophy, who remembered how eagerly in the 1920s Lewis had embraced Hoover and how loudly he had trumpeted the Coolidge administration's bogus support for the UMW. Lewis brilliantly exploited the opportunity the NRA brought, but he was in no position to vilify leaders such as Murray and Hillman who successfully used their cooperation with Roosevelt to strengthen their unions in the period of defense buildup.

All honorable labor leaders, Brophy believed, were wary of government. For Lewis to set himself apart from the others because of disagreements on specific policies was to create a Manichean world of good and evil—flattering to Lewis's ego but wide of the truth. Problems of working within the governmental and political system to maximize labor's advantages while remaining free of noxious regulation were practical problems that called for vigilance and leadership, not grandiose declarations, hopeless crusades, and persecution of those who disagreed.

Brophy understood that Lewis was sincere in his isolationism. But it was an isolation born less of thoughtful principle than of provincial ignorance. "You see," he reminded an interviewer years later, "we were all for peace, but we recognized the war danger, with Hitler on the loose, all except Lewis."[32] Lewis harbored the delusion that he could carry unionists along with him in his attacks on Roosevelt and his endorsement of Willkie. He came close to losing touch with reality. So far as Brophy was concerned, in view of the constellation of forces that prevailed in the United States and internationally in 1940–41, Lewis's savage attacks on FDR and the CIO went beyond legitimate differences of opinion. They played into the hands of reactionaries at home and fascist aggressors abroad. Lewis's neutralism, Brophy concluded, was not neutralism; it "was taking sides on the wrong side."[33]

Lewis's endorsement of Willkie was a blessing in disguise. It led to his abandonment of the CIO presidency and to replacement by Murray, a man groping toward a broader vision. Lewis failed to appear at the 1941 CIO convention, in Brophy's view, because he would have had to defend his destructive antiadministration stand and "he preferred to attack in an oblique way, rather than face up and accept the consequences of all out opposition to the defense program." In short, by 1940, Brophy believed, Lewis "had pretty much done his job. He'd exhausted his mandate." Retreat into the inner world of the UMW, where he was safe from disagreement behind his ruthless internal control and his army of sycophants, protected him from the need to expand his horizons and come to grips with the complex problems that industrial unionism faced in a war-torn world.[34]

At root, Lewis simply did not share the conviction of his counterparts in the labor movement that the United States had vital interests at stake in active opposition to the Axis powers. Perhaps as a native son of a deep midwestern state Lewis was immune to the transatlantic influences that shaped immigrants such as Hillman, Brophy, and Murray. Perhaps his most basic political values reflected a republicanism defined, as so often it was in the nineteenth-century village America, in opposition to the corruption and tyranny of Europe and the perfidy of England. Perhaps an atavistic Welsh strain choked off sympathy for the beleaguered British. In any event, whereas the great majority of labor's leaders—surely no less prideful of their country and no less committed to a vision of its libertarian and democratic traditions than he was to his—held a definition of America the very existence of which Hitler imperiled, Lewis perceived America as he perceived himself—proud, independent, unneedful of alliances with underlings who were ever capable of treachery.

By late 1942, Lewis's breaks with the Roosevelt administration and with the CIO were complete. As the District 50 and dairy farmers' organizing efforts sputtered, it became clear that the traditional realm of coal mining would once again provide the only arena for the sixty-two-year-old leader, now at war with the rest of organized labor. And even within the ranks of the coal miners, restive rank-and-file miners began to press the aging chieftain. As wartime accident rates soared and government-regulated wages lagged behind the cost of living, miners prodded their leader to translate the UMW's power into higher wages and better conditions. So once again Lewis turned to face the coal operators, free of obligations and constraints and ready to defy a wartime administration determined to bring him to heel.

6

UNDER SIEGE:
THE 1943 STRIKES

In 1943, Lewis defied the government in leading a half-million soft coal miners in a series of strikes. He stood up under a venomous campaign of public criticism and eventually negotiated significant wage increases. The Mine Workers union thus bent wartime government wage formulas and, indirectly, encouraged militant activism among tens of thousands of dissatisfied factory workers. The press, administration, officials, and many labor leaders saw Lewis as an evil genius, a wily and arrogant mastermind of discontent. These critics blasted Lewis for his seeming disregard for the national interest. Politicians and journalists viewed him as a vengeance-obsessed tyrant, using the compliant miners to punish his nemesis, FDR. The antilabor press vilified him relentlessly, while a suddenly patriotic Communist party declared him public enemy number one. Mainstream labor leaders also assailed him, even as their members began to copy the miners' militancy. Lewis, it seemed, was bent on destroying the entire wartime labor program of the government while at the same time discrediting the great majority of laborites who supported it. Would Lewis, defeated in his earlier efforts to redirect the labor movement and seize the political initiative, now translate his victories in the mine fields into a new crusade to chart labor's course?

But Lewis's battles of 1943 were not in fact the next installment in the effort to forge a new labor movement. The sixty-three-year-old chieftain had little taste now for concerns outside the coal industry and the UMW. Far from using his members to create embarrassment for FDR and for his union rivals, Lewis in reality followed the lead of the working miners. He responded to, and did not manufacture, their militancy. Moreover, despite his persona as tribune of the angry miners, Lewis actually served as a moderating force. A lifelong enemy of contract violations and wildcat strikes, he sought first to suppress and then to channel the miners' war-bred activism. Despite his harsh attacks on government "burrocrats" and their laborite lackeys, the aging union leader fought primarily to retain order in his own ranks and not to make yet another bid to recast the labor movement.

Nor did the UMW's 1943 rebellion spread very far outside the mining regions. Lewis's telling critique of wartime labor policies carried little lasting political meaning. The stridency of his attacks on fellow labor leaders and his oft-repeated scorn for allegedly reckless and overpaid industrial workers clearly indicated his priorities and precluded any possibility of mobilizing a broad antiadministration bloc. Though his 1943 campaign did implicitly raise the kinds of questions he had directly addressed in his immediate prewar dissidence, these wartime battles were fought in defense of home territory. Rank-and-file miners dictated Lewis's priorities and left him little time or energy for more ambitious initiatives.

Miners' Grievances

In 1943 the unique character of collective bargaining during World War II quickly brought Lewis and the UMW into direct conflict with the federal government. Soon after Pearl Harbor, Lewis had agreed, along with virtually all labor leaders, to a No Strike Pledge (NSP), but rank-and-file miners, first in the hard coalfields and then in bituminous, seethed with dissatisfaction. Lewis soon became convinced that the government itself had in effect rendered the NSP inoperative because of its failure to establish, as it had promised, fair and effective dispute resolution machinery. The UMW president championed the miners' claims and sought to wrest substantial wage increases from newly prosperous coal operators.

Throughout 1943, Lewis stood at the center of a complex web of negotiations, confrontations, and maneuverings. This was no simple squaring off of union and management. In addition to the coal indus-

try's basic split between anthracite and bituminous, the soft coal operators were divided into several regional and statewide associations,
which often acted at cross purposes. At least three separate agencies of
the federal government played major roles in the lengthy negotiations,
and the president himself intervened personally. Among the miners,
wildcat strikers sometimes defied even their own union leadership and
pushed Lewis into open confrontation with the government. Conducted amid intense public hostility, Lewis's fiery negotiations and the
soft coal miners' four separate work stoppages in 1943 attempted to improve basic wage rates while at the same time exposing the injustice
of federal actions, which, Lewis believed, were confused, arbitrary, and
antiworker. Thus, in mid-1943, the UMW *Journal* sneered that wartime
labor policy had been put "into the hands of political stooges [who]
have been given powers that can make the U.S.A. into one big Uncle
Tom's cabin."[1]

The main object of Lewis's displeasure was the National War Labor Board (NWLB), a twelve-member panel created by presidential order
on 12 January 1942. The board, which included four representatives
each from among employers, unions, and the public, was charged with
resolving disputes between employers and unions that the parties would
ordinarily have settled through collective bargaining and perhaps strike
action. Since organized labor had surrendered the strike weapon for the
duration, unionists looked to this panel for resolution of wage, working
conditions, and union recognition disputes. Neither employers nor unionists were happy with the performance of the board over its first fifteen
months. In a critical action in July 1942, the NWLB had handed down
a decision in a key wage case involving the United Steelworkers of
America (USWA) and the Little Steel companies that granted a modest
wage boost but ignored strong union presentations that would have permitted substantially greater increases. The resulting "Little Steel Formula" imposed sharp wage restrictions throughout the economy.
Meanwhile war production drove prices up. Since government antiinflation policies seemed weak and ineffective, laborites chafed under the
burden of this Little Steel Formula.

Mine Workers felt particularly disadvantaged. In part this was because the board had no nonmonetary inducements to offer the UMW to
sweeten the antiinflation pill. Other unions gained important union security provisions from the board, helping them solidify their positions
in defense industries and expand membership rapidly, thus at least partially compensating for wage restrictions. The UMW, however, had

gained union shop and dues checkoff provisions in the contracts negoti-ated in the 1930s and in the captive mines dispute.

For many reasons, miners believed that Labor Board rulings failed to take into account the unique circumstances of mining. Veteran min-ers had for years paid the price of poverty for remaining in a sick indus-try. Now coal production was booming and the operators reaped fat profits, but miners were forbidden from taking advantage of their newly gained market power. Nor could coal miners easily leave their jobs and find alternate employment in defense work, for the mines were often remote from centers of manufacturing. Moreover, prices were higher in the mining towns, reflecting dependency on small grocers and company stores in vast areas in which supermarkets and chain retail outlets were rare. Thus, in the judgment of one recent student, the wage and price regulation policies of wartime agencies were "patently unfair to mining labor."[2] Never seats of affluence, the mining towns sank further into poverty, despite the regular employment and high profits that the war brought.

Coal miners believed also that Johnny-come-lately urban workers benefited unreasonably from federal wage and price regulations. Labor shortages in defense-impacted cities forced up wages, which in turn fu-eled inflation. Reports from relatives now working in Detroit, Mobile, and Pittsburgh convinced mine workers that their urban counterparts—many of them women!—were profiting from wartime conditions as handsomely as were the coal operators. In the shipyards, aircraft plants, and munitions factories, they believed, the simple ability to swing a hammer or run a drill press commanded wages hitherto awarded to skilled carpenters or machinists. As coal miners tightened their belts in the face of stagnant wages and rising prices, inexperienced workers in industry and construction waxed fat. A coal miner toils beneath the earth at great risk for $7.00 a day, Lewis told a Senate committee in March, 1943, while employers "give an inferior workman across the tracks $15.50." In view of the steep increases in the cost of food, he continued, miners "are not getting enough to eat. . . . We are asking for nothing except bread."[3]

Moreover, wartime mining was dangerous work. Never models of safety, the coal mines during World War II became veritable killing fields. Production leapt upward, expanding from just over 500 million tons in 1940 to 640 million in 1942, 653 million in 1943, and 684 mil-lion tons in 1944, setting an all-time record that year, surpassing one that had stood since 1918 when 300,000 more miners toiled in the pits.

Stepped-up production, however, brought a ghastly toll of dead and injured miners. In 1942–43, cave-ins, explosions, haulage mishaps, and other accidents claimed almost 3,000 lives, the highest two-year total since 1930–31. Each week, 500 more were hurt. As of May 1943, when the first of that year's coal strikes began, U.S. armed forces in World War II had tallied 27,172 killed and wounded. During that same seventeen months, mining accidents had claimed 34,000 injured and almost 2,000 dead. Said Lewis, "That's a lot of meat, a lot of human meat, to grind up in an industry."[4] No one expected the industry to undertake expensive and time-consuming safety initiatives during the war, but Lewis and his miners believed that the men who sacrificed to dig the coal that fueled America's military power should be compensated for the risks they bore.

By the spring of 1943, Lewis had come to believe that the government's wage and price policies were a shambles of injustice, caprice, and irrationality. Corporations raked in fabulous profits, staked by the government to cost-plus contracts that fed inflation. Yet when unions sought to keep pace with the rising prices that these generous practices stimulated, they were attacked as unpatriotic and greedy. The administration, Lewis told a Senate investigating committee, was pursuing through the NWLB's arbitrary Little Steel Formula "a policy . . . that fattens industry and starves labor, and then call[s] upon labor patriotically to starve."[5] As the 1 April deadline for expiration of the UMW contract neared, Lewis became bolder in his attacks on the board, which, he said, had "befouled its own nest" through its unfair wage policies. Its greatest contribution to the war effort, he advised, would be "to resign and not cast its black shadow in the face of Americans who want to work and live and serve their country." The board's chairman, New York lawyer William H. Davis, was "a rapacious, predatory, Park Avenue patent attorney." Leaders of the AFL and CIO who continued to pin their hopes on the administration's promises of equitable labor policies and strong antiinflation measures were guilty of "cringing toadyism . . . coupled with a blind worship of the astoundingly unsound economic policies" of the administration.[6]

Although the 1943 strikes gripped the vast soft coalfields from April through October, it was in the Pennsylvania anthracite mines that strikes first erupted. At the end of December 1942, dissident hard coal miners rebelled against Lewis's leadership, protesting a dues increase of fifty cents a month, adopted over their objection at the 1942 convention. With wages lagging behind the cost of living, they argued, even a small additional fee pinched. Since the No Strike Pledge prevented the UMW from fighting for wage increases, anthracite miners lashed out against the UMW. This dues protest eventually involved at least fifteen thousand of the hard coal region's ninety thousand UMW members, as wildcat strikes spread into January, curtailing production and threatening residential, industrial, and military stockpiles.

Far from following Lewis's lead, anthracite miners had grown increasingly disillusioned with their international president. For years he had taken the declining hard coal region for granted, milking it of revenues, first to fight his interunion rivals in the late twenties and early thirties and then to finance the UMW's rebirth in bituminous coal and the building of the CIO. By 1942, the international union had accumulated a cash surplus of over $6 million, yet Lewis had pushed through a dues increase at the 1942 convention despite the deepening poverty of the coal miners. In northeastern Pennsylvania, Lewis, who had not visited the region since 1926, was widely regarded as remote, vainglorious, and ineffectual.

Of course, the UMW president would tolerate no unauthorized strike, especially one that contested the international officers. His agents quickly moved to isolate the strike leaders and to drive them out of the industry. *Journal* editor K.C. Adams soft-pedaled the dues question, which was in fact at the heart of the anthracite wildcats, and stressed the dissident unionists' other demand, a two-dollar-per-day wage increase. Even as he acted to crush the strike, Lewis recognized both the justice of the miners' complaints about their wages and the necessity to act in their behalf. He seized upon the wage increase issue, rousing delegates at the anthracite miners' March wage conference with a militant speech denouncing government wage policies and vowing to achieve the two-dollar-a-day increase in the forthcoming negotiations.

Thus, although within three weeks the UMW leadership had suppressed the hard coal strikes, these walkouts had a powerful impact on Lewis and on the union. Endorsement of wage demands totaling almost 30 percent for hard coal miners automatically meant that Lewis would have to do as well for the 400,000 bituminous miners, whose contracts also fell due in the spring. In addition, it was in this skirmish that Lewis first directly felt the brunt of the wartime government's actions. Though he and his assistants acted promptly and even harshly to end the strike and punish the dissidents, President Roosevelt, facing political embarrassment because of the strike, encouraged the public perception of Lewis as a strike-happy union boss. Indignantly, Lewis found himself used as a lightning rod, as the superpatriotic (and generally anti-labor) press crackled with hostility toward him even as resentful hard coal miners felt the lash of UMW discipline driving them back to the pits. For Lewis, the lesson was clear: cooperation with government agents was rewarded with perfidy. If he was to be pilloried as a strike-crazed strongman, he might as well align himself with the legitimate demands of his men and let the government find a way to dig coal without them.

Negotiating with the Government

Throughout the protracted soft coal controversy, all parties played complex games of bluff and thrust. Presidential statements ignored the nation's stockpiles of bituminous coal, painting a picture of imminent national emergency and whipping up public antagonism toward Lewis and the coal miners. The NWLB seemed at times more intent on forcing the union and coal operators to follow its procedures and bend to its will than on attaining a settlement. Soft coal operators hid behind the Little Steel Formula and refused during the critical weeks before the walkouts began to engage in meaningful bargaining.

But in this sort of contest, Lewis was the master. He used shock and accommodation, threats and cajolery, bluster and behind-the-scenes machinations to bend the wage formula and to gain increases for the miners. His opening demands at the first negotiation session on 10 March were breathtaking: the miners sought a two-dollar-a-day wage increase, increased allowances for vacation pay, elimination of certain paycheck deductions for miners' on-the-job expenses, and payment for the time miners spent traveling from the mine entrance to the working face (portal-to-portal pay). Added together, these items would have amounted to increases of 50 percent, shattering the Little Steel Formula.

Of course, Lewis never expected to gain all these demands. Throughout the next six months, he advanced various combinations, trying always to secure real wage increases regardless of the particular mix of concessions. Since the president stood behind the NWLB, it early became clear that the flat demand for a two-dollar daily increase could never serve as the basis of a settlement, so openly would it rupture the Little Steel Formula. Increasingly, Lewis, aided by a fortuitous court decision in a case involving metal miners, focused on the portal-to-portal issue as a means of boosting wages without openly violating the formula. Typically, miners spent anywhere from a half hour to ninety minutes traveling underground from the mine entrance to the actual site at which coal was dug. Such underground time had not traditionally been compensated, but during World War II the insatiable demand for coal forced the reopening of older mines whose tunnels stretched well back into the hills. Entrance-to-face time lengthened, lengthening in turn the work day of the miner by as much as two hours. Moreover, job site travel in a coal mine entailed danger, for the man trips and coal cars rumbling through the underground caverns fell victim to derailments and cave-ins hard to prevent in the subterranean dark. And, as miners pointed out, the analogy with the office worker or factory hand was inexact anyway, because for miners, the trip from their homes to the mine entrance was the equivalent of urban commuting. The long and perilous underground trek to the coal face had no counterpart in offices and workshops above ground.

Mine operators and the antiunion press regarded the portal-to-portal issue as a typical Lewisian outrage. The very idea that workers should receive payment for commuting seemed ludicrous. How greedy, editorialists pontificated, for coal miners to hold the nation hostage over such a trivial demand while America's sons and husbands faced death on beaches and battlefields around the world.

To Lewis, however, this public outcry was perverse. Detailed studies revealed clearly the danger of mine work and the deepening poverty of the mining communities. He had many disagreements with Roosevelt's war labor policies. He believed that the administration had forfeited its right to expect unions to observe the NSP. The Labor Board, he believed, was a meddlesome, dictatorial haven for armchair theorists, and the Little Steel Formula had been, in effect, plucked out of the air. By 1943, Lewis believed, the NWLB had revealed its true purpose: to fight inflation by suppressing wages, regardless of the justice of workers' claims. For the NWLB to proclaim its authority so piously and for Roosevelt to continue to endorse the board's actions, Lewis believed, were acts of cynicism. Wartime wage policy had become a political football, with the actions of the president and the policy of the NWLB bearing no relation to the real world of work and wages. Clearly, they were designed primarily for purposes of bureaucratic and political maneuvering.

Even so, Lewis recognized that these political and bureaucratic imperatives were real—thus the genius of the portal-to-portal plan. Here was a means by which miners could receive real increases in their take-home pay even as the board clung to the Little Steel Formula. Portal-to-portal compensation, after all, had no counterpart anywhere else in the economy. What better way of boosting the hard-working miners' income without sending inflationary signals to the mass of workers? To Lewis, then, portal-to-portal pay was a creative and responsible solution. War-profiting operators could afford it. The administration could keep its misbegotten wage program in place. Restive miners could abandon their wildcat strikes and fall back into line behind the UMW leadership. Thus when the NWLB repeatedly rejected settlements that Lewis negotiated during the course of the strike that pegged compensation gains for the miners to acceptance of various portal-to-portal formulas, Lewis was outraged. The NWLB, he concluded, and by extension the president himself, was not concerned with equity for the miners or even with preventing strikes. The goal was to curb labor and to enforce its own arbitrary dictates. He had shown a way out only to confront the government's self-serving and coercive course.

In addition to stressing the validity of portal-to-portal pay, Lewis tried other schemes as well. At one point, he agreed to abandon his original demands if the operators would guarantee miners a sixth day of work every week, pointing out that the government had authorized operators to schedule an extra day and that the operators were already enjoying price increases justified by the added nonwage expenses that an extra day's operation would have entailed, even though, in fact, the vast majority of mines continued to work only five days. On several occasions he negotiated complex agreements with Illinois coal operators who were not part of the northern bituminous operators association and who were ancient and compliant bargaining partners of Lewis. By this device, the UMW chief hoped to establish a pattern that other operators would have to follow, despite their disapproval of its terms. But the Labor Board disallowed these contracts as well.

The nation's 416,000 bituminous miners conducted four separate authorized strikes in 1943. All were short, ranging from forty-eight hours to six days in duration. In all, the coal industry lost about twelve days' production from these UMW-sanctioned stoppages. In addition, wildcat or unauthorized strikes broke out periodically, some conducted in defiance of the leadership of the union, others subtly endorsed as a means of putting pressure on operators and government officials while keeping the UMW's official skirts clean. About 200,000 bituminous miners engaged in these unauthorized strikes, most of which lasted only a few days. Despite the walkouts, in 1943, UMW soft coal miners produced over 590 million tons, the greatest figure on record. At no time were coal supplies seriously jeopardized nor did the soft coal walkouts require any significant curtailment of military production.

Of course, President Roosevelt and other government officials at the time could not know how limited the impact of the strikes would be. The specter of a half-million coal miners marching out of the pits stirred public outrage and conjured up visions of weaponless soldiers, prostrate cities, and defenseless warships. Congress rushed through punitive antilabor legislation; Roosevelt threatened to induct miners into the army; draft boards canceled occupational deferments for striking coal miners, somehow concluding that more coal would be produced without these experienced men than with them. The nation's newspapers outdid each other in thinking up new names to call Lewis. Chairman Davis of the NWLB accused him of giving "aid and comfort to our enemies."[7] Communists, once Lewis's allies, injected their particular venom, with one leading Communist union official urging the president to "make it impossible for him and his henchmen to continue to organize disruption of coal production."[8] "Speaking for the American soldier," hissed an editorial in the army newspaper *Stars and Stripes*, "John Lewis, damn your coal-black soul!"[9]

None of this seemed to affect Lewis. Perhaps because he knew that coal supplies were not really in jeopardy, perhaps because he had the clearest picture of the situation among the coal miners, or perhaps because he had been through this sort of government-orchestrated abuse before, he appeared unruffled and in command. Moreover, despite his seeming defiance of a government at war, he shrewdly calculated the limits of his dissidence. On one occasion, during the first strike in May, he announced to reporters minutes before the president was scheduled to address a nationwide audience in denunciation of the walkout that the miners would go back on Monday morning. He publicly chastised wildcat strikers, pointing to the UMW's policy of faithful contract observance. He recited the impressive production figures, the huge amounts by which war bond drives were oversubscribed in the mining regions, the numbers of gold stars appearing in the windows of coal miners' homes, each symbolizing a young miner killed in action.

Moreover, Lewis carefully refrained from linking his quarrel with the government to broader matters. He launched no political schemes; he sought out no allies in the labor movement. He made no overtures to the president's other critics. Although it is true that he blasted the

NWLB and the administration's general wage policies, he offered no general criticism of the war effort and confined his quest for settlement of the strike to those issues relating directly to the standards of the coal miners: 1943 was no reprise of 1940–41.

Settlement

Ironically, in view of his grievances against the government, Lewis eventually came to rely on federal presence in the mines to attain his goal. At the time of the original walkout, on 1 May, President Roosevelt had seized the mines and directed Solid Fuels Administrator and Secretary of the Interior Harold J. Ickes to operate them, honoring the terms of the lapsed UMW contract while doing so. Believing that the operators themselves would not bargain in good faith and utterly contemptuous of the NWLB, Lewis found in Ickes a man of common sense, eager to get on with the business of mining coal. At first, Roosevelt limited Ickes's authority to the actual operation of the mines, barring him from entering into negotiations with Lewis. For if Ickes and Lewis struck an agreement, it would have to be imposed on the operators, likely at the cost of increased coal prices. Moreover, an Ickes-Lewis agreement would discredit, perhaps fatally, the NWLB, the administration's chief instrument for restraining wages and regulating labor relations.

But all efforts to arrive at a settlement fell victim to the deepening hostility between Lewis and the board. When the government returned the mines to private owners early in October, a wave of wildcat strikes rolled through the Appalachian mines. When the NWLB on 28 October rejected an agreement arranged between the UMW and Illinois operators that might have served as the basis for an industrywide settlement, 416,000 miners once again left the pits. To critics who accused him of "ordering" miners against their will to strike in defiance of the president, Lewis replied that the strike "was the unanimous protest of men who were tired of serving as guinea pigs for Washington's campus theorists, and sick of sabotage and double-crossing," a reference to the NWLB's rejection of agreements negotiated with Illinois operators.[10] Although Lewis's depiction of the strike as a spontaneous uprising of outraged miners was an exaggeration, the frequent wildcat strikes and the swiftness with which the mines were shut down did validate the truth behind his hyperbole. Government officials, irate editorialists, and antilabor politicians might see Lewis as an evil Svengali, luring the innocent coal miners into traitorous and destructive confrontations, but careful observers knew otherwise: however autocratic Lewis might be in the day-to-day operation of the UMW, he paid careful heed to the sentiments of the rank-and-file miners. The anthracite protest had caught him off guard; it would not happen again. The miners' claims were just; the government's policies were inept; the operators were disingenuous. Seizing the banner from the militant elements in his union, Lewis reaffirmed his leadership by following their path.

The 1 November strike led directly to a settlement. President Roosevelt again ordered Ickes to seize the mines but now empowered him to negotiate with Lewis. Lewis had a high regard for the interior secretary, a veteran of progressive causes and a long-term supporter of organized labor. Though Lewis would have preferred a settlement arranged directly with the operators, using the rejected Illinois contract as a basis, he knew that as long as the NWLB remained in the picture, the operators would not meet his minimal demands. If one branch of government, the Labor Board, impeded settlement, he reasoned, he would use another agent of the same government, Ickes, to achieve his goals. Thus, on 3 November the UMW reached an agreement with Ickes in his capacity as mine administrator which gained workers increases of roughly $1.50 a day, using a version of the portal-to-portal plan as a basis. Provisions relating to increased opportunity for overtime work and recalculation of the miners' lunch period in effect boosted compensation even higher, achieving indirectly an amount that surpassed the UMW's original two-dollar-a-day demand.

Since Ickes, as the president's representative, had negotiated this settlement, the NWLB, for all its insistence on following its procedures and guidelines, had no choice but to grant approval two weeks later. In December, the northern bituminous operators reluctantly agreed to honor the contract and the mines were returned to private direction. Southern operators even more reluctantly accepted the terms, with some southern mines remaining under federal operation until the spring of 1944.

The episode of the 1943 coal strikes was one of the most controversial and divisive in the history of American industrial relations. On the face of it, the strikes by over 400,000 coal miners during a period of great national military emergency appeared monumentally self-seeking and unpatriotic. With young men daily dying under enemy bullets, how could coal miners complain of low wages or poor working conditions? Public outrage reached frenzied levels. And since the prospect of a half-million disloyal and greedy coal miners was troubling and, in the end, implausible, the hostility of government officials, journalists, and ordinary people focused on Lewis himself. The newspapers made little effort to understand the complex relationship that bound the UMW chief to his membership. "I am trying to do the thing that is in your heart," Lewis told UMW members on one occasion, saying they were bound by an "almost spiritual fealty."[11] But the press would have none of this. Its accounts depicted the miners as unwitting dupes and Lewis as a power-hungry mastermind, forcing them to abandon their critical war work to sit stolidly at home. In reality Lewis was responding to the angry activism festering in the mine fields.

Equally misleading was the interpretation of Lewis's motives that editorialists, politicians, and even his counterparts in the labor movement advanced. Defiance of the NWLB and of the president, according to this perspective, grew from Lewis's earlier estrangement from his erstwhile ally, Roosevelt, and from his growing frustration and resentment at FDR's continued popularity among workers. As leaders of the AFL and CIO drew closer to the administration and were admitted to decision-making councils, Lewis's fury mounted. Thus, the strikes of 1943 were his revenge. They sabotaged the government's antiinflation program, discredited mainline labor leaders who cooperated with the government, and struck back at the hated FDR.

The reality was quite different. For all his antagonism toward Roosevelt, Lewis had no interest in conducting a vendetta. For all his displeasure at the growth of governmental power in the realm of labor, he had no master plan of action to reverse the recent drift. He confined his attention to the coalfields. Throughout the strike crisis of 1942–43, he followed the lead of the miners. Surprised by the anthracite walkouts of January, he soon came to realize how desperate the economic plight of miners was becoming. Abstract dislike for governmental meddling became concrete when the Little Steel Formula and other NWLB rulings prevented him from gaining the increases that alone could quiet UMW dissidents. Since 1940, Lewis had suffered a series of setbacks. Miners had failed to follow his call to reject Roosevelt for Willkie. The CIO had survived his onslaught and was now flourishing. District 50 floundered. Protests at UMW conventions against provisionalism, while lacking some of the fire of earlier years, continued, encouraged, Lewis believed, by Murray and other former UMW leaders. The anthracite miners' dues protest was the latest and potentially the most severe in a string of adversities.

Even so, Lewis hardly resorted to demagoguery in the 1943 strikes. True, he did heap scorn on the NWLB, but his barbs never specifically named President Roosevelt and were usually careful to express respect for the office of president and commitment to the war effort. Indeed, from Lewis's viewpoint the government, far from making him the butt of public hatred, should rather have respected him for his responsible and, on the whole, restrained leadership. True, any strike in a nation at war was serious business, but the anger and resentment of the coal miners, fed by the unique traditions of activism and solidarity of the mining regions, might well have gotten out of hand. The wildcat strikes in anthracite in January and then in the bituminous fields in April and October voiced the bitterness of the miners. In putting himself at the head of the miners' protest, Lewis did no more than any democratically chosen leader had to do. In carefully guiding the negotiations, Lewis helped avoid a worst-case situation that might have caused the president to dispatch troops to the coalfields.

Clearly, Lewis played a shrewd game of crisis management. He bowed to the miners' militancy when he had to. He acknowledged the coercive powers of the state by halting the strike on several occasions. He proposed imaginative solutions that ultimately proved the basis of settlement. Meanwhile, the operators hid behind the NWLB, the board reiterated its tired formulas, and the president veered and tacked before finally permitting his best representative, Ickes, to reach a settlement. Yet, despite all the histrionics, the nation lost only about two weeks' worth of production; provisions in the contract that made it profitable now for operators to remain open for a sixth day would soon wipe out this deficit.

Lewis, of course, did not expect public gratitude. But he did believe that governmental officials, including especially Roosevelt and the members of the War Labor Board, had pursued actions that both impeded settlement and were designed primarily to meet political and bureaucratic, as opposed to war production, needs. In establishing rigid wage regulations, the board had encouraged the coal operators to abandon collective bargaining. When operators grew apprehensive over the duration of governmental seizure and agreed to terms, the board repeatedly rejected the results. Of all the governmental functionaries, only Ickes seemed to understand both the justice of the miners' demands and the intensity of rank-and-file determination to stop the erosion of their living standards. Ickes alone seemed to realize that Lewis was no hell-bent madman but rather a union leader attempting to steer a course between abject submission and the crisis to which continued rank-and-file rebellion might well have led.

If most government officials, however, were unfair—perhaps cynically so—to Lewis, so the ferocity of Lewis's attacks on the board distorted reality. Despite the harsh words of government officials, in the end the government pursued an accommodationist policy with regard to the striking miners. If the NWLB took the hard line, refusing to countenance the bending of its formulas and insisting that miners return to work before it would permit bargaining, the president kept options open. Threatening to draft miners into the armed forces and to send troops to the mining regions, he nonetheless vetoed punitive congressional legislation. His several radio messages were both conciliatory, praising the patriotism of miners, and minatory, hinting at the use of troops and supporting labor draft legislation. In the end, of course, FDR permitted Ickes, the one high public official whom Lewis trusted and respected, to conclude a settlement, and then stood behind the Lewis-Ickes agreement in the face of NWLB displeasure. Whether the president's course was infuriatingly contradictory or another example of FDR's vaunted administrative experimentalism depended heavily on one's basic assessment of Roosevelt the president.

In the heat of the battle, Lewis also permitted his scorn for fellow labor leaders to obscure the complexity of the wartime labor relations environment in which they—and he—operated. Miners were not the only workers bitter over NWLB regulations and rising prices. Nor were they the only strikers. By the middle of 1943, workers in war plants around the country had begun to rebel against sticky wages, harsh wartime factory conditions, and the weakness of FDR's inflation-fighting machinery. The number of strikes rose from under 2,000 in 1942 to 3,700 in 1943 and to a record-setting 5,000 in 1944. The mixture of full employment and lagging wages proved a volatile one, despite workers' strong overall support for the war and the president.

Strikes in coal mining were troublesome, but strikes in shipyards and ammunitions, aircraft, and armaments factories were downright frightening. Strike-reduced coal production, after all, could be made up with additional shifts and overtime. But much delayed military production was lost forever. In addition, oil and natural gas could, though not without difficulty, be substituted for soft coal in many industrial uses.

146

There was no substitute for fuselages, machine guns, and tanks, however. Thus, industrialists and laborites in defense production bore a special responsibility toward the war effort. The No Strike Pledge, for all its limitations, which AFL and CIO leaders continually protested, served a critical national purpose. True, unions that cooperated faithfully with government policies were rewarded with maintenance of membership contracts and burgeoning membership rolls. Within the councils of the NWLB, however, labor leaders such as the AFL's assertive George Meany and the CIO's crusty Van Bittner were hardly the tame lapdogs of Lewis's rhetoric. Like Lewis, they and their chiefs, William Green of the AFL and Philip Murray of the CIO, served as "managers of discontent" in a pressure-packed wartime environment. In each case, a balance had to be struck between rank-and-file militancy, with all its potentialities for eventual governmental repression, and the needs of the military machine. That men such as Murray, Hillman, and Meany perceived greater benefits to their memberships in a policy of critical cooperation did not warrant Lewis's vitriolic scorn.

Moreover, Lewis and the UMW benefited from the cooperation of the Murrays and the Greens with the administration. True, labor members of the NWLB agreed to board policy statements critical of Lewis. True, too, fellow labor leaders publicly criticized him, feeding the dangerous repressive climate of 1943. Still, it is equally clear that neither the AFL nor the CIO would have sanctioned a full-scale governmental assault on the Mine Workers union however much their leaders resented Lewis's actions. Threats of a labor draft or of military occupation of the coalfields were not acted out. Dependent on the cooperation and support of the national labor federations, the administration would not risk the break with organized labor that a frontal attack on Lewis's mine workers would surely have triggered. Thus, for all his fulminations against the NWLB—"These strutting little men"[12]—and against his fellow labor chiefs—Green, Hillman, and Murray were "weak-kneed" wards of "palace burrocrats"[13]—mainstream laborite support for the administration protected the UMW.

No further coal strikes shook the wartime economy. Indeed, the contract of November-December 1943, which ran until April of 1945, carried the miners peacefully through the most intense period of strike activity of the war. As thousands of aircraft, munitions, and other war industry workers defied union leaders and NWLB directives to make 1944 the most strike-torn year in American history, coal miners stayed on the job, producing an all-time record tonnage. Indeed, in a May 1945

147

article in popular *Collier's* magazine, Lewis contrasted the UMW's spotless record with the behavior of Detroit-area CIO workers, on strike "for causes shameless in their essential triviality."[14] Still railing against chaotic government policies, Lewis nonetheless signed a settlement in April, providing slight additional de facto wage increases. Once again, anthracite miners walked out of the Pennsylvania mines, but Lewis carefully avoided overt endorsement of the strike, confining his activity to suggesting to government authorities that the walkout would no doubt stop when travel-time provisions gained by soft coal miners in 1943 were extended to the hard coal miners.

The 1943 Strikes in Context

Much of the intensity of governmental and press hostility toward Lewis and the UMW sprang from the fear that coalfield strikes would trigger walkouts throughout the economy. To some extent, these fears were justified. In the industrial heartland, wildcat strikers through late 1943 and 1944 pointed to the UMW's successful defiance of government and the effectiveness of miners' militancy in bending the Little Steel Formula. With thousands of former coal miners and relatives of UMW members working in the munitions and weapons factories, Lewis became a hero to those whose inflation-ravaged paychecks and deteriorating workplaces soured them on the No Strike Pledge. Were Lewis to translate his victories for coal miners into leadership of a broad working-class movement against the policies of the government and mainstream labor leaders, war production could become chaotic. Liberal commentators added a twist to this scenario, attacking Lewis for inviting conservatism and repression, citing the passage of the antiunion Smith-Connally Act in June 1943 as evidence of the harm that Lewis and his mine workers were doing to the labor movement as a whole. "If Congress passes savage anti-union legislation," declared the *New Republic*, "Lewis will be more to blame than anyone else."[15]

Whatever the indirect encouragement the UMW's course in 1943 gave dissident workers elsewhere, however, Lewis made no overt effort to formulate a general antiadministration program, either politically or industrially. Politically, he remained on the sidelines, issuing a desultory endorsement of the Republican presidential candidate in 1944, Thomas E. Dewey, but making no particular effort in Dewey's behalf. District 50, which might have served as organizational spearhead, lan-

guished. Lewis made a bid to reenter the AFL during the height of the
strike, seemingly regarding the older federation as less supine in its deference to the president than the CIO, but when the executive council
greeted his offer of return with evasion, he quickly lost interest. His
indiscriminate attacks on labor leaders who sought to work within the
confines of the No Strike Pledge precluded alliances with those, such
as the United Auto Workers' vice-president Walter Reuther, who attempted to articulate rank-and-file protest and modify the NSP. Indeed,
far from cultivating the support of industrial workers, Lewis often spoke
of them with contempt, contrasting the faithfulness, productivity, and
skill of the mine workers with the sloth and lack of discipline of other
war workers. "I have seen plenty of morons in the Southern shipyards,"
he stated in 1944, . . . "getting twice the pay of these trained men" in
the mines.[16] Far from embracing the 1944 industrial walkouts, he criticized Detroit CIO strikes as irresponsible.

As in his warfare against Roosevelt and the CIO leadership before
the war, Lewis stood alone in 1943. Unlike the earlier episode, however, this time he sought no allies. Now in his mid-sixties, grieved by
the death of Mrs. Lewis in September 1942 and perhaps chastened by
his earlier failure to rekindle labor's dynamism, Lewis was now content
to fight on a narrower front. Responding principally to the concern of
his members, he attacked the NWLB and its laborite supporters not as a
means of reinventing a labor movement unbeholden to Roosevelt and
his party but rather as a tactic in his struggle for his members. By age
sixty-three he had concluded that the rest of his life would be spent in
the world of coal mining and the UMW. In 1943 he charted his course
with that overwhelming fact foremost in his thoughts.

7

CONFLICT AND ACCOMMODATION, 1945–60

The wartime strikes were far from John L. Lewis's last hurrah. Contentious relations with coal operators and federal authorities punctuated the latter half of the 1940s. In 1946 and in 1948, federal courts imposed sweeping injunctions on Lewis and his union, compelling mine workers to return to the pits at the behest of the government. As late as the protracted strike of 1949–50, the UMW remained in its customary position in the forefront of labor news. Building on the achievements of the 1933–43 period, Lewis negotiated ever more substantial wage increases for his members and capped this achievement with the creation of a path-breaking industry-financed health and retirement fund. Despite the emergence of new unions such as the United Steelworkers and United Automobile Workers that far eclipsed the declining UMW's membership, Lewis's boast that the mine workers' union continued to lead the way contained much substance through the remainder of the 1940s.

Nonetheless, economic and political circumstances now blunted Lewis's impact. A series of heart attacks sapped his strength, and the deaths of close associates and family members underscored his own mortality. Through the 1950s, he embraced increasingly collaborationist policies, hoping to bolster a coal industry under sharp challenge from competing energy sources. By the mid-1950s negotiations became pro forma, as the UMW cooperated with larger mining interests in a program of rapid mechanization, cooperative marketing initiatives, and restraint of rank-and-file activism.

Nor did the old Lewis presence shake the inner world of organized labor or dominate the political arena as it had once done. Brief reaffiliation with the AFL ended in 1947, leaving the UMW once again isolated from the rest of the labor movement. Traces of the old fire and assertiveness remained, but with the diminished importance of coal and the emergence of a new generation of leaders, Lewis now excited footnotes rather than headlines. Still—indeed, increasingly—fearful over the usurping power of the national security state, Lewis nonetheless left political leadership to others, quietly casting his ballot for Democrats most of the time, warning of the dangers of government meddling in labor affairs, but withdrawing ever further from the role of kingmaker and innovator.

Postwar Strikes, 1946–50

The coal strikes that erupted almost yearly in the five years after the war were the final episodes in the UMW's half century of centrality in American industrial relations. Complex bargaining, heavy governmental intervention, and mine worker solidarity again marked these tangled affairs. As other industrial unions born in the 1930s also tested their newly acquired power and learned the possibilities and limitations of the New Deal dispensation, the UMW once again led the way, this time in the establishment of health, welfare, and retirement programs. By the time Lewis and the coal operators settled the last of four postwar strikes in July 1950, the miners had enhanced their position as blue-collar wage leaders and had forced establishment of a union-governed, multimillion-dollar fund for aged and afflicted miners and their families. In fighting for these health and pension benefits, the UMW paved the way for other unions and helped establish a whole new program for modern collective bargaining.

Throughout these conflicts, the matter of pension, disability, and health care stood at the top of Lewis's agenda. The appalling safety record of American mining was widely known. In the ten years after 1935, almost 13,000 miners died on the job and 639,000 suffered disabling accidents. In addition, observers and miners alike had always known that, quite apart from the threat of accident, mining was unhealthy.

Research priorities in American medicine did not normally focus on industrial disease, but by the 1940s, many studies had documented the high rates of tuberculosis, pneumonia, and other lung diseases prevalent among miners. Certainly, people in the mining communities needed no statistics to make them aware of the chronic coughing, the coal black sputum, and the sunken chests and slack torsos of so many older miners. "Health and living conditions in most mine towns," delcared labor reporter A. H. Raskin in a 1947 article, "are so far backward that one expects to meet Jeeter Lester and Joads on the street." After a three-week sojourn in the mining communities of Pennsylvania and West Virginia, Raskin reported, "the best coal town I saw was on the level of the slum districts one sees from a pullman window on the outskirts of a big city."[1] A report of health conditions in the mining regions conducted during the period of federal operation of the mines (1945–47) documented appalling levels of ill health, infant mortality, and chronic sickness.

To be sure, poverty and ill health had always stalked the mining communities. Some of Lewis's critics believed that after years of neglect of these matters, he now focused attention on them primarily to keep the spotlight on himself and to show up leaders of other unions. No doubt Lewis relished opportunities to remind the press, the public, and those in the labor movement of his and the UMW's leadership. Indeed, he boasted of the Mine Workers' vanguard role. But, quite apart from matters of ego or vanity, the fact was that after World War II the time was ripe for bringing workers' health, disability, and pension concerns into the public arena.

For workers generally, the New Deal had created at best a quasi-welfare state. The modest Social Security benefits were, after all, financed directly or indirectly by the workers themselves. Workers' compensation programs varied sharply from state to state and provided little for residents of the poor coal-mining regions. Apart from the armed forces, there was no public provision for health and medical care. Moreover, the rising tide of conservatism, as indicated in the capture of Congress by the Republican party in the 1946 elections, guaranteed that public programs in these areas, far from being expanded, would remain under sharp attack in the foreseeable future.

Unions, including the UMW, had gained unprecedented power in the 1930s and 1940s and had driven up wage rates. Yet in the postwar environment, higher wages only led to higher prices, as employers passed along increased costs—and then some—to consumers. Of course, the UMW would have to protect its wage standards, but bargaining confined to wages would put it on a hopeless treadmill. Lewis believed that miners deserved rising standards. A health and retirement program, financed by the companies, would bypass the inflationary spiral, bring a modicum of economic security and modern medical care to the isolated valleys, and tangibly improve the quality of life.

In defending his health and retirement proposals, first introduced at the 1945 bituminous wage conferences, Lewis pointed also to the changing demographic profile of the mining labor force. The war had siphoned the younger workers out of the coalfields, drawing them into the armed forces or the great industrial centers. In 1940, half of the soft coal miners were thirty-two years of age or younger. By 1944, the average age had risen to forty-five. Only 16 percent of miners were under age thirty; eleven thousand were sixty-five or older. By 1947, the average age had risen to fifty. With rising education and wartime experiences permitting younger men to escape the danger and hardship of coal mining, the industry—still America's most basic—had to preserve the shrinking pool of aging miners.

Linking his demand for the health and retirement fund with calls for stronger mine safety legislation, Lewis introduced the demand for this innovation in collective bargaining in the spring of 1945 with a vivid account of the lives of his members. "The manpower of the coal industry," he told bituminous operators, government observers, and reporters, "is being reduced, it is being worn out by the hard work, . . . the long hours, the bad air." No machine could replace the miner, nor was a new generation available for work in the pits. "When a man is killed or taken away, or his back is broken or his flesh is burned from his bones, we have no replacements in the mines." Did it not make sense to use some of the huge profits that a booming coal market was generating to underwrite the medical care of this precious resource? Would not a modest retirement fund, providing a humble security for the miner and his family, be socially sound as well as humane? "Why not remove from their minds the horror that tomorrow they may be killed by the fall of a hanging rock or by the terrible ravages of a burning mine explosion that tears through the galleries of the mines." No human provision, of course, could guarantee against sudden death or dismemberment, but "why not remove that fear from their minds so that they will know if that occurs . . . their families will be provided with proper insurance . . . and their children will not become public charges."[2]

Perhaps an aging Lewis sought also to build a monument to himself. As a charismatic leader, he had constantly to produce for his members in a way that less spectacular personages need not. He had built his machine in the UMW on the basis of his own invincibility. He had stood as a lightning rod, justifying his suppression of dissent and his heavy-handed running of the union on the grounds of his superior abilities and his unique rapport with the miners. Of course, a powerful, wealthy UMW was his monument. High wages and reduced hours earned him gratitude. But his crowning achievement, tangibly manifested in hospitals, clinics, and monthly pension checks, would be the health and retirement program. Lewis, like many of his aging counterparts in the business world, saw perhaps a glimpse of immortality in philanthropy. In going beyond the mere achievements expressed in terms of dollars and cents, growth and power, institutions and affairs, this last great accomplishment would enshrine him forever in the hearts of miners and their families.

Lewis and the Mine Workers union gained this welfare and retirement fund through a series of work stoppages and confrontations with operators and government officials that lasted from the spring of 1945 through the summer of 1950. In March of 1945, Lewis advanced a proposal to create a fund for pensions and disability payments as a means of enabling miners to partake of wartime prosperity in the coal industry without bending NWLB wage formulas. Settling instead that year for modest compensation increases pegged to the contract's complex overtime formulas, Lewis renewed the demand more forcefully at the wage conferences beginning in March of the next year. When bituminous coal operators balked, Lewis led his miners out of the pits on 1 April, thus intensifying a strike wave that had rolled through American industry since the end of the war in September of the previous year.

The Truman administration injected itself forcefully into the coal strike, as it had in earlier walkouts in steel, autos, meat packing, and other sectors. At last on 21 May, the president ordered Secretary of the Interior Julius A. Krug to seize and operate the mines. Krug in turn quickly negotiated an agreement with Lewis, one that provided a wage increase of 18.5 cents an hour, a figure that equaled the increases gained by steel and auto workers in earlier strikes. More importantly, however, the Lewis-Krug Agreement stipulated that five cents from each ton of coal mined[3] would be placed in a welfare and retirement fund to be jointly supervised by the government and the union. The agreement also established a separate health fund, which the UMW would administer and which would be financed by diverting the deductions for health care that coal companies had been withholding from miners' pay packets.

Over the next four years, the precise contours of the welfare and retirement programs established by the Lewis-Krug Agreement constituted the main point of contention in coal industry negotiations. When collective bargaining resumed in 1947 and the mines reverted to private operation, mine owners grudgingly acceded to the fait accompli with which the Lewis-Krug Agreement had presented them. They agreed in principle to a continuation of the fund, which was to be governed by a three-member board consisting of Lewis, an operator representative, and a neutral third party. This board was to establish the operating procedures of the fund, making rules to determine eligibility, benefit levels, administration, and other basic provisions. When a deadlock developed in 1947, however, and the fund remained inoperative as 1948 negotiations loomed in the late winter, Appalachian miners conducted a series of crippling wildcat strikes that brought over 200,000 out of the pits in March 1948.

Eventually, after Lewis used contacts in the Republican party to have a new "neutral" board member favorable to him appointed, the board issued the necessary rules for the implementation of the fund. Conclusion of agreements with bituminous coal associations in the summer of 1948 confirmed the formal establishment of the fund, and on 9 September 1948, a sixty-two-year-old retired miner, Horace Alinscough of Rock Springs, Wyoming, received the first pension check, personally and ceremoniously handed to him by John L. Lewis.

Nor did the operators' acceptance of the fund and the increase in per ton royalty from ten to twenty cents in the settlement reached that year end the matter. Royalty levels and control of the fund also lay at the center of the curious and protracted 1949–50 negotiations and strike. It was a complex affair. Coal operators were determined to curb the miners' penchant for conducting wildcat strikes. At the same time, the steel industry resolved to limit the impact of pension provisions in its captive mines lest UMW gains there bolster the United Steelworkers' campaign to gain pensions in the steel mills. For his part, Lewis sought virtually exclusive control over the fund in behalf of the UMW. The eventual settlement—after nearly nine months of strikes, wildcats, operator suspensions of royalty payments, presidential intervention, and lengthy legal battles—produced a contract that boosted royalties to thirty cents a ton and all but guaranteed complete UMW (and hence

Lewis) domination of the fund's administration. In exchange, the union agreed to eliminate contract language that its leaders had used over the past several years as a means of encouraging strategic wildcat strikes without bearing direct responsibility for them. In the end, operators were willing to turn over conduct of the fund to Lewis, for they viewed the contract language issue critical in their efforts to streamline work routines, cut back on employment, and maintain steady production in the face of mounting competition from other fuels.

The Miners' Fund and the Welfare State

In one sense, these postwar bituminous strikes simply continued the troubled history of collective bargaining in the coal industry that stretched back to the 1860s. In certain respects, however, they were among the most significant in the history of American industrial relations. In regard to the central substantive issue, the establishment of the welfare and retirement fund, they did much to establish new goals for the industrial union movement that had arisen in the 1930s and thus to set the pattern of collective bargaining generally for the next generation, not only in mining, but in American industry overall. Moreover, these strikes dramatically brought the federal government into the collective bargaining process as never before and forcefully raised questions about the relationship between labor unions and governmental power adumbrated during World War II but starkly addressed now in a peacetime, and hence "normal," setting.

Before the rise of the industrial unions associated with the CIO, American workers enjoyed little if any protection from the vicissitudes of life. Unemployment compensation was virtually nonexistent until the passage of the Social Security Act of 1935. By the 1930s, a number of states had enacted workmen's compensation statutes to provide minimally for workers disabled on the job, but daunting claims procedures and niggardly benefits blunted their impact. Few workers enjoyed any sort of medical insurance, and pension programs covered only small groups of favored workers in a handful of paternalistic firms.

The legislation of the New Deal brought significant change. The Social Security Act, for example, provided directly for certain kinds of disability benefits and state-administered unemployment compensation. Since Western European countries had been developing governmentally provided medical care for their populaces since the 1880s, many supporters of the New Deal believed federally financed medical coverage was but the next step in the erection of an American welfare state.

Yet the country failed to take that step. Whereas in Britain World War II generated a commitment to expanding social services, in the United States the political climate became sharply more conservative, with the election of the Republican-controlled Eightieth Congress in 1946 clearly spelling an end to New Deal experimentation in social policy. To John L. Lewis, the lesson was clear: if government did not establish basic programs of insurance and medical support for workers, collective bargaining must—hence, the centrality of the health, welfare, and retirement funds in UMW demands after the war.

Other industrial unions were coming to the same posture. In particular, the powerful Steelworkers and Autoworkers unions sought to move beyond the traditional confines of collective bargaining, which historically had regarded questions of wages, hours, and shop conditions as the only legitimate subjects of negotiation. Frustrated in their efforts to secure enhancement of Social Security and enactment of federal medical care legislation in the conservative postwar environment, the USWA and the UAW began also to put these matters in the forefront of their bargaining demands. Thus, the UMW's breakthrough in 1946 ensured that the other industrial unions would press the auto and steel companies in the area of medical insurance and pension benefits. Indeed, the 1949–50 strike became entangled in a steel strike that focused on the Steelworkers' demand for pensions, with captive mine operators concerned lest generous benefits awarded to their miners become the norm for workers in the mills. Lewis and Steelworkers' chief Philip Murray, never reconciled since the UMW's departure from the CIO in 1942, each kept a wary eye on the other, each determined that his rival would not be able to boast of greater victories at the bargaining table.

In general, it was during this postwar period that American workers did begin to achieve pension and medical insurance rights through the collective bargaining system. By the mid-1950s even nonunion employers began to provide plans of coverage, often to forestall union organizing. The Steelworkers won their pensions in a bitter strike against the steel industry in 1949, while the UAW established its beachhead in lengthy walkouts against Ford in 1949 and Chrysler in 1950. In both cases, however, the health and pension benefits won contrasted with the programs that Lewis's protracted confrontations with soft coal operators had gained for the miners. In both the steel and the auto industries, workers gained company-paid medical insurance, not the union-administered health care networks and hospitals that the UMW soon created. In regard to pensions, the industrial unions achieved modest benefits, pegged to Social Security payment levels and provided by the companies in funds out of the control of union functionaries. In soft coal, by contrast, the UMW gained not only company financing based on a per ton royalty but, by 1950, de facto control over the character and administration of the fund itself. Lewis, of course, ignored no opportunity to proclaim the superiority of the UMW achievement. By the late 1950s, he could boast of pension benefits of a hundred dollars a month, an elaborate system of community clinics, and ten gleaming new hospitals, bringing modern medical care to the backward mining regions.

But the UMW achievement soon began to tarnish. In gaining complete control over the health and retirement funds, Lewis refused to heed actuarial principles, perhaps believing that the UMW could continue to come back to the operators for more generous per ton royalties to cover shortfalls. In a sense, his view was a principled one: the medical and economic security needs of miners and their families were not negotiable. Mine workers, their wives, and their children were entitled to the best of medical care and to adequate pensions. It was the obligation of the industry to provide them, raising payments as the need arose. But the 1950s were bad times for coal. Markets shrank, tonnage declined, and royalties diminished. Mechanization, endorsed and even sponsored by the UMW, drove miners out of the pits and weakened the UMW's collective bargaining clout. Far from using the funds established in the late 1940s as springboards for expanding benefits, the UMW had repeatedly to retrench, cutting benefits here, paring the beneficiary rolls there, juggling eligibility, and eventually, in 1964, selling off the chain of hospitals that had been Lewis's proudest achievement.

Nor was union control of the funds the blessing it originally seemed. Lewis was a brilliant bargainer and strike tactician, and a resourceful, if despotic, union leader. But he was a poor financial administrator. As he and the union became ever more deeply involved in diverse financial transactions—buying into coal companies, for example, in the late 1950s in an effort to thwart nonunion competition—the retirement and health funds became entangled in the union's complex wheeling and dealing. Huge sums were deposited in non-interest-bearing accounts, in a Washington, D.C., bank that the UMW controlled. An aging population in the mining towns imposed ever steeper demands on both funds, forcing continual redefinition of eligibility and periodic reduction of benefits. Had Lewis regarded administration of the funds as a matter for professional accountants and had he developed a competent and independent governing procedure, the great principle of union control of resources earned by the toil of workers and gained by union power at the bargaining table might have established a ruling paradigm for social benefits, wedding a new generation of workers to the cause of unionism in a society in which traditional sources of loyalty were daily weakening in the face of economic expansion, mass consumerism, and decreasing ethnic and class identity. Ultimately, however, the checkered and at times tawdry performance of the UMW in conducting the affairs of the funds discredited this approach to benefits and made the approach taken by the USWA and the UAW appear both fairer and sounder. True, these unions gained no control over the enormous amounts of money generated by the pension and health programs for which they so ably bargained and for which their members so painfully sacrificed on picket lines. True also that the purchase of medical insurance from doctor-controlled programs such as Blue Cross often resulted in driving up the cost of medical care, whereas for a time at least UMW medical programs effectively regulated the cost of health services in the mining towns. Still, in the long run Lewis's inexplicable and at times bizarre treatment of the funds' finances, along with the grim economics of the soft coal industry, served to discredit the UMW conception and to validate the more cautious route taken by his rivals in the other industrial unions. Observes medical historian Paul Starr, "no other large union achieved as much direct control over medical care"[4] as the UMW. Other observers, however, pointed to the inability of the UMW to follow through on its grandiose retirement and health care projects and the extent to which the union's long history of authoritarianism, leader worship, and lack of accountability compromised a hopeful, but deeply flawed, innovation in social services.

There were many reasons Lewis chose the route of union-controlled benefits. In multiemployer industries such as construction, garment manufacturing, and coal mining, the frequency with which workers changed employers necessitated benefits divorced from particular plants or mines. The physically isolated nature of coal-mining communities encouraged a community-union approach to health care services. Lewis's long career as steward of the miners' interests encouraged a paternalistic view of benefits, for he had made a career out of trading success in bargaining for de facto sanction for authoritarian control. In the world of coal mining, limited education, geographical provincialism, and the "us-against-them" mind set that nearly a century of fierce combat had generated also encouraged a pattern of deference to the union leadership. Now at age seventy, Lewis was a virtual demigod in the coal towns, especially among the older miners who could easily recall the despair and poverty of their lives before the rebirth of Lewis's UMW. "God bless the day John L. Lewis was born," the first recipient of a pension check was reported as saying. Remarks an investigator critical of Lewis's stewardship, "It was a comment that could hardly have seemed too effusive to anyone familiar with the conditions the welfare fund was established to combat."[5]

In addition to factors relating to the basic character of coal mining and to the paternalistic link between Lewis and many older miners, however, a political dimension also weighed. Disillusioned with the federal government's intervention in labor affairs generally, Lewis had concluded by the mid-1940s that the day of New Deal–style social policies was over. The UMW continued to support and oppose congressional and state and local candidates, but in the postwar period it withdrew from the ambitious political maneuvering that had marked the prewar period. In contrast, Lewis's counterparts in the industrial unions made the political arena central. Murray aligned himself, the Steelworkers, and the CIO ever more firmly with the Democratic party, swallowing President Truman's occasional tirades against selfish unionists during the strike wave of 1945–46, and constantly attempting to push the party to the left. Walter Reuther, elected president of the UAW in 1946, was even more active politically, enmeshing the Detroit-based Autoworkers in the Democratic party of Michigan and serving as leading liberal spokesman in the party nationally. These men, and to a lesser but important extent their counterparts in the AFL, did not share Lewis's repudiation of political action. They saw labor's involvement in the political process as the next major stage in organized labor's drive toward power and influence in American life. Committed as they were to expansion of the New Deal and eager to promote a growing governmental presence in economic and social life, they could regard the pension and health benefits they negotiated for their members as temporary expedients, providing needed support until, eventually, a revitalized and liberalized Democratic party, steeled with massive labor support, completed the New Deal agenda and established the public programs that alone could adequately meet the citizenry's health and retirement needs.

In the 1930s, Lewis had veered toward such a view. But two decades of government intervention in labor affairs, he believed, had discredited such a sanguine outlook. True, he could use government presence to cow or manipulate coal operators into making bargaining concessions. Thus, his deals with Ickes in 1943 and with Krug in 1946 established gains that private bargainers subsequently could not repudiate. Still, on the whole, government was no friend of the workingman, he now believed. As was the case in the general pattern of his activities, Lewis drew inward into the Kingdom of Coal. To be sure, as actuarial and economic realities dried up benefits, Lewis looked, usually in vain, to the federal government to supplement union-negotiated benefits. But the Mine Workers union stood largely apart from the political machinery that the merged AFL and CIO built to promote social welfare legislation. In the long run, the more limited programs that other industrial unions achieved provided a wider range of stable benefits for auto, steel, and other industrial workers than did the more ambitious UMW initiatives.

The Heavy Hand of the Law

Lewis's animus against government extended back to the years immediately preceding American entry into World War II, but events in the immediate postwar period intensified it. Though the UMW eventually benefited from government operation of the mines in that the Lewis-Krug Agreement of 29 May 1946 established the precedent for the welfare and retirement fund, Lewis's relationships with Krug and with President Truman were bitter. Attempting to reopen the contract contained in the Lewis-Krug Agreement in the fall of 1946, Lewis led his miners out on strike in October. Krug, a canny bureaucrat, secured a federal court injunction, which Lewis initially ignored. On 3 December 1946, Federal District Judge T. Alan Goldsborough handed down a ruling that assessed a fine of $3.5 million against the union and one of $10,000 against Lewis for violating the Lewis-Krug Agreement contract and for ignoring the original injunction. Though the U.S. Supreme Court later reduced the fine against the union by 80 percent, it thoroughly endorsed the ruling of Judge Goldsborough. Again, in 1948, Lewis violated a presidential back-to-work order, this one secured under the Taft-Hartley Act of 1947. And again Judge Goldsborough imposed enormous fines, assessing the union $1.5 million and Lewis personally $20,000, and once again forced Lewis to call his members back to work.

As Lewis's legal difficulties with the government mounted, so did his bitterness toward the government's representatives. In April 1947, for example, Lewis denounced Krug in the harshest terms following a ghastly mine explosion in Centralia, Illinois. One hundred and eleven miners were killed in a mine that government inspectors had cited for over five hundred safety violations. Since the mine was being operated under government auspices, in view of the 1946 seizure of the mines, Lewis blamed Krug in Senate hearings held soon after. Charging the secretary of the interior with callous ineptitude, Lewis railed against the "butchery of coal miners in Krug's slaughterhouses."[6]

The strikes of the late 1940s also brought Lewis into direct conflict with President Truman. Indeed, the fabled union chief provided a perfect target for Truman's effort to establish his public persona after the death of FDR put him in the White House. Dependent on mainstream labor leaders for political support yet sensitive to conservative criticism, he could bear down heavily on the bogeyman Lewis while enjoying cooperative relations with the likes of Philip Murray and William Green. He exulted in the 1946 ruling that forced Lewis to call off the strike. In the 1948 presidential campaign, he boasted of his victories over Lewis in the federal courts. When one wag suggested that Truman appoint Lewis ambassador to Moscow, thus punishing at once both Lewis and the implacable Russians, Truman replied that he wouldn't deign to appoint a man like Lewis dogcatcher.

Lewis replied in kind. Truman was "totally unfit" to hold the presidential office. "He has no special knowledge. . . . he is a malignant, scheming sort of an individual" who was positively "dangerous to the United States." To Truman's dogcatcher remark, Lewis riposted: "The President could ill afford to have more brains in the Dog Department than in the Department of State, and from his standpoint, his remarks . . . are eminently justified."[7]

But more was at stake than name-calling or even the heavy monetary penalties exacted against Lewis and the union. How far could a government go in bringing a private body, a union in this case, to heel? What price had the labor movement paid for the legal protections it had won in the 1930s? Could federal judges and bureaucrats, drawn from the social and economic elite, ever overcome their most basic unspoken values and assumptions to treat fairly with workers' organizations? Increasingly, Lewis answered these quesitons negatively. He charged that the attorney general was tapping the phones of UMW offices, evoking memories of the Wilson administration's repressive 1919 tactics. No, government had long since ceased being the friend of the workingman. Lewis spoke out against the "drift toward a vast centralized government and regulation by federal edict."[8] Soon he found himself agreeing with Republican conservatives, suggesting repeal of the Wagner Act and a return to the pre-1935 status of unions vis-à-vis government.

Nor were the executive and judicial branches labor's only governmental enemies. Passage by Congress in June 1947 of the Taft-Hartley Act roused him to a fever pitch of rage. Ostensibly designed by the conservative Eightieth Congress as a corrective to certain abuses allegedly caused or encouraged by the Wagner Act, Taft-Hartley in fact imposed sweeping changes in the character and implementation of federal labor policy. It strengthened employers in their ability to resist union organizing campaigns. It weakened protections earlier afforded union activists against reprisals by employers. It elaborated the administrative and legal procedures relating to union representation campaigns, thus complicating the route by which unions could gain representation rights. It permitted states to outlaw important union security devices, imposed rigorous registration requirements on unions, and, in a provision deeply resented by virtually all trade unionists, required union officers to sign affidavits denying Communist affiliation before they could make use of federal machinery in organizing and representation campaigns. Virtually to a man, America's labor leadership rose up against the Taft-Hartley Act as an outrageous, antiunion, vindictive measure. No unionist was fiercer, more vocal, or more eloquent in this opposition than John L. Lewis.

Taft-Hartley, Lewis told the 1947 AFL convention, "'is the first ugly, savage thrust of Fascism in America." It resurrected the hated labor injunction, in theory outlawed by the Norris–La Guardia Act of 1932. Provisions that permitted the president to order workers back to their jobs for an eighty-day cooling-off period brought back a form of industrial slavery, for if the government could compel men and women to work for eighty days, why could it not eventually compel them to work indefinitely? The act's detailed requirements that unions report on their memberships, finances, and deliberations threatened to turn the labor movement into an appendage of the government. The nefarious law, the product of a cynical alliance between powerful corporate interests and benighted politicians in both parties, "creates an inferior class of citizens," namely, the men and women "who toil by hand or brain for their daily bread."[9]

Nor did the passing years dim Lewis's bitterness, as he reserved a special place in the workingman's gallery of villains for the law's primary sponsor, Senator Robert A. Taft of Ohio. For the Republican senator achieved in 1947 what enemies of progress had only dreamed of doing, namely, rolling back the advance of working people and attempting to bind them with shackles. "Oh," he told the 1952 UMW convention, thinking about Taft "makes me gag." "Born in luxury," the senator—Lewis referred to him by his middle name, Alphonso— had never "lost an ounce of perspiration through a day's work." Loyal son of his labor-hating father, President and Chief Justice William Howard Taft, "Alphonso" did the bidding of the country club set and the corporate fat cats, putting the "hobnailed boot on the necks of the women and children of American workers."[10]

Lewis and the Labor Movement, 1945–55

Much of Lewis's deepening hostility toward government was based on his perception of what its transgressions were doing within the house of labor. Federal injunctions, repressive legislation, even wiretapping, could be dealt with if workers were loyal to their unions and leaders were resourceful enough. In 1945, for example, Lewis had used the Smith-Connally Act, passed in 1943 as a means of curbing union power, to embarrass the government. Since the law required unions to give thirty-day notice of possible strike action and since it required rank-and-file referenda on these strike authorizations, Lewis turned this procedure into a plebiscite on his leadership. When soft coal miners massively supported him by authorizing a strike (though in 1945 none in fact occurred), Lewis used this impressive endorsement to strengthen his hand in dealings with coal operators and government officials. Here was an example of solid ranks and skillful leadership turning an antilabor measure against its perpetrators.

Too many laborites, however, refused to so defy the government. So cozy was the relationship between the leadership of the AFL and the CIO, on the one hand, and the Democratic party on the other, that organized labor—the UMW, of course, excepted—was rapidly becoming a collection of "political company unions," he charged in a 1945 magazine article entitled "There Is No Labor Movement."[11] While the UMW defied a meddlesome government to fight for workers' rights, the Greens and the Murrays would be invited to dine at the White House "and while there," Lewis charged at the 1948 UMW convention, "they would sell out the labor movement and sell out their own Union for a lunch."[12]

The Taft-Hartley Act had brought this tendency to a head. The law contained a stipulation that union leaders seeking NLRB rights for their members had to sign affidavits pledging that they were not members of the Communist party. Virtually all unionists, Communist and non-Communist alike, attacked this section of the law. It outraged them to be singled out as suspect and to be required to pledge a specific denial of something—membership in the Communist party—that was in itself not even illegal. The vast majority of American unionists were not only not Communists but were in fact bitterly hostile to the party, yet they too were expected to sign the affidavits. This provision created consternation within the house of labor. A handful of unionists, by no means all of them Communists, refused to comply, thus depriving their unions of the right to participate in NLRB representation elections or to appeal to the federal board in cases of unfair employer practices. Workers in these nonsigning unions were thus now deprived by Congress of rights guaranteed them by acts of a previous Congress. Leaders in both the AFL and the CIO waxed eloquent in bitter denunciation of this gratuitous and offensive affront.

None more than Lewis. Moreover, while the vast majority of union leaders soon swallowed their objections and signed the required affidavits, Lewis remained steadfast. Leaders of most unions, despite their personal and principled objections, believed that failure to sign would leave their unions vulnerable. Rival unions might encroach, seeking bargaining rights that a nonsigning union could not contest through the NLRB. Leaders in both the AFL and the CIO resolved to mobilize politically, secure the defeat of Taft-Hartley incumbents, and gain repeal of the entire act, including the noxious anti-Communist affidavit provision. Meanwhile, they believed that they had no realistic alternative to signing the affidavit.

Lewis would have none of this. He proposed that union leaders refuse to sign, thus leaving the NLRB with no clientele. Bypassing the board would undercut the entire labor relations regulation machinery of the government, thus returning industrial relations to the voluntary processes that had existed before the Wagner Act—except that now there were powerful unions in place to assert workers' rights and defend their organizations. The AFL, however, rejected this strategy and at its 1947 convention approved an alternative approach. By changing its constitution, the federation could technically remove its thirteen vice presidents from formal positions of leadership, thus leaving President William Green and Secretary-Treasurer George Meany as the only remaining officers required to sign. This stratagem would protect several hundred thousand AFL members enrolled in the federation's directly affiliated unions and would obviate the necessity for all of the body's vice presidents to face signing the affidavit. Leaders in each of the AFL's eighty-odd affiliated national and international unions would decide for themselves whether or not to sign.

This evasive strategy outraged Lewis. Having reaffiliated the UMW with the AFL in January 1946, Lewis was one of the affected vice presidents. At the October 1947 convention of the federation, he rose in righteous indignation to denounce the federation's plan, dripping with contempt for its leaders. For twelve years, AFL conventions had been bereft of Lewis's scathing oratory, but now delegates got an undiluted dose.

Congress, he charged, was muzzling the labor movement. "What are you going to do about it?" he asked. "Oh, I see. You are going to change our Constitution. God help us!" Working his thesaurus overtime, Lewis trotted out his most archaic allusions. All unionists agreed as to the evil nature of Taft-Hartley, he observed, "the welkin [heavens, sky] is filled with the outcries and lamentations of our great leaders of labor . . . calling upon high heaven to witness that all indeed is lost unless they can grovel on their bellies and come under this infamous act." On and on he rolled, meting out equal punishment to "the great brains in Congress" who passed the law and the "fat and stately asses" who presumed to speak for American workers. Submission to Taft-Hartley meant the beginning of the end of a free labor movement. The next step, he suggested, might be withdrawal of the optional nature of the affidavit. Perhaps Congress would next see fit to "make it twenty years in the pen for not signing this affidavit or send out a provost-marshal guard and corral some of us." Turning his back on the AFL, the Mine Workers' chief sneered in conclusion that workers need no longer look to its leaders for direction because "I don't think that the Federation has a head. I think its neck has just grown up and haired over."[13] Shortly after the convention, Lewis sent this telegram to AFL headquarters in Washington: "Green, AFL/We disaffiliate/Lewis."[14]

Nor did this outburst exhaust his stock of rhetoric. Into the fifties, he continued to excoriate the craven labor leadership. "Even now," he told his miners in 1952, "if the leaders of the American Federation of Labor and the leaders of the CIO had the courage of a long-eared jack rabbit looking at a red boned hound they would withdraw their anti-Communist oaths and let this damnable statute fall . . . by default."[15]

Times had changed, however. In the past, Lewisian rebellion had shaken the established labor movement, rupturing it in two parts in 1935. But now, the shrinking ranks of the miners were overbalanced by the huge new industrial unions and the rebuilt older unions that had profited most from the gains of the 1930s and 1940s. In the postwar period, the marching ranks of Lewis's miners no longer set the pace. Walter Reuther's million-and-a-half Autoworkers, Philip Murray's million-member Steelworkers, an expanding Teamsters union, and even William Hutcheson's 600,000-member Carpenters surpassed the UMW.

Not only substance, but style as well was changing. After Lewis's oration at the 1947 AFL convention, Secretary-Treasurer George Meany rose to challenge him. Matching Lewis's sarcasm with a trenchant, sober assessment of the problems the AFL faced, Meany defused the tense atmosphere. It was Lewis, he declared, who brought the Communists into the labor movement in the 1930s, giving them legitimacy by using them to build the CIO. Organized labor faced real problems, dilemmas that could not be solved by orotund rhetoric and the denigration of men who sought the interests of their constituents. In the place of Lewis's improbable plan of open defiance, Meany charted a careful course of protested compliance and political action to gain repeal of the odious law. Meany's forthright attack on Lewis delighted hundreds of delegates who believed that Lewis's verbal assaults on fellow leaders who had to function in a less protected environment than the one the UMW enjoyed were unfair and yet who feared the searing Lewis tongue.

With his second departure from the AFL, Lewis's isolation from the mainstream labor movement was all but complete. He retreated into the Kingdom of Coal. District 50 remained active and even enjoyed some success in organizing disparate groups of workers ranging from taxi drivers and paper makers to chemical workers, eventually increasing its membership to 200,000. Even so, however, Lewis had long since abandoned any plans he might have had to create a rival labor center.

As the years went by, Lewis would occasionally make a foray into the established world of the AFL and CIO, setting reporters buzzing once again. In 1951, he agreed to appear as honored guest at the tenth anniversary celebration of the huge UAW Local 600, representing eighty thousand autoworkers employed at Ford's gigantic River Rouge complex. In his final days in the CIO in 1941, Lewis had given important support to these autoworkers, as he had to their counterparts in Flint in 1936–37. Rouge workers gratefully welcomed the "Father of Our Union."[16]

This was no simple celebration, however. Its organizers had an agenda that went beyond banquets, parades, and rousing speeches. The Rouge local was a center of opposition to UAW president Walter P. Reuther. It had traditionally been an outpost of the UAW's once-powerful and still vocal pro-Soviet element; now during the Korean War, the Rouge rippled with activism and dissent, much of it defiant of the international union leadership and, Reuther and his aides believed, motivated by left-wing politics rather than legitimate shop-floor complaints. Anti-Reuther forces in the large local knew, of course, that an invitation to Lewis would be provocative, for not only had Lewis regularly attacked the CIO, of which Reuther was a vice president, but he had often expressed contempt for Reuther himself, whom Lewis regarded as a self-important theorist, the darling of the Democratic party and drawing room liberals.

At the celebration on 23 June 1951, a crowd estimated at over fifty thousand gathered in the grimy Detroit suburb to hear Lewis speak. The UAW workers braved a Reuther-imposed boycott to attend. They heard Lewis lambaste the UAW president, who, he claimed, had red-baited his way to the leadership of a union that Lewis himself had done so much to found in the 1930s and early 1940s. Moreover, although he cynically impugned the loyalty and patriotism of his rivals for union office, Reuther himself had traveled to the Soviet Union in the 1930s and had absorbed the precepts of *Das Kapital*. Thus the UMW chief performed the neat trick of attacking Reuther for red-baiting *his* opponents while he, Lewis, in turn red-baited Reuther! As for Reuther's pathetic effort to derail the grand celebration of Local 600, Lewis had only scorn: "It would seem that a good way to have a successful anniversary celebration is to have some pseudo-intellectual nitwit put a boycott on it."[17]

This episode created a brief stir within the labor movement and quickly faded away. Certainly, it represented no significant challenge to Reuther's control of the UAW, his rising status as the country's most imaginative and astute labor leader, or his emerging political plans, which envisioned the UAW and the CIO as the "left wing of the possible" within the Democratic party. Lewis's fire-eating speech at the Rouge, one of the last outposts of the Popular Front radicalism so important in the 1930s and 1940s, brought to mind the alliance between the antiwar Lewis and the pro-Soviet forces in the CIO during the period of the Nazi-Soviet pact of 1939–41. During that period, the UMW chief had dominated the headlines and shaped the course of debate within the world of organized labor. Now, however, he appeared only as the avatar of the past, certainly not as a prophet of the future.

Lewis's estrangement from Meany and Reuther, each in his different way a spokesman for labor's future, sealed the UMW's isolation from organized labor. Once Lewis and the miners' union had stood at the center of all discussions of AFL-CIO unity but now they remained at the margins. In the summer of 1954, a public relations consultant hired by Lewis set up a series of meetings between him and two powerful union chiefs, each disgruntled by recent changes in leadership in the two national federations, David McDonald, the vainglorious and petulant new president of the Steelworkers, and Dave Beck, the corrupt and ruthless boss of the Teamsters. For Beck, the ascendancy of George Meany to the AFL presidency on the death of Green in 1952 was disturbing, as Meany seemed determined to single out the shady practices and questionable financial transactions of the Teamsters for special criticism. McDonald, who maneuvered his way into the presidency of the USWA after Murray's death in November 1952, detested new CIO chief Walter Reuther and threatened frequently to take the Steelworkers out of the CIO. Lewis seemingly had important interests in common with the two, quite apart from his recent clashes with their nemeses, Meany and Reuther.

At first, newspapers dignified the portentous meetings between the three labor bosses with solemn coverage. Their luncheon meetings, duly publicized but yielding little other than rumor and speculation, evoked memories of Lewis's stormy departures from the AFL in 1936 and 1947, his accouplement scheme of 1942, and indeed a generation of front-page headlines about labor's inner conflicts. Now, however, reporters and readers quickly became bored. Journalists speculated in a desultory fashion about this new, troika-headed labor leader "Lew Mc-Beck" and the possibility that "he" would create a third and rival labor federation. But by the summer, Lewis had stopped attending the gatherings and the "story" disappeared into the newspaper morgues. When the AFL and CIO engineered a merger in December 1955, Lewis stood on the sidelines, confined to issuing gloomy prognostications about the new organization's chances of success.

Elder Statesman

Estrangement from national politics and from the inner world of the labor movement combined with deepening economic crisis in the coal industry to make Lewis's last years at the helm of the UMW ones of isolation and retrenchment. As possibilities of reasserting broader national influence shrank, he looked instead to the Kingdom of Coal as his arena of leadership. As politicians and labor leaders inevitably disappointed and frustrated him, he turned more and more to coal operators, financiers, and other business leaders as his primary associates. Beginning in 1952, UMW contracts increasingly reflected the belief of both union officials and industry negotiators that survival of the soft coal industry depended on reducing labor costs, increasing mining efficiency, and establishing cooperative relations between labor and management, both at the national level and at the thousands of work sites at which mining took place. Increasingly, too, the Lewis-led UMW attempted to cope with mounting problems of nonunion coal production in the Appalachian states by resorting to coercive organizing, strong-arm tactics, under-the-table deals, and elaborate and costly schemes of buying coal properties in association with flamboyant financiers as a means of co-opting nonunion producers. With an enfeebled and often sickly John L. Lewis paying less attention to the actual conduct of UMW affairs, the union by the late 1950s had begun to sink into a cesspool of financial peculation, collusive bargaining, and gangsterish violence. Lewis's years of dictatorial rule left the union with an emerging leadership that combined sycophantic adulation of the chief with contempt for working miners, cynical views of collective bargaining, and a penchant for outright thuggery that soon made the once-proud UMW a pariah among unions.

Although Lewis's controversies with the government and with fellow union leaders continued into the 1950s, his relations with his ancient adversaries, the coal operators, grew more cordial. The 1949–50 strike was the last major walkout under his leadership. Negotiations through the decade became routine. As markets for coal tumbled and as energy conglomerates dominated the field, the UMW faced a new bargaining environment. With the establishment of the Bituminous Coal

Operators' Association (BCOA) in 1950, bituminous industry leaders resolved to reduce costs and eliminate the interruptions in production that a generation of UMW strikes had brought. Troubled too by coal's declining fortunes and willing, as always, to trade rank-and-file activism for contract security, Lewis proved an eager collaborator in their program.

In the past, Lewis had disdained making employers' ability to pay a relevant concern in advancing his demands for workers. In 1945–46, for example, he had ridiculed Walter Reuther's demand that General Motors open its books to public inspection to prove that it could not in fact absorb the UAW's demand for a 30 percent wage increase without raising auto prices. "I don't want to see the company's books," he had asserted. "We can't submerge our standard wage because of inability to pay."[18]

Now, however, when the BCOA pointed to coal's competitive disadvantage, Lewis paid heed. As coal use fell in the 1950s, large conglomerate and captive mining interests sought to cut back the labor force and achieve the unbroken production that the utilities and large corporate users who made up the bulk of the coal market demanded. They could achieve these goals only with the active participation of the UMW. For his part, Lewis realized that declining use of coal for home heating, combined with a sharp rise in nonunion strip mining, was weakening the bargaining position of the union in the traditional Appalachian and middle western areas. As he watched tonnage drop from a record high of 688 million in 1947 to a postwar low of 392 million in 1954, the BCOA's message of retrenchment and regularity made sense.

In effect, in agreements signed in 1952, 1955, 1956, and 1958, the UMW and the BCOA estabished a collaborative formula for bituminous coal. Wage rates responded to market conditions. Miners watched their leadership among blue-collar workers melt as auto, steel, and other manufacturing unions exploited the prosperity of the 1950s to surge past them. The royalties generated under the earlier agreements remained in force and reached forty cents a ton in the 1952 agreement, but declining tonnage reduced payment levels. The UMW encouraged older miners to take retirement, thus reducing the labor force. New contract language first appearing in the 1950 agreement discouraged wildcat strikes and informal job actions. Strengthened contractual grievance procedures enabled UMW officers to come down hard on dissidents, for they boasted—though often inaccurately—that smoothly running and comprehensive appeals machinery obviated the necessity for the traditional resort to direct action at the mine face. Master agreements with the BCOA reinforced traditional acknowledgment of management's right to direct the labor force, introduce new machinery and techniques, and conduct day-to-day operations free of worker harassment. In the larger mines, which claimed ever greater shares of employment and production, miners functioned as machine tenders rather than as independent producers of coal. Continuing a trend developing since the 1920s, miners and outside workers alike were increasingly paid on an hourly basis, eliminating the tonnage method of compensation that had once stood at the heart of the miner's freedom.

Lewis was willing to sanction and even collaborate in these trends for several reasons. Like the operators, he grew alarmed over the decline of coal consumption and realized that if tonnage continued to drop, it would jeopardize the entire retirement and welfare program. While wildcat strikes had been effective in achieving the UMW's goals in the 1940s, these walkouts had often been as embarrassing to the union hierarchy as they had to employers and government. Never one to welcome rank-and-file autonomy, Lewis energetically collaborated in the suppression of spontaneous activism. As far as mechanization was concerned, Lewis had always welcomed technological advance. If greater use of machinery required the use of fewer men underground, he could only hail the advance in civilization that freed a new generation from the hardship and danger of life in the mines. Passage of a federal mine safety law in 1952, he hoped, would help close down marginal mines and force the improvement of others. The welfare and retirement fund would encourage older miners to leave the pits and would, along with the health care innovations launched in the late 1940s, bring a new measure of security and decency to the hills and valleys.

Insofar as the BCOA was concerned, this program succeeded. Employment in soft coal mines fell from 350,000 in 1945 to 200,000 in 1955, to about 125,000 in 1962. After a brief walkout in 1952, directed at a government Korean War board's rejection of a BCOA-UMW contract, strikes disappeared from UMW mines. Large energy companies and captive mining operations modernized production. Continuous mining machines transformed the miner's work far beyond the changes that the mechanical cutter had earlier brought. Boasted the BCOA's director in 1952, bituminous coal mining was "the only assembly-line mass production industry carried on underground."[19] Labor costs shrank, and large energy companies found substantial profits in supplying coal to expand-

ing public utilities and generating plants, whose insatiable fuel requirements necessitated uninterrupted production.

The BCOA-UMW collaboration, however, did little for most coal
miners or retirees. Declining tonnage reduced payments to the welfare
and retirement funds and the Lewis-dominated directors slashed benefit
levels and cut eligibility lists. In a particularly cruel decision made in
1962, they decreed that a miner had to end his career in a union mine
to be able to claim pension rights. This brutal provision penalized thousands of Lewis's most loyal supporters of the battles of the 1930s and
1940s who were forced by mine closures and the needs of their families
to work in their declining years in small nonunion operations. Nor
could the health fund maintain the innovative and life-giving services
inaugurated with such fanfare in the early 1950s. The UMW-built chain
of modern hospitals that dotted Appalachia ran into immediate financial trouble and in 1964 the union sold them off at a loss of over $14
million. Benefits were cut back while UMW-employed doctors dragged
their feet in recognizing the claims of miners stricken by black lung,
the chronic disease that afflicted so many aging miners, for fear that
their claims would overwhelm the fund.

Beyond these specific injustices and failures, the Lewis-run UMW's
entire orientation toward its membership helped perpetuate the sense
of powerlessness that continued to grip Appalachia in the post–World
War II period. Energy companies, now resorting to strip mining procedures that ravaged the magnificent hills of West Virginia and
Kentucky, siphoned off huge profits and ignored or subverted environmental regulations. The huge bulldozer—its blade alone weighed five
tons—ripped into the ridges. In Kentuckian Harry Caudill's vivid de-
scription, "it shears away not only soil and trees but a thousand other
things . . . and sends them hurtling down the slope, an avalanche of
the organic and inorganic, the living and the dead." Dynamite charges
and powerful diesel-powered augers tore away at the rock. After such a
powerful assault, "all that is left of what was once a green-covered, living ridge is a vast mesa where nothing moves except the clouds of dust
on dry, windy days, . . . a New World Sahara." Spring rains washed
away the top soil, engorged the valley creeks, and, in a series of massive
and catastrophic floods in the 1950s and 1960s, carried away whole
communities and scores of people.[20]

Powerful outside-owned mining combines dominated the coal-
mining towns and counties, just as their predecessors in the 1920s had.
The UMW, a potential political force in behalf of the broad working-

class publics of these states, confined its electoral and legislative activities to narrowly defined issues relating directly to the industry and the union's interests. The UMW lobbyists often joined their industry counterparts in resisting environmental regulation, so concerned were they to maintain production and thus keep royalty payments high. In the 1950s, the UMW run by Lewis and his chief aide (and eventual successor) W. A. "Tony" Boyle was a union with little interest in serving as a broad social force. It made little effort to mobilize miners, retirees, and their families in coalition with other liberally inclined groups to work for the sorts of aggregative social reform measures increasingly characterizing the political efforts of Reuther's UAW and other progressive unions. Critics such as Kentucky writer Harry Caudill and scholar John Gaventa underscored the political failures of the UMW. Gaventa found that in District 19, in the heart of the Appalachian fields, the Lewis and Boyle leadership had exploited the "powerlessness of the miners and their families," thus encouraging "a dependency upon the union organization" and a fear of democratic action. Caudill, in his poignant 1963 lament for the impoverished mining families of Kentucky, believed that the UMW had become so discredited that its members were "more likely to oppose than to support a candidate" endorsed by the union.[21]

The multiple catastrophes that afflicted the Appalachian mining regions in the 1950s affected the UMW as such only marginally. Even though the percentage of coal mined in nonunion pits edged upward, reaching one-quarter of soft coal tonnage in 1962, the UMW as an organization remained prosperous. Union reports filed in 1960 in compliance with a new federal labor law revealed that the organization had assets—cash reserves, investments, physical facilities—of over $110 million. By way of comparison, the same source showed that the *combined assets* of three of the largest American unions, the Autoworkers, the Steelworkers, and the Teamsters, were only marginally higher, although these three giants embraced at least twenty times more members than the shrinking UMW.

Indeed, the Mine Workers' union had the wherewithal to embark on a number of risky financial ventures, ostensibly designed to reduce nonunion competition. Lewis had always been fascinated with the world of high finance. His bitter attacks on the financial cabals he perceived to be dominating the country's economic and political life in the 1930s suggested at times as much envy as they did outrage. In a series of shadowy maneuvers he arranged in 1949 for the purchase in behalf of the UMW of controlling interest in a large Washington, D.C., bank. With the huge infusions of assets created by the bourgeoning welfare and retirement funds, the National Bank of Washington expanded rapidly, and by 1964, had become the national capital's second largest bank, with assets of $432 million. With a board of directors controlled by Lewis, the bank invested heavily in loans to modernizing coal operators, thus contributing directly to the mechanization of the industry and the shrinkage of the labor force. It bought into the electrical power generating sector as well, for utilities were enormous consumers of UMW-dug coal. Until forced to reveal the full scope of the union's financial activities by the 1959 Landrum-Griffin Act, UMW officials kept much of this phase of their activities secret. Even after public disclosure of the enormous extent of the union's holdings brought sharp questioning from rank-and-file miners and from the press, the union hierarchy issued only the vaguest and most unrevealing reports.

The most spectacular of Lewis's financial adventures in behalf of the union in the 1950s derived from his close association with Cyrus Eaton, a wealthy Cleveland financier and industrialist. Always attracted to wealth, Lewis found in Eaton something of a soulmate. The two men shared a belief that financial power provided the key to economic efficiency and social progress. Lewis reveled in being entertained at Eaton's grand estate in Ohio, developing an intimate friendship that revolved around their mutual desire to bring stability to the soft coal industry. Eaton, a major investor in Cleveland financial and utilities enterprises, soon became an unofficial financial adviser to Lewis, nodding with approval as the National Bank expanded and UMW assets mushroomed.

As they looked to the troubled Appalachian bituminous fields, the two men soon realized that the Tennessee Valley Authority (TVA), an independent government corporation created in 1933, provided an important key to soft coal's crisis in production and employment. Relentlessly pursuing a policy of buying the enormous quantities of coal needed to fire its vast generators as cheaply as possible, the TVA, despite its progressive role in bringing electrical energy to the remote valleys, was in effect encouraging nonunion coal production. In a region so poverty-stricken as Appalachia, miners, even loyal UMW members, proved willing to work for wages far below union scale. Coal operators exploited this surplus of labor and passed along the savings in labor costs to the TVA in the form of lower prices for the coal they sold. The efforts of the UMW to organize these nonunion producers had met repeatedly with failure. A successful campaign often had the result of closing a mine down, thus throwing the miners out of work while the operator moved to another nearby facility and began producing coal again, under a different name perhaps but with the same lower-than-union-wage scales. These nonunion mines bled the UMW two ways: they deprived union miners of employment, and the tonnage they produced, of course, did not generate royalty payments to the welfare and retirement funds.

Eaton and Lewis sought to solve this problem. In 1951, Lewis engineered a loan of $6 million to Eaton, some of it drawn from the National Bank, some of it from the UMW treasury. The union also bought stock in a large nonunion firm in Kentucky, assigning the voting rights to Eaton as its proxy. Using the loans and the UMW-ceded voting power, Eaton soon became chairman of the company's board of directors. In 1953, he directed that the company now recognize the union, an action that in turn brought hundreds of new dues-payers into the UMW and large sums in royalty payments into the welfare and retirement funds. The UMW remained a pipeline for this company, West Kentucky Coal, to tap when it needed large sums for capital investment for the purpose of mechanization of operations. In 1955, the Lewis-Eaton combine gained control of another large Appalachian producer. Indeed, calculating the combined tonnage of these two firms along with that produced by others in which Eaton had a direct individual interest, industry analysts found that "the Eaton-Lewis empire [was] the third-largest bituminous producer in the country."[22]

Not all the UMW's dealings with Appalachian operators in these years were so profitable. As recession struck the region in the late 1950s, small "dog-hole" mines began opening up, employing jobless UMW members. In impoverished Appalachia, work at any wage was welcome. Lax enforcement of federal minimum-wage regulations and the fact that the loosely drafted Federal Mine Safety Act of 1952 did not apply to mining operations employing fewer than fifteen workers left these submarginal operators free to claim a rising share of the coal market through nonunion, cut-rate coal. In southwestern Virginia, never a union stronghold, other nonunion mines began to flourish. By 1960 as much as 25 percent of the country's bituminous tonnage was being produced in nonunion holdings.

Apart from buying into some of the larger nonunion operations, the UMW tried two expedients in meeting this competition. Beginning in the late 1940s and continuing through the 1950s, it sought to organize nonunion operations in Kentucky, Tennessee, and Virginia. At the same time, it entered into secret arrangements with dog-hole operators wherein parts of the national UMW contract would be ignored. Wages below the UMW scale would be tolerated, or operators would get rebates, reducing the forty-cent-per-ton royalty paid to the welfare and retirement fund. The result had some short-range benefits for the union. The figures reflecting nonunion tonnage looked less bad, and at least some dues and royalty payments were coming in from dog-hole mines. In the long run, however, the miners suffered. Not only did their union collaborate in a system of substandard wages and safety provisions but secretive arrangements regarding the welfare and retirement fund put them in jeopardy as potential recipients of the funds' benefits. When the funds' trustees—led, as always, by Lewis—in 1962 cut off benefits to miners whose employers had not made normal royalty payments, thousands of dog-hole miners, victimized for years in the mines, were now cruelly victimized again, this time by their own union. The sweetheart contracts that permitted these arrangements, notes UMW critic Brit Hume, "soon became an established fact of industrial life in southern Appalachia. They did not stop the growth of nonunion mining, but they contributed mightily to the disillusionment and bitterness that were later to spread through the union's entire membership."[23]

The UMW did make efforts to organize some of the nonunion operations. From the late 1940s onward, the union waged a bitter campaign against a growing number of nonunion mines in eastern Kentucky, southwestern Virginia, and Tennessee. Lewis himself preferred to remain ignorant of the details of this protracted campaign, relying heavily on Tony Boyle, his administrative assistant. According to a disaffected UMW organizer, Lewis had directed his men to "organize these small mines and damn the law suits." Organizers, he allegedly told one field representative, should give nonunion operators and miners alike "a good taste of rough stuff."[24] "Rough stuff," much of it apparently orchestrated by Boyle and his underlings in Kentucky and Tennessee, Albert Pass and William Prater, rumbled through the valleys through the 1950s. Shootings, dynamitings, and vigilante squadrons carried on, although in a lower key, the bloody traditions of labor conflict of the Appalachian hills. Although a spate of lawsuits in the late 1950s caused Lewis to order a pullback from this violent and largely unsuccessful campaign, none came to judgment. Reporters and on-site observers were convinced that the UMW had indeed waged a lethal, brutal campaign against its adversaries, and they were convinced as well that

Boyle and his henchmen often functioned as little more than hired killers. But no definitive exposé or trial ever proved these allegations.

By the late 1950s Lewis was paying little attention to such matters. Having long since driven from the UMW virtually every forthright and independent voice, he could rely only on Boyle to keep the machine running. He played little role in the bargaining sessions of 1955, 1956, and 1958, turning over negotiations to vice president Thomas Kennedy. Even the welfare and retirement fund, which he continued to head, claimed less and less of his attention as it ran into problems of underfunding that brought a chronic need to reduce benefits, tighten eligibility rules, and cover shortfalls. Lewis drew ever closer to his counterparts in the coal industry. With them, he bombarded the federal government with demands for assistance for the declining industry, calling for stiff tariffs on imported oil, subsidized exports of American coal, and rigorous enforcement of mine safety provisions, by means of which the union and large-scale operators could force the shutdown of many marginal, nonunion competitors.

In May 1958, Lewis appeared for the first time at the coal section of the annual meeting of the American Mining Congress. Addressing his erstwhile rivals at the bargaining table, the seventy-eight-year-old unionist extolled the virtues of cooperation and advanced a plan that would bring the union, coal operators, coal-carrying railroads, and mine equipment manufacturers together in a National Coal Policy Conference (NCPC), a body designed to serve as the industry's public relations, legislative, and lobbying arm. "It makes quite a formidable aggregation," he told an interviewer the next year, "all dedicated to seeking to promote a national coal policy that will recognize the importance of the coal industry."[25] His election in 1962 to the presidency of the NCPC crowned his career as industrial statesman, and he basked in the glow of the accolades awarded him by the industry's representatives.[26]

The UMW *Journal* of 15 December 1959 informed the membership that effective 14 January of the new year, Lewis would retire as UMW president. Heart attacks in 1956 and 1959, along with assorted other health problems, helped him make the decision. He would still draw a salary of fifty thousand dollars a year as president emeritus, and he would continue as chairman of the welfare and retirement fund. But, he informed a reporter in 1958, "the time has come now for other leadership to develop."[27] Actually, through the years Lewis had devoted virtually no time or effort to the cultivation of a new generation of leaders in the UMW. The loyal Kennedy, to be sure, would succeed him, but he and secretary-treasurer John Owen were both in their eighth decade. Lewis had no heir apparent beyond Kennedy, whose interim presidency would obviously be short-lived. Boyle, his administrative assistant since 1948, waited in the wings, but Lewis regarded him as little more than a henchman. It was almost as if Lewis, as was the case with so many miners, could not, despite his retirement announcement, truly imagine the UMW under any other hand but his own.

EPILOGUE

John L. Lewis lived out his final decade, that of the 1960s, in relative isolation. He continued as director of the welfare and retirement fund until his death on 11 June 1969, a month before Neil Armstrong's moon walk and two months before the Woodstock rock festival. He faded from the public arena, granting only a handful of interviews, refusing all requests that he speak out about the mounting evidence of corruption and violence in the UMW, spending more and more of his time in the seclusion of his Alexandria home. In the early sixties, his limousine took him several times a week to UMW headquarters, but thereafter age and infirmity kept him largely at home. The passing of his brothers and sister, along with daughter Kathryn's death in 1962, added to his isolation. Son John maintained nominal contact. Toward the end, only his friend and associate Josephine Roche and a couple who attended to his household and transportation needs remained to see after him. His death came as something of an anticlimax. "In the field of labor he was the greatest Roman of them all," intoned Steelworkers' president David McDonald, but the more common reaction was "I thought he was already dead."[1]

To the end, Lewis rejected the claims of history and historians. Other laborites of his generation might regale interviewers with accounts of their exploits, but Lewis rebuffed requests for interviews. John Brophy, Lee Pressman, and labor activist Gardner Jackson cooperated with Columbia University's oral history project, each generating hundreds of pages of reminiscences, many of them featuring John L. Lewis. But the UMW chief would have none of it. The record, he believed, was clear; it existed in the files of newspapers and in the records of conventions and meetings spanning three-quarters of a century. "The moving finger [of events] has made a record," he told a hopeful historian.[2] So be it.

Through the sixties, he received all too frequent reminders of mortality. The deaths of Myrta in 1942 and his mother in 1950 were but the first in a long catalog of family sorrows. In January 1962, daughter Kathryn, long victimized by overweight and emotional instability, died in New York City at a time of at least temporary estrangement from her father. Barely two weeks later, brother Dennie, John L.'s closest sibling, followed. Sister Hattie died a year later and brother Howard passed away in April of 1968. Nor did remaining kin provide much comfort. Brother Raymond, president of UMW District 17, fell out with his older brother over John L. Lewis's conduct of the welfare and retirement fund. Son John, always aloof from his father's world, remained distant, both physically and psychologically, carefully limiting his children's contact with their famous and controversial grandfather. Indeed, John eventually destroyed most of the family records and correspondence he inherited on the death of John L. Lewis.

Declining years brought no religious conversion and no revision of the working assumptions of a lifetime. If there was a divine plan, weak humanity could not know it. If there was a dialectic to history, moving man toward some new height of consciousness and achievement, its workings were perverse and obscure. Ideologues and preachers came and went. The wheel of history rumbled onward, crushing the unwary and the dogmatic, providing occasional opportunities for the diligent and practical. In the world we knew—the only world we could know—power and power alone ultimately counted. A man strove to achieve what he could. He made the most of the limited opportunities presented, perhaps at least marginally increasing the sum of human happiness. "How many blocks of seven years do you think one man has to give?" he abruptly asked one of his rare interviewers in 1963.[3]

No doubt this life-view helped to sustain him as the Boyle-led UMW reeled from disaster to disaster in the 1960s. He remained silent as critics called his attention to mounting evidence of fraud and coercion emanating from the top leadership. Collusive in his dealings with coal operators and brutal in his suppression of internal dissent, Boyle continued the pattern of leadership he had practiced at Lewis's side for twelve years. Lewis, however, had coupled his ruthlessness with a genuine concern for miners' welfare and with a knowledge that ultimately his power rested on the allegiance of the men in the pits, but Boyle exhibited only disdain for working miners. "Tough Tony" Boyle surrounded himself with gun-toting goons and turned the UMW *Journal*, which during the Lewis imperium had retained a modicum of objectivity, into a leader-worshiping rag.

The Boyle style was most glaringly displayed in November 1968, when an explosion ripped through a Farmington, West Virginia, mine, killing seventy-eight miners. Veteran observers recalled Lewis's responses to similar disasters that had punctuated his reign. He would rush to the mine site, don a hard hat, and climb down into the shaft. Invariably, he would emerge to hurl fiery denunciations at federal mine inspectors and mine operators. Eloquently, he identified with the mangled victims and the weeping families. True, throughout his tenure, mine accident rates remained high. Only late in his career did he award the safety problem sustained attention, and even then he relied on a weak federal mine safety law rather than risk rank-and-file empowerment at the point of production. Still, there could be no doubt as to the sincerity of Lewis's response. At the very least, a mining disaster could be used to pry concessions from bargaining opponents and to cultivate public sympathy for the courageous men who ventured into the earth to dig the nation's coal.

Boyle's response to the Farmington disaster, however, was cold and even callous. "As long as we mine coal," he lectured the stunned relatives of the dead, "there is always this inherent danger." He then praised the company in whose holding the explosion occurred. Consolidated Coal was, he ventured, "one of the best companies to work with as far as cooperation and safety are concerned."[4]

Rank-and-file miners and social critics asked Lewis to speak out against Boyle. Privately the old chief did grumble that appointing Boyle as his assistant in 1948 was "the worst mistake I ever made."[5] But Lewis made no public criticism. As the UMW careened toward disaster and as Boyle plunged ever deeper into murderous schemes to destroy his rivals, Lewis remained silent.

No doubt this was partly because much of the criticism of the current UMW regime centered on the handling of the welfare and retirement fund. One controversial ruling in 1962 stopped benefits to members who toiled in mines whose operators did not contribute full royalty payments. Since these arrangements had been tolerated and even at times arranged by the UMW while Lewis was president, the old leader had no desire to become involved in public controversy. Indeed, Raymond Lewis, president of UMW District 17, publicly rebuked his brother for the welfare and retirement fund's actions against these miners, breaking three-quarters of a century of family loyalty. Mishandling of welfare and retirement fund reserves, laid at the doorstep of Boyle, also implicated John L. Lewis in his capacity as head of the fund's board of trustees. Thus, much of the criticism of Boyle's UMW was criticism aimed, in effect, at Lewis himself.

Even the more sinister aspects of the Boyle regime hit too close to the Lewis record to make the old leader comfortable with public denunciation. All the devices that Boyle used to maintain power—thuggery, control of information, shady dealings with operators, stifling of dissent—were, after all, prominent elements in the Lewis repertoire of command. Boyle's collusive bargaining posture, for example, grew directly from the agreements of the 1950s. No, despite the pleas of victimized miners and public-spirited reformers, the grand old man of the UMW, whatever his private misgivings, kept quiet.

On 22 May 1969, reformer Ralph Nader made public a letter he was sending to Lewis. It called upon him to repudiate Boyle and to sanction a rank-and-file revolt against the UMW leadership. Doubtless Nader had no illusion about Lewis's response, hoping only that through the device of publicizing such a letter, he might stir rank-and-file opposition to Boyle. But if Lewis did not respond to Nader, neither did he issue the ringing declaration of support that Boyle expected. "They built that cesspool over there," Lewis reportedly remarked. "Let them drown in their own slime."[6] Such a judgment, of course, acknowledged no responsibility of Lewis's in creating the conditions that made the UMW's sorry state possible.

Vice President Joseph "Jock" Yablonski thought that he might secure his old chief's blessing in his campaign to replace Boyle. A Lewis loyalist of the 1950s, Yablonski got favorable signs from Lewis's confidante, Josephine Roche. He spoke with the ailing Lewis several times on the phone, delaying a visit to Alexandria until the old man felt better.[7] On 8 June 1969, before the two men could meet, however, Lewis entered a Washington hospital, suffering from internal bleeding. Three days later he died.

When he retired in 1963 as chair of the National Coal Policy Conference, Lewis received an oil portrait of himself as a token of esteem from the businessmen and coal operators who were his colleagues. The portrait drew from him a rare gesture of uncertainty. His words, uttered at the ceremony, might serve as his epitaph. "I value this portrait," he assured his benefactors. But, looking on his own visage, he added, "I am going to have a hard time reading all the facets of his character."[8]

CHRONOLOGY

12 February 1880	John Llewellyn Lewis born, Lucas County, Iowa.
22 January 1889	Brother Alma Dennie (Dennie) Lewis born.
ca. 1894–1897	Lewis family in Des Moines.
1897–1901	Works as miner, manages opera house, Lucas County, Iowa.
1901–1905	Works and travels in American west.
1907	Defeated in election for mayor.
1907	Feed and grain business fails.
5 June 1907	Marries Myrta Edith Bell
Spring 1908	Moves to Panama, Illinois
1908–1909	Elected president of Panama Local 1475.
1909	Appointed legislative agent for District 12 (Illinois), UMW.
Early 1910	Birth of daughter, Mary Margaret.
January 1911	Defends incumbents at UMW convention.
14 April 1911	Birth of daughter, Kathryn.
23 October 1911	Appointed AFL representative.
1915	AFL representative in Ohio, Pennsylvania, and West Virginia.

18 January–February 1916	Plays key role in defending incumbents at UMW convention.
1 February 1917	Appointed UMW Statistician.
6 April 1917	United States declares war on Germany.
Late summer 1917	Named UMW *Journal* business manager.
8 September 1917	Death of daughter, Mary Margaret.
October 1917	Appointed UMW vice president.
October 1917	Washington Agreement concluded.
11 November 1918	Armistice ends World War I.
25 November 1918	Birth of son, John Llewellyn Lewis, Jr.
December 1918	Elected UMW vice president.
March 1919	Assumes duties of UMW president.
October–December 1919	Bituminous strike.
1 January 1920	Becomes acting president of UMW.
December 1920	Elected UMW president.
Fall 1920–1921	Armed conflict rages in West Virginia coalfields.
June 1921	Loses bid to defeat Gompers for AFL presidency.
April–August 1922	Anthracite and bituminous strikes.
February 1924	Jacksonville Agreement.
Summer–fall 1924	On Advisory Committee, Republican National Committee.
1925	Publishes *The Miners' Fight for American Standards*.
1925–1926	Anthracite strike.
Fall 1926	Defeats John Brophy for UMW presidency.
1927–1928	Bituminous strike; Central Competitive Field dismantled.
Fall 1928	Vigorously supports Herbert Hoover.
March 1930	Reorganized UMW formed.
1 September 1932	Progressive Miners of America formed.

17 February 1933	Gives testimony before Senate Finance Committee.
16 June 1933	National Industrial Recovery Act passed.
Summer–fall 1933	UMW launches massive organizing drive.
7 September 1933	NRA coal code promulgated.
21 September 1933	Appalachian bituminous agreement signed.
1934	UMW (and Lewis family) move to Washington, D.C.
31 March 1934	Improved Appalachian bituminous agreement signed.
5 July 1935	National Labor Relations (Wagner) Act signed.
30 August 1935	Guffey-Snyder Bituminous Coal Stabilization Act signed.
16 October 1935	Punches William Hutcheson at AFL convention.
9 November 1935	First formal meeting of Committee for Industrial Organization (CIO).
March 1936	Rubber Workers' victory in Akron, Ohio.
April 1936	Labor's Non-Partisan League formed.
4 June 1936	Steel Workers Organizing Committee (SWOC) established.
3 August–5 September 1936	AFL executive council suspends CIO unions.
3 November 1936	Roosevelt elected to second term.
30 December 1936– 11 February 1937	Flint sit-down strike.
2 March 1937	SWOC and U.S. Steel sign agreement.
26 April 1937	Guffey-Vinson Bituminous Coal Act signed.
30 May 1937	Republic Steel massacre.
Fall 1937–spring 1939	"Roosevelt" recession.

15 November 1938	Committee for Industrial Organization becomes Congress of Industrial Organizations.
23 August 1939	Nazi-Soviet Pact announced.
1 September 1939	World War II begins.
May–June 1940	Fall of France.
August–November 1940	Battle of Britain.
16 September 1940	Selective Training and Service Act signed.
25 October 1940	Endorses Wendell Willkie.
5 November 1940	Roosevelt reelected.
22 November 1940	Steps down as CIO president; succeeded by Philip Murray.
11 March 1941	Lend-Lease Act signed.
22 June 1941	Germany attacks the Soviet Union.
15 September–7 December 1941	Captive mines dispute.
Fall 1941	Reorganizes District 50.
7 December 1941	Pearl Harbor attack.
18 December 1941	No Strike Pledge.
12 January 1942	National War Labor Board (NWLB) created.
17 January 1942	Announces "accouplement" plan.
15 April 1942	NWLB establishes maintenance of membership rule.
25 May 1942	Murray expelled from UMW.
16 July 1942	NWLB promulgates "Little Steel Formula."
9 September 1942	Myrta Lewis dies.
January 1943	Anthracite strike.
26 March 1943	Testifies before Truman Committee.
April–June, November 1943	Bituminous strikes.
25 June 1943	Smith-Connally Act passed.
15 August 1945	V-J Day.
November 1945–March 1946	Postwar strike wave.

24 January 1946	UMW reaffiliates with AFL.
1 April 1946	Bituminous strike begins.
21 May 1946–30 June 1947	Federal government operates bituminous mines.
29 May 1946	Lewis-Krug Agreement establishes welfare and retirement fund.
4 December 1946	Judge Goldsborough fines UMW $3.5 million, Lewis $10,000.
25 March 1947	Centralia, Illinois, mine disaster; 111 killed.
23 June 1947	Taft-Hartley Act passed.
October 1947	Confrontation with George Meany at AFL convention.
12 December 1947	Disaffiliates UMW from AFL.
1948	Names W. A. "Tony" Boyle his assistant.
March–April 1948	Bituminous "pension" strike.
9 September 1948	First pension check issued.
Spring 1949–1960	Gains control of National Bank of Washington for UMW.
June 1949–March 1950	Bituminous strikes.
July 1950	Bituminous Coal Operators' Association (BCOA) formed.
Early 1951	Begins long association with Cyrus Eaton.
June 1951	Criticizes Walter Reuther at anniversary celebration of UAW Local 600.
October–December 1952	UMW strike against Wage Stabilization Board rulings on contract with BCOA.
1954 (also 1958, 1960)	Welfare and retirement benefits cut.
5 December 1955	AFL and CIO merge.
2 June 1956	UMW Appalachian hospitals dedicated.
5 May 1958	Addresses Coal Section of American Mining Congress.
14 January 1960	Retires as UMW president.

Spring 1960	Reports under terms of 1959 Landrum-Griffin Act put UMW assets at $110 million.
1962–1963	Chairs National Coal Policy Conference.
7 January 1962	Kathryn Lewis dies.
24 January 1962	Dennie Lewis dies.
January 1963	Tony Boyle becomes UMW president.
1964	UMW sells off Appalachian hospitals.
11 June 1969	Dies in Alexandria, Virginia.
30 December 1969	Joseph A. Yablonski and family murdered.
December 1972	Arnold Miller defeats Boyle for UMW presidency.
December 1973	Boyle convicted of conspiracy to murder Yablonski.

NOTES AND REFERENCES

INTRODUCTION

1. Quoted in "Strategic Position," *Fortune*, June 1949, p. 181.
2. Quoted in Melvyn Dubofsky and Warren Van Tine, *John L. Lewis: A Biography* (New York: New York Times Co., Quadrangle, 1977), p. xvi.

CHAPTER 1

1. Dubofsky and Van Tine, *Lewis*, p. 15.
2. John L. Lewis, *The Miners' Fight for American Standards* (Indianapolis: Bell Publishing Co., 1925), p. 168.
3. Ibid., p. 171.
4. Ibid., pp. 98–99.
5. Ibid., pp. 100–101.
6. Carter Goodrich, *The Miner's Freedom: A Study of the Working Life in a Changing Industry* (Boston: Marshall Jones, 1925), pp. 56–57.
7. These Canadian districts entitled the United Mine Workers to claim status as an "international" union. The term international union or simply international was (and is) commonly used to indicate a union under discussion with Canadian as well as American membership. In this book, it serves as a synonym for the United Mine Workers.
8. Lewis, *Miners' Fight*, p. 92.
9. United Mine Workers of America, District 12, *Report of the Proceedings of the 1909 Convention* (1909), p. 270, in Edward Wieck Papers, Archives of Labor and Urban Affairs, Wayne State University (hereafter cited as ALU-AWSU), Box 15.
10. Quoted in Robert H. Zieger, *Republicans and Labor, 1919–1929* (Lexington: University of Kentucky Press, 1969), p. 8.
11. Quoted in Dubofsky and Van Tine, *Lewis*, p. 38.
12. Ibid., p. 38.

CHAPTER 2

1. UMW, *Report of Proceedings of the 26th Convention*, 15–26 January, 1918 (Indianapolis, 1918), p. 666 (hereafter UMW convention proceedings will be cited: UMW, *Proceedings*, year, page).

2. Quoted in Dubofsky and Van Tine, *Lewis*, p. 59.

3. UMW, *Proceedings*, 1918, p. 42.

4. Quoted in David Alan Corbin, *Life, Work, and Rebellion in the Coal Fields: The Southern West Virginia Miners, 1880–1922* (Urbana: University of Illinois Press, 1981), p. 188.

5. Quoted in ibid., p. 208.

6. Quoted in ibid., p. 198.

7. Quoted in ibid., p. 206.

8. Lewis, *Miners' Fight*, pp. 170–71.

9. Quoted in Goodrich, *The Miner's Freedom*, p. 132.

10. Lewis, *Miners' Fight*, pp. 40–41, 47.

11. Ibid., p. 52.

12. Ibid., pp. 85, 110.

13. Quoted in Zieger, *Republicans and Labor*, p. 232.

14. David A. McDonald and Edward A. Lynch, *Coal and Unionism: A History of the American Coal Miners' Unions* (Silver Spring, Md., and Indianapolis: Cornelius, 1939), p. 167.

15. McAlister Coleman, *Men and Coal* (New York: Farrar & Rinehart, 1943), p. 132.

16. Quoted in Zieger, *Republicans and Labor*, p. 233.

17. Coleman, *Men and Coal*, p. 89.

18. *New York Times*, 3 February 1924.

19. John Brophy, letter to the editor, *New Republic*, 25 December 1929, pp. 145–46.

20. McDonald and Lynch, *Coal and Unionism*, p. 159.

21. Benjamin Stolberg, "King Coal's Boss," *Independent*, 11 July 1925, p. 45.

22. Lewis, quoted in Dubofsky and Van Tine, *Lewis*, p. 128.

23. UMW, *Proceedings*, 1927, pp. 447–51, 452–59.

24. *New York Times*, 24 January 1924.

25. John L. Lewis radio address, 17 October 1928, John L. Lewis Papers, Reel 1, Speeches File, State Historical Society of Wisconsin.

26. Brophy letter, *New Republic*, 25 December 1929, p. 146.

CHAPTER 3

1. Quoted in Dubofsky and Van Tine, *Lewis*, p. 297.

2. UMW, *Proceedings*, 1936, p. 503.

3. Ibid., 1930, pp. 685–86.

4. Coleman, *Men and Coal*, p. 141.

5. UMW *Journal*, 15 March 1930.

6. Coleman, *Men and Coal*, p. 141.

7. Malcolm Brown and John N. Webb, quoted in ibid., p. 142.

8. Dubofsky and Van Tine, *Lewis*, p. 72.

9. UMW, *Proceedings*, 1936, p. 122.

10. Ibid., p. 123.

11. Ibid., p. 123.

12. Ibid., 1934, p. 487.

13. Ibid., 1936, pp. 50, 55, 122.

14. Ibid., pp. 50, 123.

15. Dubofsky and Van Tine, *Lewis*, p. 286.

16. John W. Hevener, *Which Side Are You On?: The Harlan County Coal Miners, 1931–1939* (Urbana: University of Illinois Press, 1978), p. 47.

17. W. Jett Lauck to Lewis, 5 May 1933, W. Jett Lauck Papers, Alderman Library, University of Virginia, Box 39.

18. Ibid.

19. Edward Wieck, notes of interviews with William Thompson, Williamson Field, West Virginia, 17 February 1934, George Hudson, War Eagle, West Virginia, c. February 1934, in Wieck Papers, ALUAWSU, Box 14.

20. Wieck interview with Jesse Aquino, 4 March 1934, ibid.

21. Hevener, *Which Side?*, p. 94.

22. Wieck interview with P. F. Buckley, "Mononger" [sic], West Virginia, 26 January 1934, Wieck Papers, Box 14.

23. James Wechsler, *Labor Baron: A Portrait of John L. Lewis* (New York: William Morrow, 1944), p. 96.

24. Quoted in Dubofsky and Van Tine, *Lewis*, p. 191.

25. Ibid., p. 199.

26. Lauck to Lewis, 22 October 1934, Lauck Papers, Box 39.

27. UMW, *Proceedings*, 1934, pp. 205ff.

28. Ibid., 1940, p. 102.

29. Brophy quoted in Coleman, *Men and Coal*, pp. 162–63.

30. Wieck quoting Hapgood in Decatur (Ill.) *Herald* of 5 January 1936, in Wieck to Oscar Ameringer, 8 February 1936, Wieck Papers, Box 15.

31. Wieck to Ameringer, 8 February 1936, ibid.

CHAPTER 4

1. The initials "CIO" refer to two discrete, but continuous, organizations. Between 9 November 1935 and 15 November 1938, they stand for "Committee for Industrial Organization." After 15 November 1938, they stand for "Congress of Industrial Organizations." The earlier embodiment of the CIO functioned, at least nominally, as an adjunct to the AFL, whereas the second

was an entirely separate, autonomous organization. In reality, the earlier CIO had no meaningful ties to the AFL as early as June 1936. In this book, the designation "CIO" refers to both incarnations.

2. John Burke quoted in Robert H. Zieger, *Rebuilding the Pulp and Paper Workers' Union, 1933–1941* (Knoxville: University of Tennessee Press, 1984), p. 69.

3. Goodrich, *The Miner's Freedom*, pp. 154–55.

4. Lewis speech, 7 December 1934, reprinted in UMW *Journal*, 15 December 1934.

5. Benjamin Stolberg, "King Coal's Boss," *Independent*, 11 July 1925, p. 45.

6. Lewis remarks at CIO meeting, 7 and 8 November 1936, John Brophy Papers, Catholic University of America, Box for 1934–36.

7. American Federation of Labor, *Report of the Proceedings of the 1935 Convention* (1935), p. 534.

8. Green quoted in Dubofsky and Van Tine, *Lewis*, p. 215.

9. AFL, *Proceedings*, 1935, pp. 534, 535, 537.

10. Ibid., p. 538.

11. Ibid., pp. 539–40.

12. Ibid.

13. Ibid., p. 542.

14. Dubofsky and Van Tine, *Lewis*, p. 220.

15. Heywood Broun, "Mr. Lewis and Mr. Green," *Nation*, 28 November 1936, p. 634.

16. Lewis to Green, 7 June 1936, American Federation of Labor Papers, State Historical Society of Wisconsin, Series 11C.

17. UMW, *Proceedings*, 1936, p. 211.

18. Lewis release, 20 September 1936, Lewis Papers, Reel 2, Releases, UMW papers.

19. Lewis radio address, "Industrial Democracy," 31 December 1936, ibid., Reel 2, Speeches.

20. Dubofsky and Van Tine, *Lewis*, p. 252.

21. Lewis remark, 7 November 1936, as reported by Katherine Pollock Ellickson, Ellickson Papers, ALUAWSU, Box 14.

22. Wechsler, *Labor Baron*, p. 72.

23. Dubofsky and Van Tine, *Lewis*, p. 217.

24. Clinton Golden to Katherine Pollock Ellickson, 3 June 1937, CIO Secretary-Treasurer Papers, ALUAWSU, Box 59.

25. Irving Bernstein, *The Turbulent Years: A History of the American Worker, 1933–1941* (Boston: Houghton Mifflin Co., 1970), p. 447.

26. Gordon Carroll, "John L. Lewis: His Labor Record," *American Mercury*, June 1937, p. 138.

27. Wechsler, *Labor Baron*, p. 71.

28. Edward Levinson, quoted by Wechsler, *Labor Baron*, p. 69; Dubofsky and Van Tine, *Lewis*, p. 271.

29. Lewis, quoted in Wechsler, *Labor Baron*, p. 69.

30. Membership figures for the cio are notoriously unreliable. Since many swoc and cio organizing campaigns waived initiation fees and initial dues payments and since some unions included in their membership totals the number of workers covered by their contracts (not all of whom actually belonged to the union), it is wise to be skeptical about a figure this large. Moreover, membership in the new affiliates, such as the uaw, urw, and ue fluctuated rapidly in their early days, responding to victories and defeats. The core membership of the cio derived from the older, established unions, notably the umw, the acwa, and the ilgwu, which had a combined membership of just over 1 million. The swoc claimed 500,000, but its membership was to fluctuate severely during its first five years of existence, as was that of the uaw, which claimed 375,000 in August 1937.

31. Dubofsky and Van Tine, *Lewis*, pp. 278, 279.

32. Levinson, quoted in Wechsler, *Labor Baron*, p. 76.

CHAPTER 5

1. Lee Pressman interview, 19 March 1957, Columbia Oral History Collection (herefter cited as cohc), p. 189.

2. Quoted in Dubofsky and Van Tine, *Lewis*, p. 327.

3. Quoted in *New York Times*, 16 March 1937.

4. Ibid., 3 September 1940.

5. UMW, *Proceedings*, 1940, pp. 312, 314.

6. Typescript of Lewis speeches, 26 April and 18 June 1940, Lewis Papers, Reel 1, Speeches.

7. UMW, *Proceedings*, 1940, p. 104.

8. Typescript of Lewis speech, 1 April 1940, Lewis Papers, Reel 1, Speeches.

9. Typescript of Lewis speech, 18 June 1940, ibid.

10. *New York Times*, 26 October 1940.

11. Ibid., 26 and 27 October 1940.

12. CIO, *Proceedings of the Third Constitutional Convention* (1940), p. 192.

13. Ibid., pp. 271–74.

14. John Brophy, interview, 23 May 1955, cohc, pp. 840, 850.

15. Quoted in Dubofksy and Van Tine, *Lewis*, pp. 400–401.

16. Ibid., p. 404.

17. Ibid., p. 405.

18. Dale Kramer, "John L. Lewis: Last Bid?" *Harper's*, August 1942, p. 275.

19. Ibid., p. 283.

20. Ibid.

21. *New York Times*, 19 and 21 November 1941.

22. CIO, Proceedings of the Executive Board, 24 January 1942, ALU-AWSU.

23. Ibid., 24 March 1942.

24. Ibid.

25. Dubofsky and Van Tine, *Lewis*, p. 411.

26. UMW, *Proceedings*, 1942, p. 191.

27. Ibid., pp. 190–91.

28. Benjamin Stolberg, "Lewis Fights Labor Peace," *American Mercury*, March 1940, p. 349.

29. James Wechsler, "Can Lewis Wreck the C.I.O.?" *Nation*, 11 April 1942, p. 422.

30. Pressman interview, 12 December 1957, COHC, p. 356.

31. Ibid., p. 395.

32. Brophy interview, 23 May 1955, COHC, p. 840.

33. Ibid., p. 851.

34. Ibid., pp. 914, 927.

CHAPTER 6

1. Quoted in Coleman, *Men and Coal*, p. 241.

2. Makoto Takamiya, *Union Organization and Militancy: Conclusions from a Study of the United Mine Workers of America, 1940–1974* (Meisenheim am Glan: Hain, 1978), p. 55.

3. Lewis testimony before Senate Committee to Investigate the National Defense Program, 26 March 1943, reprinted in UMW, *Proceedings*, 1944, pp. 132, 134.

4. U.S. Department of Commerce, Bureau of the Census, *Historical Statistics of the United States, 1789–1945* (Washington, D.C.: U.S. Government Printing Office, 1949), p. 154; John C. Cort, "Lewis and the Miners," *Commonweal*, 21 May 1943, p. 119.

5. Lewis testimony, 26 March 1943, reprinted in UMW, *Proceedings*, 1944, p. 131.

6. Quoted in Coleman, *Men and Coal*, pp. 239, 242.

7. Davis quoted in Dubofsky and Van Tine, *Lewis*, p. 430.

8. Julius Emspak, secretary-treasurer of the United Electrical, Radio, and Machine Workers, CIO, telegram to Roosevelt, 10 June 1943, CIO Secretary-Treasurer Papers, ALUAWSU, Box 62.

9. Quoted in Coleman, *Men and Coal*, p. 268.

10. Lewis, "Not Guilty!" *Collier's*, 15 July 1944, p. 49; Dubofsky and Van Tine, *Lewis*, p. 438.

11. UMW, *Proceedings*, 1948, p. 338.

12. Lewis, quoted in Takamiya, *Union Organization and Militancy*, p. 49.

13. K. C. Adams, quoted in Dubofsky and Van Tine, *Lewis*, p. 417.

14. Lewis, "There Is No Labor Movement," *Collier's*, 5 May 1945, p. 63.

15. Editorial, *New Republic*, 24 May 1943, p. 688.

16. Lewis, "Not Guilty!" p. 12.

CHAPTER 7

1. A. H. Raskin, "How Miners Live," *American Mercury*, April 1947, p. 422.

2. UMW, *Proceedings*, 1946, pp. 86–87.

3. Ironically, the royalty per ton method of payment was inserted at the insistence of the operators. Lewis had favored a royalty based on the number of working miners, a method that would have crippled the fund by the mid-1950s as machines replaced men in the mines. Although tonnage dropped sharply from the peak year of 1947, employment dropped even more swiftly and irrevocably.

4. Paul Starr, *The Social Transformation of American Medicine: The Rise of a Sovereign Profession and the Making of a Vast Industry*, softbound ed. (New York: Basic Books, 1982), p. 315.

5. Brit Hume, *Death and the Mines: Rebellion and Murder in the United Mine Workers* (New York: Grossman, 1971), p. 30.

6. Lewis testimony, 17 April 1947, U.S., House of Representatives, Committee on Labor and Education, Subcommittee on Miners' Welfare (pamphlet published by Labor's Non-Partisan League), p. 47, in Lewis Papers, Reel 1, Speeches and Reports.

7. Quoted in Dubofsky and Van Tine, *Lewis*, pp. 469–70.

8. Lewis testimony, 23 April 1953, U.S., Senate, Committee on Labor Public Welfare, in Lewis Papers, Reel 2, Speeches and Reports.

9. AFL, *Proceedings*, 1947, p. 486.

10. UMW, *Proceedings*, 1952, pp. 336–43.

11. *Collier's*, 5 May 1945.

12. UMW, *Proceedings*, 1948, p. 11.

13. AFL, *Proceedings*, 1947, pp. 486–92.

14. Dubofsky and Van Tine, *Lewis*, p. 475.

15. UMW, *Proceedings*, 1952, p. 339.

16. Banner inscription, photographs, c. 23 June 1951, Lewis Papers, Reel 4, Photographs.

17. United Mine Workers *Journal*, 15 July 1951; pamphlet, c. 1 July 1951, "Auto Rank and File Hail 'Mr. Organized Labor,' " Lewis Papers, Reel 1, Speeches.

18. Quoted in Dubofsky and Van Tine, *Lewis*, p. 457.

19. Quoted in ibid., p. 494.

20. Harry M. Caudill, *My Land Is Dying* (New York: Dutton, 1971), pp. 104–7.

21. John Gaventa, *Power and Powerlessness: Quiescence and Rebellion in an Appalachian Valley*, softbound ed. (Urbana: University of Illinois Press, 1980), p. 201; Harry M. Caudill, *Night Comes to the Cumberland: A Biography of a Depressed Area* (Boston: Little, Brown & Co., 1963), p. 332.

22. Dubofsky and Van Tine, *Lewis*, p. 509.

23. Hume, *Death and the Mines*, p. 23.

24. Quoted in ibid., p. 27.

25. *U.S. News and World Report*, 9 November 1959, p. 64.

26. Lewis "Response," on the occasion of his leaving the presidency of the NCPC, 3 April 1963, Lewis Papers, Reel 3.

27. Quoted in Dubofsky and Van Tine, *Lewis*, p. 516.

EPILOGUE

1. Dubofsky and Van Tine, *Lewis*, p. 528.

2. Quoted in ibid., p. 523.

3. John Herling remarks, 22 June 1984, typescript in author's files.

4. Quoted in Dubofsky and Van Tine, *Lewis*, p. 527.

5. Quoted in ibid., p. 526.

6. Quoted in ibid., p. 527.

7. Yablonski followed through in his challenge to Boyle. On 9 December 1969, Boyle defeated him by a vote of 81,056 to 45,872. Three weeks later, Yablonski, his wife, and his daughter were murdered. In 1972, after a federal court invalidated the 1969 election, Arnold Miller defeated Boyle and replaced him as UMW president. In December 1973, Boyle was convicted of conspiring to murder Yablonski.

8. Quoted in ibid., p. 521.

BIBLIOGRAPHIC ESSAY

John L. Lewis was controversial in life and has remained so among historians and biographers. Lines of debate, however, have shifted with a changing intellectual and social environment and with the emerging concerns of a new generation of scholars and activists. For years, two contemporary accounts dominated the Lewis literature. James Wechsler (*Labor Baron: A Portrait of John L. Lewis* [1944]) offers a shrewd and pungent critique of Lewis from a liberal journalist who sympathized with New Deal–oriented laborite opponents of Lewis. While crediting the UMW chief with a key role in launching the CIO, Wechsler stressed Lewis's cynicism and egomania, common roots, he believed, of such disasters as the UMW's descent in the 1920s, the penetration of the CIO by Communists, and Lewis's destructive confrontations with Roosevelt during the war.

Saul Alinsky (*John L. Lewis: An Unauthorized Biography* [1949]) acknowledged Lewis's personal faults but saw him as a virtually omniscient actor in the drama of the 1930s and 1940s. Alinsky, a populist/radical organizer and social critic in his own right, stressed Lewis's grasp of the danger that the powerful modern state posed for popular social movements such as organized labor. Prefiguring some of the central concerns of the young radicals of the 1960s—for whom Alinsky himself was one of the few older radicals meriting respect—the activist-biographer made Lewis into a sort of superhuman oracle. This biography seemed to rest on extensive exclusive interviews with Lewis himself. Thus, for years it enjoyed a kind of authority that ill fit with the mainstream of scholarship on the CIO–World War II period, as reflected in such industrial relations standards as Walter Galenson, *The CIO Challenge to the AFL: The Conflict in American Labor, 1935–1941* (1960), and Joel Seidman, *American Labor from Defense to Reconversion* (1953).

More recently, scholars have shifted focus from Lewis's personal attributes to his role in the structural underpinnings of the modern labor movement. Thus, Paul A. C. Koistinen in "Mobilizing the World War II Economy: Labor and the Military-Industrial Alliance," *Pacific Historical Review* (1973), and Nelson N. Lichtenstein in *Labor's War at Home: The CIO in World War II* (1982) are impressed with the perspicacity and courage of Lewis's challenge to the Roosevelt administration and view the postwar relationship of the labor movement with the national security apparatus as vidication of Lewis's course in the 1940s. These publications reflect the authors' dissent from the cold war–liberal consensus and their criticism of the labor movement of the Vietnam era.

Other recent thrusts in labor historiography, however, have been less generous toward Lewis. As Lichtenstein, for example, readily acknowledges, Lewis's often principled and perceptive opposition to Roosevelt and his labor allies in the World War II period rested upon ruthless and authoritarian control of the UMW. Informed by recent "workers' control" perspectives, some scholars have linked Lewis's antidemocratic conduct of the UMW directly to his role as a modernizing destroyer of miners' autonomy and job-site power. Thus, Keith Dix in *Work Relations in the Coal Industry: The Hand-Loading Era, 1880–1930* (1978) couples Lewis's rise in the UMW with his ready acceptance of mechanization and the leaching away of power in the union from the pit committees, local unions, and UMW districts to Lewis's office. Alan Jay Singer, " 'Which Side Are You On?': Ideological Conflict in the United Mine Workers of America, 1919–1928" (Ph.D diss., Rutgers University, 1982), expands upon this theme. Singer extrapolates Lewis's domination of the UMW into the CIO period, arguing that the lack of rank-and-file autonomy and prevalence of top-down governance of the modern labor movement owes much to Lewis's UMW formula of the twenties. Mark Naison, *The Southern Tenant Farmers' Union and The C.I.O.* (pamphlet reprint from *Radical America* [1968]), castigates Lewis for his important role in the failure of the uprising of American workers in the 1930s to achieve genuinely innovative and democratic forms. Staughton Lynd, "The Possibility of Radicalism in the Early 1930's: The Case of Steel," *Radical America* (1972), brings a similar perspective to a key industry.

The standard biography of Lewis now is Melvyn Dubofsky and Warren Van Tine, *John L. Lewis: A Biography* (1977). This authoritative life is exhaustive in research, balanced in judgment, and keenly attuned to the public controversies and many of the historiographical debates surrounding Lewis. Dubofsky and Van Tine are definitive on Lewis's early life and their book supplants all previous (and some subsequent) accounts, virtually all of which purvey unsubstantiated myths and public relations puffs as truth. *John L. Lewis: A Biography* is particularly devastating in its critique of Alinsky's biography, demonstrating that Alinsky may well have created many of his "interviews" with Lewis out of thin air. The authors, although often impressed with Lewis's intelligence and contributions, are far from uncritical. They amply document his shadowy financial arrangements, his questionable association with coal operators, and his arrogance and insensitivity. This splendid book is a landmark of American labor historiography. An abridged edition (1987) and the authors' biographical chapter on Lewis in Dubofsky and Van Tine, eds., *Labor Leaders in America* (1987) make their work readily available, although neither of these recent publications takes into account the extensive literature on the UMW and the labor movement that has appeared since 1977.

Other biographical works on Lewis are of limited use. J. B. S. Hardman, "John L. Lewis, Labor Leader and Man: An Interpretation," *Labor History* (1961), is a spirited commentary from a veteran labor journalist. Charles Madison, "John Mitchell and John L. Lewis: The Moses and Samson of the Miners," in *American Labor Leaders: Personalities and Forces in the Labor Movement*, rev. ed., (1962), contains a clear outline of Lewis's major public activities. Wechsler's *Labor Baron* remains useful for its contemporary flavor, but Cecil Carnes, *John L. Lewis: Leader of Labor* (1936), and John Hutchinson, "John L. Lewis: To the Presidency of the UMWA," *Labor History* (1978), rest on dated materials. Alinsky's biography remains interesting as a document in the intellectual life of the American Left but cannot be relied upon for scholarly purposes.

Lewis himself wrote relatively little. Articles and speeches appearing under his name were usually the work of assistants such as K. C. Adams and W. Jett Lauck. His one book, *The Miners' Fight for American Standards* (1925), was based largely on material gathered by Lauck and was actually written by Lauck and Adams but is, nonetheless, a reliable guide to Lewis's basic views. Over the years, Lewis published many articles in popular magazines and the United Mine Workers *Journal*. The W. Jett Lauck Papers at the Alderman Library, University of Virginia, contain copious materials that show the process by which many a Lewis-bylined article came into print. Specific citations to particularly useful Lewis articles and records of his testimony at congressional hearings appear in the notes to this book, especially those for chapters 4 through 7. Rare is the issue of the UMW *Journal* between 1917 and 1969 that does not contain articles by Lewis, excerpts from his speeches, or similar material. In addition, of course, the proceedings of UMW conventions contain pages and pages of Lewis's speeches, along with officers' reports and records of exchanges on the convention floor. Here again, note citations provide a good guide to characteristic utterances.

The actual papers of John L. Lewis, like much else associated with the man, are the subject of some mystery and much controversy. A small collection, consisting largely of drafts and reprints of articles and speeches, many of which are cited in the notes, is at the State Historical Society of Wisconsin and is available on microfilm. Office files in the UMW headquarters in Washington contain important material on the union during the Lewis era but virtually nothing distinctive about Lewis himself. A large body of UMW records is now being processed in Alexandria, Virginia, in conjunction with a centennial history of the union being written. These records contain invaluable information on the history of the UMW, the CIO, the labor movement in general, and the mining industry. Archivists, however, fear that John L. Lewis's son, John L. Lewis, Jr., may have been extraordinarily thorough in culling from these records all but official and public materials relating to his father.

Since John L. Lewis's career is virtually synonymous with the history of the labor movement in the twentieth century, other archival collections contain critical information. The bibliographical essay in Dubofsky and Van Tine, *John L. Lewis*, provides basic citations. See also the fall 1982, issue of *Labor History*, which consists of essays describing major labor archives in the United States. The Van A. Bittner Collection at the West Virginia University Library in Morgantown is a particularly rich repository of unpublished and photographic materials on the pre-1930 struggles of the miners and the UMW. The records of UMW District 50, as yet unprocessed, are at Pennsylvania State University and document the course of one of Lewis's most important initiatives.

Those interested in pursuing study of Lewis must consult the copious materials available in the National Archives and presidential libraries. Of particular importance are the records of the United States Conciliation and Mediation Service (Record Group 280), the United States Coal Commission (RG 68), the National War Labor Board (RG 202), and other federal agencies dealing with labor, energy, and legal matters.

Presidential libraries also contain substantial Lewis and UMW material. The Herbert Hoover Presidential Library in West Branch, Iowa, has rich material illuminating the relationship between these two sons of Iowa, especially for the period 1919–33. Papers in the Franklin D. Roosevelt Presidential Library in Hyde Park, New York, help document Lewis's role in developing the National Industrial Recovery Act and contain a record of Roosevelt's stormy involvement with the UMW chief during the CIO and World War II years. The Gardner Jackson Papers, part of the Roosevelt Library collections, help document Lewis's ideas and goals in the critical late 1930s and early 1940s. The wealthy and well-born Jackson was one of the few people active in the labor movement with whom Lewis maintained a close social relationship. The Harry S. Truman Presidential Library in Independence, Missouri, contains detailed records of the numerous coal crises of the late 1940s. The recently opened John Steelman Papers there are illuminating on the post–World War II political economy and especially on the strikes that loomed so large in these years.

Although Lewis himself never submitted to a formal oral history, a number of his associates, allies, and enemies did, and several of these provide extensive commentary on Lewis. Virtually all the archives described in the fall 1982 issue of *Labor History* house oral histories, with Wayne State University and Penn State containing those most directly pertinent to the study of Lewis's era. In addition, the Columbia Oral History Collection's interviews with key CIO-era labor leaders are available on microform. The voluminous transcripts of the interviews with Lee Pressman, John Brophy, and Gardner Jackson, all part of this collection, abound with recollections and assessments of Lewis.

C. L. Sulzburger's *Sit Down with John L. Lewis* (1938) is useful more as a record of Lewis's view of himself at the height of his reputation than as an independent document.

Despite the great importance of the coal industry and the UMW, there is no adequate history of either. The diligent student, however, can piece together a coherent picture from monographs, biographies, and specialized studies. Government reports are also useful.

The best general introduction to labor in the American coal industry is McAlister Coleman, *Men and Coal* (1943), a sensitive yet unsentimental account based on published sources and personal observations. Lewis looms large in this spirited account of the period through the 1943 strikes. Dix, *Work Relations in the Coal Industry*, cited above, is an uncommonly insightful monograph with excellent pictorial and statistical material. Carter Goodrich, *The Miner's Freedom: A Study of the Working Life in a Changing Industry* (1925), is a splendid example of social observation, published as the world of the miner was being transformed. John Brophy, *A Miner's Life*, edited and supplemented by John O. P. Hall (1964) is derived from Brophy's Columbia Oral History interview and is a rich account of the mining industry, the crisis in coal in the 1920s, and the rise of the CIO, in all of which Brophy's enemy/ally Lewis is at center stage. David A. McDonald and Edward A. Lynch, *Coal and Unionism: A History of the American Coal Miners' Unions* (1939), is an in-house account but is sometimes surprisingly candid about the UMW's tribulations and Lewis's authoritarian methods of control. Morton S. Baratz, *The Union and the Coal Industry* (1955), contains useful statistical material and a good outline of collective bargaining in the twentieth century. Glen Lawhon Parker, *The Coal Industry: A Study in Social Control* (1940), is an able overview of the industry on the eve of World War II.

Specialized studies on coal abound. Some of the more useful include U.S., Federal Works Agency, Works Progress Administration, National Research Project, *Mechanization, Employment, and Output per Man in Bituminous Coal Mines*, 2 vol. (1939), and C. L. Christenson, *Economic Redevelopment in Bituminous Coal: The Special Case of Technological Advance in United States Coal Mines, 1930–1960* (1962), both of which stress the substitution of machines for men in the wake of UMW gains in the 1930s. William Graebner, *Coal-mining Safety in the Progressive Period: The Political Economy of Reform* (1976), highlights business control of safety initiatives and the relative lack of interest in safety by wage-maximizing coal miners and their unions. Carlton Jackson, *The Dreadful Month* (1982), provides vivid and often gruesome details of mine disasters, large and small. James P. Johnson, *The Politics of Soft Coal: The Bituminous Industry from World War I through the New Deal* (1979), is a detailed account of the coal industry's failure to achieve order and provides a lucid record of the disappointing Lewis-instigated coal legislation of the 1930s.

Thus far, writing on the social character of coal-mining areas has been episodic and impressionistic. There is vivid material in Coleman, *Men and Coal*, and Brophy, *A Miner's Life*, both previously cited. The Edward Wieck papers at the Archives of Labor History and Urban Affairs, Wayne State University, Detroit, abound with interviews, reports, and notes drawn from a lifetime of observing coal communities. Herman R. Lantz, *People of Coal Town* (1958), is a poignant study of a post–World War II community based on extensive interviews.

Government reports provide illuminating information. See, for example, U.S., Congress, Senate 64th Cong., 1st Sess., *Final Report and Testimony . . . Commission on Industrial Relations*, 11 vols. (1916), vols. 7–9, for conditions in the pre–World War I Colorado coal camps and for the social background of the Ludlow Massacre. U.S., Congress, Senate, Committee on Education and Labor, 67th Cong., 1st Sess., *Senate Hearings*, vol. 181, "The West Virginia Coal Fields" (1922); U.S., Congress, Senate, Committee on Interstate Commerce, 70th Cong., 1st Sess., *Conditions in the Coal Fields of Pennsylvania, West Virginia, and Ohio*, 2 vols. (1928); and United States Coal Commission, *Report*, 5 parts (1925), describe living and working conditions in the 1920s. See also Edward Eyre Hunt and others, *What the Coal Commission Found* (1925). U.S., Department of the Interior, Coal Mines Administration, *A Medical Survey of the Bituminous-Coal Industry* (1947), is an important and telling document.

Recent books and articles describe the lives of coal miners and help place Lewis and the UMW in the diverse geographic contexts in which they operated. Rowland Berthoff, "The Social Order of the Anthracite Region, 1825–1902," *Pennsylvania Magazine of History and Biography* (1965), is a splendid overview of the geographically fractured and ethnically diverse hard coal region. See also Harold W. Aurand, *From the Molly Maguires to the United Mine Workers: The Social Ecology of an Industrial Union, 1869–1897* (1971). Joe Gowaskie, "John Mitchell and the Anthracite Mine Workers: Leadership Conservatism and Rank-and-File Militancy," *Labor History* (1985–86), and John Cerullo and Gennaro Delena, "The Kelayres Massacre," *Pennsylvania Magazine of History and Biography* (1983), add important twentieth-century material, stressing anthracite miners' dissidence. The standard account of the key 1902 hard coal strike is Robert J. Cornell, *The Anthracite Coal Strike of 1902* (1957).

Dorothy Schwieder, *Black Diamonds: Life and Work in Iowa's Coal Mining Communities, 1895–1925* (1983), examines the social and ethnic character of the region that produced the Lewis family. The key Illinois mines have long attracted attention. Paul M. Angle, *Bloody Williamson: A Chapter in American Lawlessness* (1952), chronicles the 1922 massacre, and Eric D. Wietz, "Class Formation and Labor Protest in the Mining Communities of Southern Illinois and the Ruhr, 1890–1925," *Labor History* (1985–86), adds a comparative perspective. Chapter 2, "Coal Mines: Unionism as a Tradition," in Joel Seidman, Jack London, Bernard Karsh, and Daisy L. Tagliacozzo, *The Worker*

Views His Union (1958), pp. 15–41, is derived from extensive interviews with Illinois coal miners in the 1950s and documents the combination of awe and cynicism with which post–World War II miners regarded Lewis.

There are insightful observation on Pennsylvania bituminous miners' lives in Brophy, *A Miners' Life*, and Singer, "Which Side Are You On?," which contains fascinating oral history material from miners active in central Pennsylvania in the 1920s. See also Heber Blankenhorn, *The Strike for Union: A Study of the Non-Union Question . . . Based on the Somerset Strike* (1924).

Ronald D. Eller, *Miners, Millhands, and Mountaineers: Industrialization of the Appalachian South, 1880–1930* (1982), presents a good overview of the intrusion of mining into Kentucky, West Virginia, and Tennessee. David Alan Corbin, *Life, Work, and Rebellion in the Coal Fields: The Southern West Virginia Miners, 1880–1922* (1981), and Winthrop D. Lane, *Civil War in West Virginia: A Story of the Industrial Conflict in the Coal Mines* (1921), chronicle one of the UMW's bloodiest episodes during Lewis's reign. Cabell Phillips, a prominent journalist and son-in-law of West Virginia UMW hero Frank Keeney, brings a vivid and personal focus in "The West Virginia Mine War: Union versus Management, 1921," *American Heritage* (1974). The Phillips article includes photographs of the mining communities. John W. Hevener, *Which Side Are You On?: The Harlan County Coal Miners, 1931–1939* (1978), analyzes social conditions and recounts the UMW's eventual triumph in a notoriously anti-union area. George S. McGovern and Leonard L. Guttridge, *The Great Coalfield War* (1972), depicts conditions in the infamous southern Colorado fields of the early twentieth century. The distinctive world of Canadian UMW members is portrayed in Paul MacEwan, *Miners and Steel Workers: Labour in Cape Breton* (1976), and David Frank, "Contested Terrain: Workers' Control in Cape Breton Coal Mines in the 1920s," in Craig Heron and Robert Storey, eds., *On the Job: Confronting the Labour Process in Canada* (1986), pp. 102–23. Both document the clash between dissident Canadian miners and Lewis's autocratic control of the international union. Donald T. Barnum, *The Negro in the Bituminous Coal Industry* (1970), is an able monograph.

Lewis and the UMW loom large in general accounts of the twentieth-century labor movement. Standard chronicles include Philip A. Taft, *Organized Labor in American History* (1964), Taft, *The A.F. of L. in the Time of Gompers* (1957), and Taft, *The A.F. of L. from the Death of Gompers to the Merger* (1959). More interpretive perspectives can be found in James Green, *The World of the Worker: Labor in Twentieth Century America* (1980), Ronald Filippelli, *Labor in the USA: A History* (1984), and Robert H. Zieger, *American Workers, American Unions, 1920–1985* (1986).

Bruno Ramirez, *When Workers Fight: The Politics of Industrial Relations in the Progressive Era, 1898–1916* (1978), contains a provocative account of the UMW's early twentieth-century efforts to bring collective bargaining to the soft coalfields. Dubofsky and Van Tine, *Lewis*, previously cited, is the best guide to Lewis and the UMW in the World War I period. For the dismal 1920s, see Corbin, *Life, Work, and Rebellion*, previously cited, and Singer, "Which Side Are You On?" also cited above. The anthracite strikes of the decade are treated in Howard K. Kanarek, "The Pennsylvania Anthracite Strike of 1922," *Pennsylvania Magazine of History and Biography* (1975), Kanarek, "Disaster in Hard Coal: The Anthracite Strike of 1925–1926," *Labor History* (1974), and Robert H. Zieger, "Pennsylvania Coal and Politics: The Anthracite Strike of 1925–1926," *Pennsylvania Magazine of History and Biography* (1969).

Lewis's efforts to stabilize the soft coal industry are treated in Edmond Beame, "The Jacksonville Agreement," *Industrial and Labor Relations Review* (1955), and Ellis Hawley, "Secretary Hoover and the Bituminous Coal Problem, 1921–1928," *Business History Review* (1968). See also Johnson, *The Politics of Hard Coal*, cited above, and Robert H. Zieger, *Republicans and Labor, 1919–1929* (1969). Irving Bernstein, *The Lean Years: A History of the American Worker, 1921–1933* (1960), contains important material on Lewis and his miners. See also Coleman, *Men and Coal*, and Brophy, *A Miner's Life*, both cited above.

Lewis's struggles with the Illinois dissidents are graphically described in Coleman, *Men and Coal*. Lorin Lee Cary, "The Reorganized United Mine Workers of America, 1930–31," *Journal of the Illinois Historical Society* (1973), and Harriet Hudson, *The Progressive Mine Workers of America: A Study in Rival Unionism* (1952), are standard. See also Oscar Ameringer, *If You Don't Weaken: The Autobiography of Oscar Ameringer* (1940), for a key dissident's view of the UMW under Lewis.

Standard works on the New Deal include William E. Leuchtenburg, *Franklin D. Roosevelt and the New Deal* (1963), Arthur M. Schlesinger, Jr., *The Age of Roosevelt*, 3 vols. (1957–60), and James MacGregor Burns, *Roosevelt: The Lion and the Fox* (1956). Irving Bernstein, *New Deal Collective Bargaining Policy* (1950), is standard, and Milton Derber and Edwin Young, eds., *Labor and the New Deal* (1957), remains useful. Bernstein, *Turbulent Years: A History of the American Worker, 1933–1941* (1970), is the standard overview, but Dubofsky and Van Tine, *Lewis*, supplants it in important matters relating to Lewis. Galenson, *The CIO Challenge*, cited above, chronicles the rebirth of the UMW and the genesis of the CIO. The essays on the 1930s in David Brody, *Workers in Industrial America: Essays on the Twentieth Century Struggle* (1980), put Lewis in an illuminating context. Sidney Fine, *Sit-Down: The General Motors Strike of 1936–1937* (1969), and James O. Morris, *Conflict within the AFL: A Study in Craft versus Industrial Unionism, 1901–1938* (1958), chronicle two key Lewis battlegrounds. Melvyn Dubofsky, "John L. Lewis and American Isolationism," in John N. Schacht, ed., *Three Faces of Midwestern Isolationism: Gerald P. Nye, Robert E. Wood, John L. Lewis* (1981), pp. 23–34, explores the roots of Lewis's conflict with FDR. C. K. McFarland, *Roosevelt, Lewis, and the*

New Deal, 1933–1940 (1970), adds little. See also the works by Taft and by Dubofsky and Van Tine cited above.

James MacGregor Burns, *Roosevelt: Soldier of Freedom* (1970), remains the best general account of the World War II mobilization. See also Richard Polenberg, *War and Society: The United States, 1941–1945* (1972). David Brody, "The New Deal and World War II," in John Braeman, Robert H. Bremner, and Brody, eds., *The New Deal*, vol. 1, *The National Level* (1975), pp. 267–309, and Koistinen, "Mobilizing the World War II Economy," cited above, are important overviews. Joel Seidman, *American Labor from Defense to Reconversion*, cited above, is the standard account of labor during war, but Lichtenstein, *Labor's War at Home*, also cited above, offers a challenging reinterpretation.

J. R. Sperry, "Rebellion within the Ranks: Pennsylvania Anthracite, John L. Lewis, and the Coal Strikes of 1943," *Pennsylvania History* (1973), is an important article. Thomas C. Clapp, "The Bituminous Coal Strike of 1943" (Ph. D. diss. University of Toledo, 1974), chronicles the soft coal strikes. Makota Takamiya, *Organization and Militancy: Conclusions from a Study of the United Mine Workers of America, 1940–1970* (1978), contains illuminating documentary and statistical information on Lewis and the UMW during the war.

Waldo E. Fisher, *Collective Bargaining in the Bituminous Coal Industry* (1948), and Colston E. Warne, "Industrial Relations in Coal," in Warne, ed., *Labor in Postwar America* (1949), pp. 367–86, are sober introductions to the controversial history of Truman-Lewis confrontations. See also the three-part *Fortune* magazine series (March-May 1947), "Coal." Joanna Healey Shurbet, "John L. Lewis: The Truman Years" (Ph. D. diss. Texas Technological University, 1975), provides a detailed account based on UMW and Truman Library files. "Day by Day, 1946: The Sargent Family," in Marc S. Miller, ed., *Working Lives: The "Southern Exposure" History of Labor in the South* (1980), pp. 111–19, contains a sampling of the eight thousand photographs of Appalachian mining families that Russell Lee took for the Department of the Interior during the 1946–47 period of government operation. Together with the Coal Mines Administration, "A Medical Survey of the Bituminous-Coal Industry," cited above, they document the conditions that impelled Lewis to fight for the establishment of the UMW health and retirement funds. Paul Starr, *The Social Transformation of American Medicine: The Rise of a Sovereign Profession and the Making of a Vast Industry* (1982), contains a brief assessment of the UMW's health program and regional hospitals. See especially Starr's citations to Janet E. Ploss, "A History of the Medical Care Program of the United Mine Workers of America Welfare and Retirement Fund" (M.A. thesis, John Hopkins University, 1980). Robert I. Myers, "Experience of the UMWA Welfare and Retirement Fund," *Industrial and Labor Relations Review* (1956), and Myers, "The

Mine Workers' Welfare and Retirement Fund: Fifteen Years Experience," *Industrial and Labor Relations Review* (1967), provide statistical background.

The dismal history of the UMW in the last years of Lewis's presidency and in the final decade of his life is well documented. Dubofsky and Van Tine, *Lewis,* provides the clearest account. Harry M. Caudill, *Night Comes to the Cumberland: A Biography of a Depressed Area* (1963), is a classic of protest literature. See also Caudill, *My Land is Dying* (1971), which contains gruesome photographs of the havoc wrought by strip mining. Joseph Finley, *The Corrupt Kingdom* (1972), Treavor Armbrister, *Act of Vengeance* (1975), and Stuart Brown, *A Man Named Tony: The True Story of the Yablonski Murders* (1976), chronicle and document the UMW's sordid activities under Boyle. Brit Hume, *Death and the Mines: Rebellion and Murder in the United Mine Workers* (1971), is an example of outstanding reportage informed by a shrewd historical sense. The shadow of Lewis looms large in Paul F. Clark's account of the union's re-awakening in the 1970s, *The Miners' Fight for Democracy: Arnold Miller and the Reform of the United Mine Workers* (1981). John Gaventa, *Power and Powerlessness: Quiescence and Rebellion in an Appalachian Valley* (1980), is a brilliant piece of social investigation whose union of social theory and historical research suggests the tragic legacy of Lewis's rule of the UMW.

SELECTED BIBLIOGRAPHY

Alinsky, Saul D. *John L. Lewis: An Unauthorized Biography*. New York: Putnam, 1949.

Angle, Paul M. *Bloody Williamson: A Chapter in American Lawlessness*. New York: Alfred A. Knopf, 1952.

Armbrister, Treavor. *Act of Vengeance: The Yablonski Murders and Their Solution*. New York: Dutton/Saturday Review Press, 1975.

Baratz, Morton. *The Union and the Coal Industry*. New Haven, Conn.: Yale University Press, 1955.

Beame, Edmond. "The Jacksonville Agreement: Quest for Stability in Coal." *Industrial and Labor Relations Review* 8 (January 1955):195–203.

Bernstein, Irving. *The Lean Years: A History of the American Worker, 1921–1933*. Boston: Houghton Mifflin, 1960.

————. *The New Deal Collective Bargaining Policy*. Berkeley and Los Angeles: University of California Press, 1950.

————. *Turbulent Years: A History of the American Worker, 1933–1941*. Boston: Houghton Mifflin, 1970.

Berthoff, Rowland. "The Social Order of the Anthracite Region, 1825–1902." *Pennsylvania Magazine of History and Biography* 89 (July 1965):261–91.

Brody, David. "The New Deal and World War II." In *The New Deal*. Vol. 1. *The National Level*, edited by John Braeman, Robert H. Bremner, and David Brody, pp. 267–309. Columbus: Ohio State University Press, 1975.

————. *Workers in Industrial America: Essays on the Twentieth Century Struggle*. London and New York: Oxford University Press, 1980.

Brophy, John. *A Miner's Life*. Edited and supplemented by John O. P. Hall. Madison: University of Wisconsin Press, 1964.

Brown, Stuart. *A Man Named Tony: The True Story of the Yablonski Murders*. New York: W. W. Norton, 1976.

Carnes, Cecil. *John L. Lewis: Leader of Labor.* New York: Robert Speller, 1936.

Cary, Lorin Lee. "The Reorganized United Mine Workers of America, 1930–1931." *Journal of the Illinois State Historical Society* 66 (Autumn 1973):245–70.

Caudill, Harry M. *My Land Is Dying.* New York: E. P. Dutton, 1971.

Caudill, Harry M. *Night Comes to the Cumberland: A Biography of a Depressed Area.* Boston: Little, Brown, 1963.

Cerullo, John, and Delena, Gennero. "The Kelayres Massacre." *Pennsylvania Magazine of History and Biography* 107 (July 1983):331–61.

Christenson, C. L. *Economic Development in Bituminous Coal: The Special Case of Technological Advance in United States Coal Mines, 1930–1960.* Cambridge: Mass.: Harvard University Press, 1962.

Clapp, Thomas C. "The Bituminous Coal Strike of 1943." Ph.D. dissertation, Toledo University, 1974.

Coleman, McAlister. *Men and Coal.* New York: Ferrar and Rinehart, 1943.

Corbin, David. *Life, Work, and Rebellion in the Coal Fields: The Southern West Virginia Miners, 1880–1922.* Urbana: University of Illinois Press, 1981.

Cornell, Robert H. *The Anthracite Coal Strike of 1902.* Washington, D.C.: Catholic University of America Press, 1957.

Dix, Keith. *Work Relations in the Coal Industry: The Hand-Loading Era, 1880–1930.* Morgantown: Institute for Labor Studies, West Virginia University, 1977.

Dubofsky, Melvyn. "John L. Lewis and American Isolationism." In *Three Faces of Midwestern Isolationism: Gerald P. Nye, Robert E. Wood, John L. Lewis,* edited by John N. Schacht, pp. 23–34. Iowa City: Study of the Recent History of the United States, 1981.

Dubofsky, Melvyn, and Van Tine, Warren. *John L. Lewis: A Biography.* New York: New York Times / Quadrangle, 1977.

———. *John L. Lewis: A Biography,* abridged edition. Urbana: University of Illinois Press, 1987.

———. "John L. Lewis and the Triumph of Mass Production Unionism." In *Labor Leaders in America,* edited by Melvyn Dubofsky and Warren Van Tine, pp. 185–206. Urbana: University of Illinois Press, 1987.

Fine, Sidney. *Sit-Down: The General Motors Strike of 1936–1937.* Ann Arbor: University of Michigan Press, 1969.

Finley, Joseph. *The Corrupt Kingdom: The Rise and Fall of the United Mine Workers.* New York: Simon & Schuster, 1972.

Fisher, Waldo E. *Collective Bargaining in the Bituminous Coal Industry.* Philadelphia: University of Pennsylvania Press, 1948.

Frank, David. "Contested Terrain: Workers' Control in the Cape Breton Coal Mines in the 1920s." In *On the Job: Confronting the Labour Process in Canada,* edited by Craig Heron and Robert Storey, pp. 102–23. Kingston and Montreal: McGill–Queen's University Press, 1986.

Galenson, Walter. *The CIO Challenge to the AFL: The Conflict in American Labor, 1935–1941.* Cambridge, Mass.: Harvard University Press, 1960.

Gaventa, John. *Power and Powerlessness: Quiescence and Rebellion in an Appalachian Valley.* Urbana: University of Illinois Press, 1980.

Goodrich, Carter. *The Miner's Freedom: A Study of the Working Life in a Changing Industry.* Boston: Marshall Jones, 1925.

Gowaskie, Joe. "John Mitchell and the Anthracite Mine Workers: Leadership Conservatism and Rank-and-File Militancy." *Labor History* 27 (Winter 1985–86):54–84.

Graebner, William. *Coal-Mining Safety in the Progressive Period: The Political Economy of Reform.* Lexington: University Press of Kentucky, 1976.

Hardman, J. B. S. "John L. Lewis, Labor Leader and Man: An Interpretation." *Labor History* 2 (1961):3–29.

Hawley, Ellis. "Secretary Hoover and the Bituminous Coal Problem, 1921–1928." *Business History Review* 48 (Autumn 1968):247–70.

Hevener, John W. *Which Side Are You On?: The Harlan County Coal Miners, 1931–1939.* Urbana: University of Illinois Press, 1978.

Hudson, Harriet D. *The Progressive Mine Workers of America: A Study in Rival Unionism.* Urbana: University of Illinois Press, 1952.

Hume, Brit. *Death and the Mines: Rebellion and Murder in the United Mine Workers.* New York: Grossman, 1971.

Hutchinson, John. "John L. Lewis: To the Presidency of the United Mine Workers." *Labor History* 19 (Spring 1978):185–203.

Jackson, Carlton. *The Dreadful Month.* Bowling Green, Ohio: Bowling Green State University Popular Press, 1982.

Johnson, James P. *The Politics of Soft Coal: The Bituminous Industry from World War I through the New Deal.* Urbana: University of Illinois Press, 1979.

Kanarek, Harold K. "Disaster for Hard Coal: The Anthracite Strike of 1925–1926." *Labor History* 15 (Winter 1974):44–62.

Koistinen, Paul A. C. "Mobilizing the World War II Economy: Labor and the Industrial-Military Alliance." *Pacific Historical Review* 42 (November 1973):443–78.

Lane, Winthrop D. *Civil War in West Virginia: A Story of the Industrial Conflict in the Coal Mines.* New York: B. W. Huebsch, 1921.

Lewis, John L. *The Miners' Fight for American Standards.* Indianapolis: Bell Publishing Company, 1925.

Lichtenstein, Nelson. *Labor's War at Home: The CIO in World War II.* Cambridge, U.K.: Cambridge University Press, 1982.

McDonald, David, and Lynch, Edward A. *Coal and Unionism: A History of the American Coal Miners' Unions.* Silver Spring and Indianapolis: Cornelius, 1939.

MacEwan, Paul. *Miners and Steelworkers: Labour in Cape Breton.* Toronto: A. M. Hakkert, 1976.

McFarland, C. K. *Roosevelt, Lewis, and the New Deal, 1933–1940.* Fort Worth: Texas Christian University Press, 1970.

Madison, Charles A., ed. "John Mitchell and John L. Lewis: The Moses and the Samson of the Miners." In *American Labor Leaders: Personalities and Forces in the Labor Movement,* 2nd rev. ed., pp. 157–98. New York: Ungar, 1962.

Morris, James O. *Conflict within the AFL: A Study in Craft versus Industrial Unionism, 1901–1938.* Ithaca, N.Y.: Cornell University Press, 1958.

Naison, Mark. *The Southern Tenant Farmers' Union and the C.I.O.* Pamphlet. Boston: New England Free Press, ca. 1968.

Parker, Glen Lawhon. *The Coal Industry: A Study in Social Control.* Washington, D.C.: American Council on Public Affairs, 1940.

Phillips, Cabell. "The West Virginia Mine War: Union versus Management, 1921." *American Heritage* 25 (August 1974):58–61, 90–94.

Ramirez, Bruno. *When Workers Fight: The Politics of Industrial Relations in the Progressive Era, 1898–1916.* Westport, Conn.: Greenwood, 1978.

Schwieder, Dorothy. *Black Diamonds: Life and Work in Iowa's Coal Mining Communities, 1895–1925.* Ames: Iowa State University Press, 1983.

Seidman, Joel. *American Labor from Defense to Reconversion.* Chicago: University of Chicago Press, 1953.

Shurbet, Joanna Healey. "John L. Lewis: The Truman Years." Ph.D. dissertation, Texas Technological University, 1975.

Singer, Alan Jay. " 'Which Side are You On?': Ideological Conflict in the United Mine Workers of America, 1919–1928." Ph.D. dissertation, Rutgers University, 1982.

Sperry, J. R. "Rebellion within the Ranks: Pennsylvania Anthracite, John L. Lewis, and the Coal Strikes of 1943." *Pennsylvania History* 40 (July 1973):293–312.

Sulzberger, C. L. *Sit Down with John L. Lewis.* New York: Random House, 1938.

Taft, Philip A. *The A. F. of L. from the Death of Gompers to the Merger.* New York: Harper, 1959.

———. *The A. F. of L. in the Time of Gompers.* New York: Harpers, 1957.

———. *Organized Labor in American History.* New York: Harpers, 1964.

Takamiya, Makoto. *Union Organization and Militancy: Conclusions from a Study of the United Mine Workers of America, 1940–1974.* Meisenheim am Glan, W. Ger.: Hain, 1978.

Warne, Colston E. "Industrial Relations in Coal." In Warne, ed. *Labor in Postwar America.* Brooklyn: Remsen Press. 1949.

Wechsler, James A. *Labor Baron: A Portrait of John L. Lewis.* New York: William Morrow. 1944.

Zieger, Robert H. *American Workers, American Unions, 1920–1985.* Baltimore: Johns Hopkins University Press. 1986.

————. "Pennsylvania Coal and Politics: The Anthracite Strike of 1925–1926." *Pennsylvania Magazine of History and Biography* 92 (April 1969): 244–262.

————. *Republicans and Labor, 1919–1929.* Lexington: University of Kentucky Press. 1969.

INDEX

ABOUT THE AUTHOR

Robert H. Zieger is professor of history at the University of Florida. His previous books are *Republicans and Labor, 1919–1929* (University of Kentucky Press, 1969); *Madison's Battery Workers* (New York State School of Industrial and Labor Relations, 1977); *Rebuilding the Pulp and Paper Workers' Union, 1933–1941* (University of Tennessee Press, 1984); and *American Workers, American Unions, 1920–1985* (Johns Hopkins University Press, 1986). He was co-winner of the Philip A. Taft Prize for Labor History, 1985, and is currently working on a history of the CIO. His wife, Gay, is a teacher and writer. Their son, Robert, is a recent graduate of the University of Michigan.